ETHICS IN QUALITATIVE RESEARCH

SECOND EDITION

ETHICS IN QUALITATIVE RESEARCH

edited by
TINA MILLER, MAXINE BIRCH,
MELANIE MAUTHNER & JULIE JESSOP

Los Angeles | London | New Delhi
Singapore | Washington DC

Los Angeles | London | New Delhi
Singapore | Washington DC

SAGE Publications Ltd
1 Oliver's Yard
55 City Road
London EC1Y 1SP

SAGE Publications Inc.
2455 Teller Road
Thousand Oaks, California 91320

SAGE Publications India Pvt Ltd
B 1/I 1 Mohan Cooperative Industrial Area
Mathura Road
New Delhi 110 044

SAGE Publications Asia-Pacific Pte Ltd
3 Church Street
#10-04 Samsung Hub
Singapore 049483

Editor: Jai Seaman
Assistant editor: Anna Horvai
Production editor: Ian Antcliff
Copyeditor: Jeremy Toynbee
Proofreader: Danielle Hart
Indexer: Henson Editorial Services
Marketing manager: Ben Griffin-Sherwood
Cover design: Wendy Scott
Typeset by: C&M Digitals (P) Ltd, Chennai, India
Printed and bound by CPI Group (UK) Ltd,
Croydon, CR0 4YY
Printed on paper from sustainable resources

MIX
Paper from
responsible sources
FSC
www.fsc.org   FSC® C013604

Introduction © Maxine Birch, Tina Miller, Melanie Mauthner and
Julie Jessop 2012
Chapter 1 © Rosalind Edwards and Melanie Mauthner 2012
Chapter 2 © Tina Miller 2012
Chapter 3 © Val Gillies and Pam Alldred 2012
Chapter 4 © Tina Miller and Linda Bell 2012
Chapter 5 © Linda Bell and Linda Nutt 2012
Chapter 6 © Maxine Birch and Tina Miller 2012
Chapter 7 © Jean Duncombe and Julie Jessop 2012
Chapter 8 © Andrea Doucet and Natasha S. Mauthner 2012
Chapter 9 © Pam Alldred and Val Gillies 2012
Chapter 10 © Natasha S. Mauthner 2012
Chapter 11 © Melanie Mauthner, Maxine Birch, Tina Miller
and Julie Jessop 2012

First edition published November 2002; reprinted in 2007 and
2008 (twice)

Library of Congress Control Number: 2012932218

British Library Cataloguing in Publication data

A catalogue record for this book is available from
the British Library

ISBN 978-1-4462-1088-8
ISBN 978-1-4462-1089-5 (pbk)

Contents

Contributors' biographies

Editors

Tina Miller is a Professor of Sociology at Oxford Brookes University. Her research and teaching interests include motherhood and fatherhood constructions and transitions, gender and identities, issues around maternity and fertility in a development context, narrative and qualitative research methods and ethics. She is the author of *Making Sense of Motherhood: A Narrative Approach* (Cambridge University Press, 2005) and *Making Sense of Fatherhood: Gender, Caring and Work* published by Cambridge University Press in 2011.

Maxine Birch is a Senior Lecturer with the Faculty of Health and Social Care at The Open University. Maxine's teaching and research interests centre on experiences of health and well-being, qualitative research methods ethnography, and narrative. Maxine's interest in ethics and feminist research, developed in the first edition (Mauthner et al., 2002), has led to facilitating workshops to encourage ethical thinking for qualitative researchers.

Melanie Mauthner spent 15 years as a social science lecturer teaching and researching gender issues before becoming a translator and poet. She has written books about sibling relationships including *Sistering: Power and Change in Female Relationships* (Palgrave, 2005) and co-edited *Waterwords: Lido Poems* (BLU Press, 2008) She translates articles for *Justice Spatiale/Spatial Justice* (www.jssj.org), writes short stories (www.etherbooks.com) and belongs to Malika's Kitchen Poetry Collective. Her ethical thinking has influenced her community activism. She was Chair of Trustees at the Women's Therapy Centre (www.womenstherapycentre.co.uk) and Chair of BLU, campaigning for 10 years to save an outdoor pool from closure and oversee its regeneration as a partnership between users, Lambeth Council and a not-for-profit leisure company (www.brockwelllido.com).

Julie Jessop completed her PhD into the psychosocial dynamics of post-divorce parenting at the Centre for Family Research, University of Cambridge in 2001. She went on to become a Senior Research Associate at the Centre and worked on various research projects in the field of family sociology, including divorce, interventions and support services for children and the ethical implications of organ donation. During this time she was a member of the Cambridge Socio-legal Group, and contributed to several of their publications. She also worked with Jane Ribbens McCarthy on a Joseph Rowntree Foundation project 'Young People, Bereavement and Loss: Disruptive Transitions?' (2005). For the last five years she has been travelling and living in the Caribbean where she has worked as a consultant for an international leadership agency looking into family business dynamics.

Authors

Pam Alldred is Senior Lecturer at Brunel University, in the Centre for Youth Work Studies and her research interests include sexualities education, equalities interventions, young parents and interprofessionalism. *Get Real About Sex: The Politics and Practice of Sex Education* (co-authored with M. E. David, Open University Press) was published in 2007 and 'Obstacles to "good"sex education: International angles' (a special issue of the *Journal of Sex Education*) will be published in 2012. She contributed to the two previous Women's Workshop books, and also to previous book collectives (Burman, E., Alldred, P., Bewley, C., Goldberg, B., Heenan, C., Marks, D., Marshall, J., Taylor, K., Ullah, R. and Warner, S., *Challenging Women: Psychology's Exclusions, Feminist Possibilities*, Open University Press, 1996; and Burman, E., Aitken, G., Alldred, P., Allwood, R., Billington, T., Goldberg, B., Gordo Lopez, A. J., Heenan, C., Marks, D. and Warner, S., *Psychology, Discourse, Practice: From Regulation to Resistance*, Taylor and Francis, 1996).

Linda Bell is Principal Lecturer in the School of Health and Social Sciences, Middlesex University. She teaches research methods to students in social work and health and also works extensively with research students. She has chaired a departmental ethics committee and from a research perspective is interested in decision making within such committees. Her recent research has focused around issues of professional identity including gender. Between 1991–1995 she was based at King's College, University of London, where she researched inter-professional and organizational aspects of social work education and women's experiences of a therapy centre concerned with male violence. She completed her Phd entitled 'My child, your child; mothering in a Hertfordshire town in the 1980s' in 1994. Her publications include journal articles and book chapters relating to mothering and to health and social care. She is co-reviews editor for the *International Journal of Social Research Methodology* (Routledge).

Andrea Doucet is the Canada Research Chair in Gender, Work and Care and Professor of Sociology at Brock University. She has published widely on themes of gender and care work, mothering and fathering, parental leave policies, embodiment, reflexive sociology, feminist philosophy and epistemological issues, and knowledge construction processes. Her book *Do Men Mother?* (University of Toronto Press, 2006) was awarded the John Porter Tradition of Excellence Book Award from the Canadian Sociology Association. She is also co-author of *Gender Relations: Intersectionality and*

Beyond (with Janet Siltanen, Oxford, 2008) and a forthcoming book entitled *Narrative Analysis: The Listening Guide Approach* (with Natasha Mauthner, Sage). She is the current Editor of the international journal *Fathering*.

Jean Duncombe, formerly Senior Research Officer at Essex University, is now Senior Lecturer in Social Studies at University College Chichester. Her interests include the sociology of the emotions (love and intimacy); family; childhood; and qualitative research. Her work on the gendered division of emotional labour has been published widely in academic journals and in *The Sociology of the Family: A Reader* (Blackwell, 1999).

Rosalind Edwards is Professor of Sociology at the University of Southampton. Her interest is in family lives and relationships, on which she has researched and published widely. Her most recent publications include: *Researching Families and Communities: Social and Generational Change* (Routledge, 2008); *Teenage Parenting – What's the Problem?* (with S. Duncan and C. Alexander, the Tufnell Press, 2010); *Key Concepts in Family Studies* (with J. McCarthy, Sage, 2011) and *International Perspectives on Racial and Ethnic Mixedness and Mixing* (with S. Ali, C. Caballero and M. Song, Routledge, 2012). Ros also maintains an interest in methodology, and is a founding and co-editor of the *International Journal of Social Research Methodology*.

Val Gillies is a Professor of Social Research and a co-director of the Families and Social Capital Research Group at London South Bank University. She has researched and published in the area of family, social class and marginalized children and young people, producing a wide range of journal articles and book chapters on parenting, young people at risk of school exclusion, home school relations as well as qualitative research methods. Her book: *Marginalized Mothers: Exploring Working Class Parenting* (Routledge) was published in 2007.

Natasha Mauthner is a Reader at the University of Aberdeen Business School. Her research interests lie in the areas of health and well-being; gender, work and family; and knowledge-making in the academy (including interpretive, collaborative and data sharing practices). She is author of *The Darkest Days of my Life* (Harvard University Press, 2002) and is writing a book on the Listening Guide method of data analysis with Andrea Doucet for Sage. Her current work explores the performativity of digital methods, and the philosophical, legal, ethical and moral issues that arise in digital data sharing. Her work in this area is funded by a grant from the Society for Research Into Higher Education.

Linda Nutt is an independent child care consultant. She completed her doctoral research when employed by the National Foster Care Association (now the Fostering Network). While there is an established body of research on children who are fostered, there is little work on the views of foster carers. Her research 'Foster carers' perspectives: the dilemmas of loving the bureaucratized child' therefore makes an original contribution to the field.

Introduction to second edition

MAXINE BIRCH, TINA MILLER,
MELANIE MAUTHNER AND JULIE JESSOP

In the first edited collection of this book (2002) we set out to address the perplexing area of ethics in qualitative research from our positions as feminist researchers. We examined the ethical dilemmas we had encountered at a time when less attention had been paid to ethics when conducting qualitative research. We argued that the complexities of researching private lives and placing accounts in the public arena raised multiple ethical issues for the researcher that could not be solved solely by the application of abstract rules, principles or guidelines, and that the kind of ethical issues encountered when doing qualitative research were empirical and theoretical and *permeated* the qualitative research process. As researchers we had found that we were faced with the inherent tensions that characterize qualitative research – fluidity and inductive uncertainty – and that could not be met by ethical guidelines, which were static and increasingly formalized. In this new edition we continue to integrate the theoretical and practical aspects of ethical dilemmas in qualitative research studies to highlight the ways in which ethical decision processes and 'thinking ethically' throughout the qualitative research process have become ever more necessary in a changing research environment. We also reiterate our call for a contextual, situational, and practice-based approach to ethics in qualitative research that is increasingly conducted in more technologically sophisticated and globally immediate circumstances. The translation of the first edition of this book into Mandarin provides just one example of this dynamic and rapidly changing sphere.

The first edition proved to be a timely publication that encouraged ethical thinking as awareness and attention towards ethical research became heightened, alongside the growing acceptability of qualitative methods and the use of mixed methods in larger scale research. During the 10-year period between editions the production of professional ethical frameworks and formal processes to gain ethics research approval from regulatory committees – before commencing data collection – have been established and is now observed widely. Ethics approval processes scrutinize the familiar ethical principles of protection, informed consent, confidentiality and anonymity across the research design that in turn provide new ways to justify and judge the integrity and quality of social research. Ten years on, as both the ethical and methodological choices that face qualitative researchers increase, the ethical dilemmas we raised regarding research boundaries, informed consent, participation, rapport and data interpretation, have become even more significant for qualitative researchers.

The new landscape of ethical research: regulation and new technologies

Ethical questions in the research relationship, the use of data and the interpretative and analytical processes have all become more significant as the landscape of qualitative research continues to change and researchers face new issues when using new tools to produce knowledge. Ethical dilemmas about how much information to disclose to whom and in what contexts, the blurring boundaries of privacy, access to and sharing of information, face so many more of us, not only within research worlds but in multiple layers of connection and communication with others. This means that suddenly we have all become more responsible for looking after and for caring about what we reveal and under what conditions. When we published the first edition in 2002 we could not have foreseen the importance of ethical thinking and its application beyond the preserve of experts and professionals: but behaving ethically has become a much broader concern.

This changing research landscape has been accompanied by a rapid increase in research ethics regulation and governance. The consequence of this for social researchers has evoked a range of, sometimes polarized and heated responses, which will be explored in more detail below. In the first edition of this book attention was drawn to the momentum that had 'grown apace' in relation to regulation and ethics in social research. This was at a time when academic institutions were, individually, in the process of 'setting up ethics committees to which researchers … should submit their projects for approval' (Edwards and Mauthner, 2002: 14). Ten years on, it is commonplace (taken-for-granted even) that academic researchers must gain ethics approval from a university (or other) research ethics committee (UREC/REC) before commencing their research: but this does not mean it is universally accepted or welcomed.

Remonstrating against this significant turn to regulation and capturing the mood of some researchers, Dingwall notes that 'we have not suddenly developed new techniques that can kill people' (2006: 53). The growth of ethical jurisdiction in social research (which now encompasses other bodies such as research funding councils) has raised further concerns about the remit and reach of research ethics regulation (Dingwall, 2006; Haggerty, 2004; Hammersley, 2009; Stanley and Wise, 2010). And although most researchers would agree that research should be carried out in ways that are ethical, and which do not wilfully exploit, harm or coerce (potential) participants, the extent to which research ethics committees are best placed or able to 'ensure that research is conducted ethically' remains highly contested (Richardson and McMullan, 2007: 1116). There is no doubt then that in the intervening years since the first publication of this text, issues of research ethics have come to the fore as concerns over the regulation of 'knowledge production endeavours' are increasingly expressed (Haggerty, 2004: 391; Hedgecoe, 2008). Questions over whether increased ethics regulation and standardization lead to, or can 'ensure', research practice that is more ethical – and importantly who decides these issues and when – has provoked a potent and, sometimes, divided debate among research communities (Dingwall, 2006; Hammersley, 2009; Richardson and McMullan, 2007).

Developments in the regulation of research ethics across the UK, mainland Europe and North America has resulted in greater external control exerted at the institutional, organizational and funding body levels over research projects and processes. Through this process there has been a discernible shift from a discourse of moral integrity and researcher self-regulation guided by professional codes of practice, to one of external regulation and governance (Haggerty, 2004; Miller and Boulton, 2007). The landscape in which this external control operates has become progressively congested as professional ethics guidelines have been augmented (and so supplanted?) by funding body, as well as university and health RECs, ethics requirements. These shifts have not surprisingly provoked concerns that universal research ethics and 'generalist criteria', which are 'context free', are being (inappropriately) applied (at times) by those who lack an understanding of qualitative research approaches (Mattingly, 2005:453; Reissman, 2005; Stanley and Wise, 2010).

There is then a sense that 'a form of ethics creep' has changed the research landscape for social scientists, potentially compromising – or at least reconfiguring – research endeavours (Haggerty, 2004: 391). But the context in which this 'creep' is evident has become more complex in other ways too, for example, concern over litigation (at the institutional and individual level) as well as legislative changes (for example, the Data Protection Act 1998; Freedom of Information Act 2000) that have changed aspects of research practice. But perhaps of greater significance have been developments in technologies that have provided new research tools, for example, the use of web-based/online forums including chat rooms, social networking sites and email. These new ways of researching the social world have created new research sites in virtual spaces and new possibilities for collecting and sharing digital data (see Chapters 2 and 10, this volume). They can provide 'ethical benefits' for example when researching 'sensitive or potentially taboo subjects' anonymously via Internet forums (Rundall, forthcoming), but they also provoke new ethical concerns and questions too about what should – or can – be regulated.

Ethics guidelines and research governance in the social sciences have been significantly influenced by statements of ethical principles and standards for medical research put in place following the Second World War and Nazi experiments on human subjects (Miller and Boulton, 2007; Weindling, 1994). Subsequently, the legacy of biomedical research ethics regulation has patterned models of ethics review practice in social research too, prompting critical comment on the appropriateness and (mis)fit between biomedical and social science research practices (Aldred, 2008; Dingwall, 2006). Yet these debates have not stemmed the regulatory tide and since the millennium there has been 'a rapid increase in research ethics activity' marked by the introduction of both health and social science ethics governance frameworks

(Alderson and Morrow, 2005: 406). The first of these in the UK, which was acknowledged to have implications for social science researchers working in areas related to health, was the Department of Health *Research Governance Framework* (RGF) introduced in 2001 (Alderson and Morrow, 2005: 406). This framework, among other things, 'specified the responsibilities of funders and sponsors of research which included ensuring that research protocols were reviewed by an appropriate REC' (Miller and Boulton, 2007: 2203). This led UK universities, which relied upon biomedical and health funding research support, to strengthen their research ethics review mechanisms in order to meet these new RGF requirements (Tinker, 2004). In response in part to these developments, four years later the Economic and Social Research Council (ESRC) in 2005 published its own *Research Ethics Framework* (REF) (Webster et al., 2004; see Alderson and Morrow, 2005 for an overview of research ethics governance developments during this period). The ESRC has more recently published an enhanced *Framework for Research Ethics* (FRE) which combines elements of the ESRC's 2005 *Research Ethics Framework* with new requirements for researchers.

The entry of the principal UK research funding body – the ESRC – into the arena of ethics review was seen to mark a 'watershed' (Aldred, 2008: 889), requiring British institutions to put in place 'internal processes equivalent to those of Institutional Review Boards (IRB) in the US' (Dingwall, 2006: 51). Not surprisingly, it has elicited a range of responses from expressions of broad support to concern about academic freedom and surveillance. The more recent iteration of the framework (FRE) published in 2010 extends the provisions of the earlier document including the role of the RECs that is now to be responsible for 'reviewing all research proposals accepted by the ESRC and other funding bodies … funding will depend on the REC review, with its purview extending through a project's life' (Stanley and Wise, 2010). The document has been declared 'not fit for purpose' in a recent article, and the debate will surely continue (Stanley and Wise, 2010).

Increased regulation can be seen, in part, as a response to the growth in new technologies and an attempt to oversee the use of these technologies in social research. Social networking is a good example of a new virtual space where some of these issues come to the fore in questions about who decides and who censors what information users have access to and share. In some countries of course the state operates as a censor. This brings us to consideration of our own 'ethical responsibility' as researchers and how it is connected to that of 'thinking ethically'. For example, in the film that charts the development of the social networking space, Facebook (*The Social Network*, 2010) the dichotomy between caring and not caring about ethical issues is concretely presented. In the film the ethical issues surface in the context of business entrepreneurship, capitalism, leisure and the increasing use by social actors of these new, virtual spaces in which as users they had to decide what actions to take and what level of responsibility to accept for any potential ethical consequences. In this changing environment we are all then increasingly faced with more complex – ethical – challenges as researchers, activists and citizens.

In this second edition we suggest that ethics matter now more than they did a decade ago when we identified a 'turn to ethics' in the first edition of this book. This is because of the impact of new information and apparently borderless, digital technologies on our daily lives and the ways in which these have now seeped into everyday life making ethical dilemmas, and questions on right and wrong actions more visible and transparent, or contrarily, more invisible and fraught. Recent abuses of power and unethical actions on the part of professionals entrusted with managing national financial systems provides a pertinent example of more public concerns with ethical behaviours. Such individual concerns can also now be collected, shared and mobilized, using internet based technologies and other mediums and so this becomes a more ethically complex period – but also an exciting one because of the new possibilities for engagement in political and social change. And finally, 'thinking ethically' has become a more urgent concern in our daily lives as it falls upon citizens to detect and confront more readily than before abuses of power they may witness. Making our voices heard in this way reminds us of the links between ethics and power, an examination of which has occupied feminist researchers for many years. Alongside these specific shifts, the growth and popularity of qualitative research over the last ten years together with the new possibilities for dialogue and the democratization of research spaces and the sharing (archiving) of data make this an exciting time to once again contemplate ethics in qualitative research.

Being a feminist researcher

In our continued interest in the interplay between public, social knowledge and private and personal lived experiences we describe ourselves as 'feminist researchers' (Edwards and Ribbens, 1995; Mauthner et al., 2002; Ribbens and Edwards, 1998; Weller and Rogers, 2012). This reflects our concern with conducting research about personal lives, grounded in individual experiences and from a particular theoretical and methodological perspective that we continue to call 'feminist' despite the breadth and evolution of the term (Hesse-Biber and Leavy, 2007; Hughes and Cohen, 2010; Letherby, 2003; McRobbie, 2008; Ramazanoglu and Holland, 2002). The arguments we present here affirm our identities as feminist researchers as we understand and employ the term within our research practices. As Bell notes, 'feminism has been an articulation, set of demands, forces and strategies, the success of which I for one have inherited and benefited from' (1999: 1), an inheritance that continues to have resonance for our professional lives, our epistemological perspective and the qualitative research we undertake (Denzin and Lincoln, 2008).

Our personal and research experiences reveal how ethical concerns are increasing in our everyday lives and arise at all stages of the research process and how our responses to them may not, on reflection, have always been ethical. Nevertheless a feminist perspective provides a key starting point for us and enables us to re-examine and challenge the assumptions that underpin feminist research practices. We argue that researchers need to invoke contextualized reasoning and not just appeal to abstract rules and principles. While all ethical models contribute to ethical knowing our feminist perspectives draw more upon a reflexive model of ethics as identified within Hegelian philosophy to examine ethical practice. Here the negotiation of ethics moves beyond a model of reasoning and rationality and enables the acknowledgment of feelings and emotions. The reflexive self becomes a key constituent in enabling ethical reflection through evaluation and reconsideration in the research process (Fraser, 2000). Thus ethics become part of our relationships, our interactions and our shared values portrayed in the sense of belonging to a community (Benhabib, 1992). It is apparent then that ethics in qualitative research require a combination of theoretical models to enable us to make sense of ethical decision making and a reflexive self to develop and guide ethical thinking. Most vital to the feminist discussions developed here is the theoretical development of the ethics of care. Rosalind Edwards and Melanie Mauthner's chapter establishes a helpful review of ethics and feminist research: theory and practice. Against the deontological, consequential, virtue and justice ethical models, the ethics of care framework can provide practical guidance for ethical thinking in research practice and endorses a feminist, communitarian approach to forge 'collaborative, trusting and non-oppressive relationships between researchers and those studied' (Denzin and Lincoln, 2008: 53).

This edition continues to question the emergence of a professional ethical and 'caring' researcher as an 'ideal type' and explores whether the feminist contribution to this 'ideal type' leads to a perception of ethics as a promise to be a 'caring' professional demonstrated through being a committed and responsible researcher. We are concerned that if the label 'feminist perspective' has become synonymous with ethical ways of working, then it can be misleading and offer more than it can deliver (Mauthner, 2000). Corresponding to the shifts in ethical research and qualitative methods the ethics of care has also received increasing academic attention during the past 10 years and its theoretical application is far reaching (Gilligan, 2011; Held, 2006). At the heart of care ethics is the negotiation between people in caring relationships and this association with the research relationship is questioned in this book in Duncombe and Jessop's chapter on 'faking friendship'. The philosophical position underpinning care ethics view caring relationships as essential for life to flourish and for individuals, groups and communities to reach their potential and achieve a sense of well-being (Held, 2006; Sevenhuijsen, 2002). Within networks of relationships ethical dilemmas arise where varying dimensions of care are negotiated and balanced 'for the self, for others and for relations between these' (Sevenhuijsen, 2002: 132). This perspective does not imply notions of care as altruistic acts or involve judgments on selfish or selfless acts, but looks at the complexity of care as sets of feelings, activities and resources that enable a caring relationship to support one another (McCarthy and Edwards, 2011). Therefore a caring relationship 'involves cooperative well-being of those in the relation and well-being of the relation itself' (Held, 2006: 12). Importantly, it encourages the 'capacities that constitute our humanity and alerts us to the practices that put them at risk' as we strive for ethical responsibility in our research endeavours in increasingly complex times (Gilligan, 2011: 177).

The writing process

This second edition continues the collaboration of members of the Women's Workshop on Qualitative/Household Research and its successful publication record of five edited collections that prioritize exploration of the gap between public and private, and the tensions between personal experiences and the practices of creating academic knowledge. If we trace the history of this research and writing group we can chart the different concepts that we have explored: from research dilemmas (Edwards and Ribbens, 1995; Ribbens and Edwards, 1998), to ethics (Mauthner et al., 2002), power dynamics in academia (Gillies and Lucey, 2007), and understanding caring relations, identities and cultures (Weller and Rogers, 2012). As a group of women working as researchers and lecturers in higher education the workshop provides space to critically appraise and interrogate contemporary 'social problems' alongside in-depth exploration of subjectivity and personal experiences. Currently the workshop consists of 43 members, ranging from doctoral students to professors from over 20 institutions who are based not only in the UK but also in Canada, Denmark, France and Switzerland. The members research and teach from different disciplinary backgrounds that include Anthropology, Geography, Psychology, Sociology and Social Policy and these disciplinary perspectives are applied to areas which include Education, Health and Social Care, Family, Childhood and Youth studies (Weller and Rogers, 2012). The regular meetings and discussions in the Workshop continue to explore ways of investigating and making sense of 'lived experiences' and the meanings of these experiences for both those being researched and the researchers.

All authors in the edited collections are members of the Women's Workshop, but membership styles – for example, attending the workshops – vary. Previous edited collections have established the model of inviting all members to participate in book discussions, irrespective of authorship, and contribute to the development of the book. In this way membership has been likened to the serving of an apprenticeship (Wellers and Rogers, 2012) where the multifaceted experiences, skills and knowledge of writing and research are shared. The initial meetings to develop our ethical thinking for this book provided a supportive forum for us to question standard practice or admit uncertainties and doubts about our own research practice. We could reflect on our actions and discuss practical ways forward. In the first edition we emphasized the contributions that all members of the group made to the development of our ethical thinking; it is important to acknowledge this vital aspect once again, the value of this collective and 'safe' thinking space should not be underestimated.

As a working group it is also interesting to see how our writing collaborations have increasingly benefited from new technologies. In the next Workshop book on Care (Weller and Rogers, 2012), the editors have fostered inclusive collaboration through the use of a shared, members only Internet-based, electronic folder into which recordings of workshop discussions and work-in-progress are uploaded. Interestingly the ethical questions posed by digital data sharing are explored by Natasha Mauthner in a significant new chapter in this edition of the ethics book (Chapter 10). We have benefited from the use of internet conferencing and data sharing in the production of this book too and note this here in order to make visible, explicit and transparent our reliance on different technological tools to facilitate collaborative working and writing. Clearly these new technologies are having an impact on us and our way of working has evolved as a consequence of these developments and possibilities. At the same time, our shared history permits an intimacy that can transfer to the videoconferencing medium – by virtue of web cams virtually 'stepping into' each other's personal writing spaces at home. Such technological tools are being increasingly used in all areas of education and research, prompting questions about the ways in which boundaries between public and private spheres are becoming increasingly disrupted/reconfigured: some of the consequences of these shifts are examined in a new chapter in this edition by Tina Miller (Chapter 2).

In the first edition we chose to write each chapter with a co-author to promote collaboration and cohesion in the practice of sharing and developing our ideas and experiences. During this period of working on the book we held a series of book meetings where our discussions stimulated and provided much food for thought. We valued these precious spaces for 'talk', away from the pressurized working environments of higher education. This second edition – which has been undertaken to address specific changes in the research environment occurring since the first edition – was initially instigated by one of the editors (approaching SAGE Publications with the idea) and the collaboration has been led by the existing editors. The project this time around has involved notifying all the workshop members of the new edition and requesting updated biographies as well as information about any publications or other experiences relevant to this new edition. References (and other changes for example in relation to professional requirements) have also been updated by authors of chapters in the first edition. Our decision to request additional chapters from specific authors has been led by academic and pragmatic reasoning and editorship of the new edition reflects who did the work to get the contract as well as recognition of institutional research demands – rather than ideal notions of collaboration.

This second edition, although presented within the established academic framework of named authors and editors, deemed necessary for our professional credibility, still seeks to challenge academic writing conventions and be more imaginative and radical in our collective writing. We hope that our continued use of personal pronouns and personal research experiences succeed in making this an accessible research text. By presenting our personal, private research stories we seek to get inside research practices and to interrogate, illuminate and share the ethical dilemmas we have encountered.

Outline

The key themes of the book concern ethical responsibility and accountability in applied feminist research practice within offline and online research communities in contexts that increasingly have global reach. The contributors approach the themes of responsibility and accountability from several angles: some challenge the practical reality and desirability of achieving such elevated ethical standards, others question whether being a feminist researcher requires such a caring responsible identity, others propose some practical frameworks for doing things differently, while others explore the implications of new technologies for researcher and participant relationships and the consequences of digital data sharing. The book is intended for a wide readership including all those who want to understand and/or carry out qualitative research in ways that are ethically, theoretically and practically informed. It is divided into 11 chapters that between them interrogate in different ways aspects of ethical research practice: spanning theoretical and practical research examples and concluding by drawing attention to the ethical benefits and costs associated with qualitative research in a more regulated and technologically more democratized era.

In the first chapter Rosalind Edwards and Melanie Mauthner establish the practical and theoretical context for a focus on ethics in conducting feminist research. They consider the growing interest in ethical issues among health, medical and social research as well as legal frameworks and implications from distinct epistemological perspectives. They review current ethical concerns and assess prevalent models. They then consider political approaches to theories of ethics and morality, and feminist theorizing of an ethic of care, and their respective value bases. Finally, they bring a feminist ethics of care to bear on the research process and explicitly elaborate some practical guidelines for researchers to contemplate. Below are outlined the questions they pose, which are implicitly and explicitly addressed across the subsequent chapters.

Questions

1   Who are the people involved in and affected by the ethical dilemmas raised in the research?
2   What is the context for the dilemma in terms of the specific topic of the research and the issues it raises personally and socially for those involved?
3   What are the specific social and personal locations of the people involved in relation to each other?
4   What are the needs of those involved and how are they interrelated?
5   Who am I identifying with, who am I posing as other, and why?
6   What is the balance of personal and social power between those involved?
7   How will those involved understand our actions and are these in balance with our judgement about our own practice?
8   How can we best communicate the ethical dilemmas to those involved, give them room to raise their views, and negotiate with and between them?
9   How will our actions affect relationships between the people involved?

These questions share a concern with care and attention to relationships when doing research (Weller and Rogers, 2012) and have become even more pertinent in the changing research environments in which we find ourselves.

In the next chapter Tina Miller discusses ethical issues related to new technologies and how these have redrawn the contours of research relationships and practices during the last decade. She uses recent research examples to ask how the parallel developments in institutional ethics regulation alongside new (unregulated) research forums pose new questions about ethical research practices as well as configure research relationships in new ways. This is followed by Val Gillies and Pam Alldred who engage with theoretical debates among post-structuralist feminists who have problematized the notion of 'truth' as a justificatory foundation underpinning statements, claims or actions. They argue that this epistemological shift necessitates scrutiny of the intentions underlying feminist research. Focusing in particular on feminist efforts to represent women's voices, initiate personal change and to undermine oppressive knowledge structures, they identify potential ethical dilemmas contained within each approach.

Next, several authors examine in detail the ethical implications of using qualitative methods in the field and how viable or desirable a feminist ethic of working towards a responsible committed research relationship is. Tina Miller and Linda Bell examine notions of what constitutes 'informed' consent. They explore the interplay between access, coercion and motive/motivation in three research projects that encompass issues of gender, power and ethnicity. They examine the role of the gate-keeper in relation to access being granted to those who may be in less powerful positions. They suggest that consent should be ongoing and renegotiated throughout the research process and that researchers need to continually reflect on what it is that research participants have consented to. In a chapter updated to capture more recent professional requirements, Linda Bell and Linda Nutt explore how professional and occupational responsibilities translate into empirical research dilemmas. They focus on the ethical difficulties that accompany divided loyalties towards research and employment, specifically in the health and social care fields. They draw on two examples from different parts of the social work 'practitioner spectrum' to explore issues of 'confidentiality' and 'negotiation'. Maxine Birch and Tina Miller question the dimensions of participation encouraged in research to show how difficulties are encountered during the various phases of their projects. Maxine and Tina argue that carrying out ethically responsible research requires the researcher to negotiate these different levels of participation at the outset of a project. Jean Duncombe and Julie Jessop pick up on the themes of consent and negotiation. They evaluate the idea of 'rapport' that supposedly promotes empathy, genuineness, authenticity and disclosure in 'the good interview', particularly where women talk to women. They argue that as the emotions and emotion work of 'doing rapport' become professionalized and commercialized, the 'skills' of negotiating rapport become a substitute for the awkward ethical problems of negotiating consent.

Wider ethical implications of conducting qualitative research are then explored across the following chapters. Inspired by the Canadian philosopher Loraine Code's writings on ethics and feminist approaches to epistemologies and methodologies Andrea Doucet and Natasha Mauthner describe a research practice aimed at 'knowing well' and 'knowing responsibly'. Drawing on Code's idea that one way of grounding a theoretical discussion on the inseparability of epistemology and ethics into actual research practice is to seek ways of conducting and then presenting 'responsible knowledge of human experience' (Code, 1993: 39), they ask what it means to 'know responsibly' or to 'know well'. In their chapter Pam Alldred and Val Gillies argue that researchers construct participants as modernist subjects through both the interview interaction and in research accounts because conventional ways of negotiating, conducting and transcribing interviews rest on this understanding of 'the individual'. Unsurprisingly, interviewees, as well as researchers, re/produce themselves through the dominant individualist subjecthood, and ethical practice rests on this. This means that we reinforce the Western model of the subject, with its exclusions and oppressive view of its Others, even as we strive to do 'ethical research'. But elements of such constructs may be set to shift as new technologies can enable our participants to 'answer back' (to position the researcher as 'subject') in public forums such as 'blogs' (see Miller, Chapter 2).

In the penultimate chapter Natasha Mauthner explores our ethical and moral responsibilities as researchers to study and not just to use, methods: to understand what they do and what else they are entangled with and to contest and rework the moralisms and normativities that they are situated within. Natasha demonstrates the ways in which (new) digital data sharing methods are being promoted as good science and good research practice on scientific, ethical, moral and political grounds, but she asks good for whom? From whose perspective and on whose terms? This chapter importantly contextualizes contemporary debates about what happens once we collect and analyse our data, and we are reminded that just as in the physical material world, our concerns with pervasive issues of care, control and power remain relevant in virtual electronic spheres too (Gillies and Lucey, 2007). In the concluding chapter, co-written by the editors, the ethical issues of accountability and responsibility are returned to both retrospectively and prospectively as new digital horizons are contemplated.

The ethical issues discussed in this book, while informed by a broadly feminist perspective, are obviously applicable to other aspects of social science research. Although they represent the particular ethical dilemmas that we encountered as researchers working mainly within family and household studies, they are relevant for any research, which aims to increase knowledge using qualitative, personal experience methods. While our endeavour has not been to provide a comprehensive account of ethical dilemmas which may arise, we believe that drawing attention to areas which are not always seen as problematic will open up and expand much needed ethical debates. In the intervening years since publication of the first edition, societies have become ever more complex, and researchers must be able to act reflexively and practice ethically as research dilemmas are set to increase alongside new research possibilities and processes. The nine questions posed earlier in this introduction provide a way of grounding reflections and thinking and acting ethically through aspects of our research plans and practices. Indeed increased research ethics regulation has not diminished the need to formulate guidelines for research, which take a much broader ethical stance and are borne of practice – and it is hoped that the new edition of this book provides a further step towards that goal.

References

Alderson, P. and Morrow, V. (2005) 'Multidisciplinary research ethics review: is it feasible?', *International Journal of Social Research Methodology, 9* (5): 405–17.

Aldred, R. (2008) 'Ethical and political issues in contemporary research relationships', *Sociology,* 42: 887–902.

Bell, V. (1999) *Feminist Imagination.* London: Sage.

Benhabib, S. (1992) *Situating the Self.* Cambridge: Polity Press.

Code, L. (1993) 'Taking subjectivity into account', in L. Alcoff and E. Potter (eds), *Feminist Epistemologies.* New York: Routledge.

Denzin, N.K. and Lincoln, Y.S. (2008) *The Landscape of Qualitative Research: Theories and Issues,* 3rd edn. Thousand Oaks, CA: Sage.

Dingwall, R. (2006) 'Confronting the anti-democrats: the unethical nature of ethical regulation in social science', *Medical Sociology Online,* 1: 51–8.

Edwards, R. and Mauthner, M. (2002) 'Ethics and feminist research: theory and practice', in M. Mauthner, M. Birch, J. Jessop and T. Miller (eds), *Ethics in Qualitative Research.* London: Sage. pp. 14–31.

Edwards, R. and Ribbens, J. (1995) 'Women in families and households: qualitative research', *Women's Studies International Forum,* 18 (3): 247–386.

Fraser, N. (2000) 'Recognition without ethics', in M. Gaber, B. Hanssen and R.L. Walkowitz (eds), *The Turn to Ethics.* London: Routledge.

Gillies, V. and Lucey, H. (eds) (2007) *Power, Knowledge and the Academy. The Institutional is Political.* Basingstoke: Palgrave MacMillan.

Gilligan, C. (2011) *Joining the Resistance.* Cambridge: Polity Press.

Haggerty, K.D. (2004) 'Ethics creep: governing social science research in the name of ethics', *Qualitative Sociology,* 27 (4): 391–414.

Hammersley, M. (2009) 'Against the ethicists: on the evils of ethical regulation', *International Journal of Social Research Methodology,* 12 (3): 211–25.

Held, V. (2006) *The Ethics of Care Personal, Political, and Global.* Oxford: Oxford University Press.

Hedgecoe, A. (2008) 'Research ethics review and the Sociological research relationship', *Sociology,* 42 (5): 857–70.

Hesse-Biber, S.N. and Leavy, P.L. (2007) *Feminist Research Practice. A Primer.* Thousand Oaks, CA: Sage.

Hughes, C. and Cohen, R.L. (2010) 'Feminists really do count: the complexity of feminist methodologies', *International Journal of Social Research Methodology,* 13 (3): 189–96.

Letherby, G. (2003) *Feminist Research Theory and Practice (Feminist Controversies).* Buckingham: Open University Press.

Mattingly, C. (2005) 'Towards a vulnerable ethics of research practice', *Health, 9* (4): 453–71.

Mauthner, M. (2000) 'Snippets and silences: ethics and reflexivity in narratives of sistering', *International Journal Social Research Methodology,* 3 (4): 287–306.

Mauthner, M., Birch, M., Jessop, J. and Miller, T. (2002) *Ethics in Qualitative Research.* London: Sage.

McCarthy, J.R. and Edwards, R. (2011) *Key Concepts in Family Studies.* London: Sage.

McRobbie, A. (2008) *The Aftermath of Feminism; Gender, Culture and Social Change.* London: Sage.

Miller T. and Boulton, M. (2007) 'Changing constructions of informed consent: qualitative research and complex social worlds', *Social Science & Medicine,* 65 (11): 2199–11.

Ramazanoglu, C. and Holland, J. (2002) *Feminist Methodology Challenges and Choices.* London: Sage

Reissman, C.K. (2005) 'Exporting ethics: a narrative about narrative research in South India', *Health,* 9 (4): 473–90.

Ribbens, J. and Edwards, R. (eds) (1998) *Feminist Dilemmas in Qualitative Research, Public Knowledge and Private Lives.* London: Sage.

Richardson, S. and McMullan, M. (2007) 'Research ethics in the UK: what can sociology learn from health?', *Sociology,* 41 (6): 1115–32.

Rundall, E. (2012) 'Ethics in the field: key ethical considerations which inform the use of anonymous asynchronous websurveys in "sensitive" research', in J. MacClancy and A. Fuentes (eds), *Ethics in the Field.* Oxford: Berghahn

Sevenhuijsen, S. (2002) 'A third way? Moralities, ethics and families: an approach through the ethic of care', in A. Carling, S. Duncan and R. Edwards (eds), *Analysing Families: Morality and Rationality in Policy and Practice.* London: Routledge.

Stanley, L. and Wise, S. (2010) 'The ESRC's 2010 framework for research ethics: fit for research purpose?', *Sociological Research Online,* 15 (4): 12.

Tinker, A. (2004) 'National survey of university ethics committees: their role, remit and conduct', *Newsletter, The Association of Research Ethics Committees,* 14: 9–11.

Webster, A., Lewis, G., Brown, N. and Boulton, M. (2004) *Developing a Framework For Social Science Research Ethics: Project Update for ESRC.* York: SATSU, University of York and School of Social Sciences and Law and Oxford Brookes University.

Weindling, P. (2004) *Nazi Medicine and the Nuremberg Trials: From Medical War Crimes to Informed Consent.* Basingstoke: Palgrave Macmillan.

Weller S. and Rogers, C. (2012) *Critical Approaches to Care Understanding Caring Relations, Identities and Cultures.* London: Routledge.

1

Ethics and feminist research: theory and practice

ROSALIND EDWARDS AND MELANIE MAUTHNER

Introduction

Ethics concerns the morality of human conduct. In relation to social research, it refers to the moral deliberation, choice and accountability on the part of researchers throughout the research process. General concern about ethics in social research has grown apace. In the UK, for example, from the late 1980s on, a number of professional associations developed and/or revised ethical declarations for their members. The guidelines available from these bodies include: the Association of Social Anthropologists of the UK and Commonwealth's Ethical Guidelines for Good Research Practice; the British Educational Research Association's Ethical Guidelines for Educational Research; the British Sociological Association's Code of Ethics and Conduct; and the Social Research Association's Ethical Guidelines. Indeed, it would be interesting to trace the genealogy of these statements as they all seem to acknowledge drawing on each other's declarations. Research funders may also produce ethical statements, such as the Economic and Social Research Council (see www.esrc.ac.uk/_images/Framework_for_Research_Ethics_tcm8–4586.pdf), which is the UK's largest organization for funding social research. Academic institutions have set up ethics committees to which academics and students should submit their projects for approval, and research ethics committees have been a feature for social (not just medical) researchers working with and through statutory health organizations for some time now (see www.corec.org.uk). In addition, ethical guidelines have been published that address particular social groups on whom researchers may focus, such as children (see Priscilla Alderson and Virginia Morrow, 2004).

Researchers themselves have written extensively on ethics in social research. While feminist researchers certainly have not been the only authors to undertake reflexive accounts of the politics of empirical research practice, it is fair to say that such reflections have done and do form a substantial feature of feminist publications on the research process. Indeed, some have characterized feminist ethics as a 'booming industry' (Jaggar, 1991). These pieces, however, are not usually explicit investigations of ethics per se. In discursive terms, they are posed in terms of politics rather than ethics. Nonetheless, they represent an empirical engagement with the practice of ethics. As such, they pose the researcher as a central active ingredient of the research process rather than the technical operator that can be inferred by professional ethical codes.

Mary Maynard (1994) has characterized feminist work in this area, in the early stages of second wave scholarship, as being concerned with a critique of dominant 'value-free' modes of doing social research, the rejection of exploitative power hierarchies between researcher and researched, and the espousal of intimate research relationships, especially woman-to-woman, as a distinctly feminist mode of enquiry (see also Jean Duncombe and Julie Jessop, Chapter 7, this volume). In particular, detailed attention was given to the empirical process of collecting data for analysis.

In this chapter we are concerned with ethical perspectives on qualitative social research, from a feminist perspective in particular. We start from the position that an explicit theoretical grounding in a feminist ethics of care would enhance many feminist and other discussions of the research process where such discussions are concerned with ethical dilemmas. Such work, however, rarely draws on these theories, although authors may often implicitly work within or towards just such an ethics. In turn, though, few feminist analyses and elaborations of an ethics of care at the epistemological level (a vibrant feature of feminist political philosophy) pay attention to the empirical process of conducting social research. We feel, however, that feminist discussions of the research process and of the ethics of care have a lot of concerns in common.

Our focus is on philosophical theories of ethics and the difficulties we face as researchers in applying these models in our practice when we conduct research projects. There are clear tensions among the range of models of ethics that we can draw on to negotiate our way through the competing demands of research, both practical and theoretical. We are often left in isolation to ponder and plot our decisions about how best to draw on these perspectives. This chapter connects theoretical ethical models with the complex dilemmas we encounter in the 'doing' of research. We begin our exploration of such issues by laying out explanations for the rise of concern about the practice of ethics in social research. We then pinpoint ethical concerns in social research, which subsequent chapters explore in more depth. We review specific ethical models including deontology, consequentialism, virtue ethics of skills, rights/justice ethics and the ethics of care. After considering some of the care-based ethical debates we suggest some practical guidelines for researchers to consider rooted in a feminist ethics of care.

Why the rise in concern with ethics in social research?

Martyn Hammersley has argued that what he calls 'ethicism' is one of the four main tendencies operating in contemporary qualitative social research. The others are empiricism, instrumentalism and postmodernism. Although not explicitly referring to feminist researchers, he perhaps has them, among others, in mind when he points to:

> ... a tendency to see research almost entirely in ethical terms, as if its aim were to achieve ethical goals or to exemplify ethical ideals ... Whereas previously ethical considerations were believed to set boundaries to what researchers could do in pursuit of knowledge, now ethical considerations are treated by some as constituting the very rationale of research. For example, its task becomes the promotion of social justice. (Hammersley, 1999: 18)

Hammersley sees this posing of research as ethics as leading to the neglect of research technique – the better or worse ways of carrying out the processes of research in terms of the quality of research knowledge that they generate (see also Hammersley and Traianou, 2012). He also sees the dominance of ethicism as attributable to the effects of the tendencies of instrumentalism – the idea that the task of research is to relate to policymaking and practice (on which see also Hammersley, 2004; Simons, 1995) – and of postmodernism, especially the 'turn' to irony and scepticism. For Hammersley, they both lead to the down-playing or questioning of the possibility and desirability of knowledge, and he argues that a concern with ethics has expanded to fill this space. We feel, however, that there may well be other factors at work in the rise in concern with research ethics. In its institutionalized form we see this as, at least in part, related to a concern with litigation.

An overt and similar preoccupation in professional ethical statements or guidelines, given the way they draw on each other, is with the contract between research funder, or sponsor, and the researcher. There are two main linked issues here. First, there is a concern that researchers should retain their academic freedom. They should not accept contractual conditions that conflict with ethical practice, such as confidentiality of data and protection of participants' interests, and should consider carefully any attempt to place restrictions on their publication and promotion of their findings. Indeed, there has been concern about the way that government departments can place restrictions on research that they fund, requiring researchers to submit draft reports, publications and so on, so that the department in question can vet these (for examples, see *Times Higher,* 31 March 2000, 31 March 2001), and the way that government priorities and policy concerns are driving research funding (see, for example, http://www.newstatesman.com/blogs/cultural-capital/2011/03/society-research-ahrc-cuts).

Second, and conversely, we can also detect a concern that researchers need to protect themselves from any legal consequences that might arise if they unwittingly contractually agree to research funders' restrictions and then break that agreement. It is here that we also see the possibility of litigation concerns on the part of the academic institutions that employ researchers: this is why these institutions have a vested interest in these posed ethical issues, for they are implicated in the contractual obligations. Institutional preoccupations with ethics can sometimes appear to be more premised on avoiding potentially costly litigation than with ethical practice itself. Moreover, the pressures of time, bureaucratic administration and funding, our training as social scientists and the prevailing ethos of professional detachment can all militate against our giving ethical dilemmas the focused attention that they require in the research process.

There are no laws (at least in the UK) requiring researchers to submit their proposals and modes of practice to ethics committees, and professional association guidelines hold no legal status. Like journalists, however, researchers do not enjoy the protection of the law if they seek to keep their data confidential when its disclosure is subpoenaed (see discussion in Feenan, 2002). Furthermore, as Linda Bell and Linda Nutt discuss in Chapter 5, where researchers work within, or are associated with, a welfare professional context where disclosure of certain types of data is mandatory, such as social work and an interviewee revealing child abuse, they may be required to reveal their source.

Institutional concerns about legal redress being pursued by research participants are equally an issue, especially in the UK with untested – in this area at least – copyright, designs and patents acts (http://www.qualidata.essex.ac.uk/). This legislation concerns breaching interviewees' copyright in their spoken words in publication of data collected from them. Professional association ethical statements also place an emphasis, in an absolutist way, on researchers' responsibilities for ensuring informed consent to partici-pation in research, protecting research participants from potential harm (and some-times also wider society), and ensuring their privacy by maintaining confidentiality and anonymity. The research ethics policies at UK universities thus usually require researchers to obtain written ethical approval from any collaborating organizations involved in the research and to ask research participants to sign a consent form basi-cally stating that they have had the nature and purpose of the research explained to them and that they fully and freely consent to participate in the study. Such an approach implies an either/or position: either consent is informed, participants are protected, and so on, or they are not, as Tina Miller and Linda Bell (Chapter 4), and Maxine Birch and Tina Miller (Chapter 6) write about in this volume. It also implies that all the ethical issues involved in a research project can be determined at the start of the project being carried out, that any potential harm may be offset by research participants' stated willingness, and that an ethics committee sanctioned project is by definition an ethical one. The aim appears to be to avoid ethical dilemmas through asserting formalistic principles, rather than providing guidance on how to deal with them. Indeed, while some pose codes of ethical practice as alerting social researchers to ethical issues (for example, Punch, 1986), others argue that they may have the effect of forestalling rather than initiating researchers' reflexive and continuing engagement with ethical research practice (for example, Mason, 1996).

We are not suggesting, however, that such institutionalized concerns with litiga-tion are necessarily what motivates social researchers in their considerations about, and reflections on, ethics, both here in this book and elsewhere. Nor would we agree with Hammersley that their/our focus on ethics is driven by instrumentalism or by postmodernism in the terms in which he poses the latter, as ironic scepticism. Rather, we would see it as rooted in a genuine and legitimate concern with issues of power. We acknowledge that research is a political, rather than neutral, process – as Val Gillies and Pam Alldred describe in Chapter 3 – in a world that is characterized by awareness of difference and a questioning of the motives and rights of 'experts' to define the social world and to proscribe templates for what constitutes the 'correct' course of action (see Edwards and Glover, 2001).

Ethical concerns in social research

As we noted earlier, there is an extensive literature on ethics in social research. The Social Research Association Ethical Guidelines, for example, contains over 120 key references (www.the-sra.org.uk/). These cover a range of aspects of ethical practice. There are numerous other examples of publications concerned with ethics in social research as well, including a strand of feminist pieces. Indeed, discussions of the research process related to ethical issues have become a feature of feminist research, especially qualitative empirical work.

Ethical decisions arise throughout the entire research process, from conceptualization and design, data gathering and analysis, and report, and literature on the topic reflects this. Regarding access, the issue of informed consent has been subject to fierce debate among qualitative social researchers generally: in particular the ethics of carrying out covert research (see Calvey, 2008; Spicker, 2011) and the nature and time frame of consent (David et al., 2001; Edwards and Weller, 2012). The time frame involved in assessing the benefits or harm of social research has also been an issue in discussion (for example, Wise, 1987). There have also been debates among feminists concerning the ethical merits and consequences of qualitative versus quantitative methods (see review in Maynard, 1994), and the ethical problems involved in archiving qualitative data for secondary analysis have been raised (Parry and Mauthner, 2008; as well as Mauthner, Chapter 10, this volume).

The epistemologies of the theoretical perspective informing research have also been discussed as generating ethical questions, allied to debates around research as involved empowerment or distanced knowledge production (see Andrea Doucet and Natasha S. Mauthner, Chapter 8). The issue of the ethics of epistemology has been the focus of much debate within feminism, and feminists have also engaged in debate with other perspectives on this topic (see, for example, Maynard 1994). Feminist work in this vein include arguments that ethical issues are inherent in the researcher's definition of social reality; that is the epistemologies of the theoretical perspective framing research questions, analysis of data, and writing up of findings. Sue Wise (1987), for example, argues that the 'cognitive authority' of the researcher's view in producing knowledge, and assessments as to whether or not that knowledge is empowering, are knotty ethical issues. She poses a series of questions, including: who decides, and how, what counts as knowledge? What if one research group's empowerment is another's disempowerment? Hilary Rose (1994) has unpacked the way the scientific knowledge system is entwined with other power systems, and shaped by a masculinist instrumental rationality that denies emotion. In contrast, Rose puts forward a feminist epistemology that 'thinks from caring' and that is 'centred on the domains of interconnectedness and caring rationality' (1994: 33). Underlying these sorts of discussions and debates over ethical concerns in the research literature are various models of how to understand and resolve ethical issues.

Ethical models

Professional association ethical guidelines and textbook discussions of social research ethics usually pose the sorts of ethical issues outlined above as being formed around conflicting sets of rights claims and competing responsibilities. Steiner Kvale (1996, 2008) outlines three ethical models that provide the broader frameworks within which researchers reflect on these issues. These are derived from mainstream political philosophy and draw out their implications for conducting social research.

In the 'duty ethics of principles' or deontological model, research is driven by universal principles such as honesty, justice and respect. Actions are governed by principles that should not be broken, and judged by intent rather than consequences. As Kvale points out, however, 'carried to its extreme, the intentional position can become a moral absolutism with intentions of living up to absolute principles of right action, regardless of the human consequences of an act' (1996: 121).

The 'utilitarian ethics of consequences' model prioritizes the 'goodness' of outcomes of research such as increased knowledge. Thus the rightness or wrongness of actions is judged by their consequences rather than their intent. This model is underlain by a universalist cost-benefit result pragmatism. In extremis, though, as Kvale notes, such a position can mean that 'the ends come to justify the means' (1996: 122).

In contrast to the two universalist models above, a 'virtue ethics of skills' model questions the possibility of laying down abstract principles. Rather, it stresses a contextual or situational ethical position, with an emphasis on the researchers' moral values and ethical skills in reflexively negotiating ethical dilemmas: 'Ethical behaviour is seen less as the application of general principles and rules, than as the researcher internalising moral values' (Kvale, 1996: 122). Researchers' ethical intuitions, feelings and reflective skills are emphasized, including their sensibilities in undertaking dialogue and negotiation with the various parties involved in the research.

Feminist writers on ethics, however, have put forward another basis for reflecting on ethical issues (although not specifically in relation to research), with an emphasis on care and responsibility rather than outcomes, justice or rights. In other words, this is a model that is focused on particular feminist-informed social *values*. Elisabeth Porter (1999) argues that there are three interrelated features of feminist thinking on ethics: personal experience, context and nurturant relationships. Daily life dilemmas are shaped by social divisions of gender, class and ethnicity: experiences of these dilemmas generate different ethical perspectives. These perspectives are not only obtained in particular contexts, but those contexts also alter and inform the ethical dilemmas that we face as researchers and the range and appropriate choices in resolving them. These dilemmas are not abstract but rooted in specific relationships that involve emotions, and which require nurturance and care for their ethical conduct.

While some, such as Elisabeth Porter, see a clear distinction between the virtue ethics of skills and the value-based feminist model, our own stance is that there are some overlaps as well as distinctions between the two. Both stress context and situation rather than abstract principles, and dialogue and negotiation rather than rules and autonomy. A virtue skills model, however, can imply that the skills that researchers acquire through practice in making ethical decisions are impartial and neutral 'good' (virtue) research standards, even with awareness of particular context. In contrast, a value-based model explicitly advocates a 'partial' stance based on analysis of power relations between those involved in the research and society more broadly, and admits emotion into the ethical process. Here, partiality refers to the importance of acknowledging power relations and taking up a position:

> Ethics encourages partiality, the specific response to distinctiveness ... partiality does not preclude impartiality ... partiality varies according to the [relationships] involved ... responding to this particularity is fundamental to ethics. (Porter, 1999: 30)

A contingent virtue and/or value, rather than universalist approach has become predominantly advocated in texts discussing ethics in social research (Blaxter et al., 2010; Davidson and Layder, 1994). Professional association guidelines, however, often weave a difficult balance between various models. So, for example, the British Sociological Association's Statement of Ethical Practice 'recognises that it will be necessary to make ... choices on the basis of principles and values, and the (often conflicting) interests of those involved'. While difficult balancing acts will always remain, it may be that some awkward tensions would be eased by a theoretical and feminist approach to ethical dilemmas, as we elaborate later.

Tensions between different ethical models or situational shades of grey, however, do not often seem to be apparent on the part of ethics committees who vet research proposals. Moreover, some researchers seem to want them to apply abstract universalistic principles. Ann Oakley (1992), for example, in discussing her experiences with hospital and health authority ethics committees, points to evidence concerning inconsistencies in their judgements. Such criticism may well be fairly made, but it also implies that there are universal principles and abstract criteria that can be applied regardless of situational context. This is a puzzling stance for researchers such as Oakley, whose research practice has been informed by feminism. Indeed, much feminist work addressing aspects of ethical research practice that we discuss below draws on complex situationally informed debates.

There are, nonetheless, contrasts and tensions between positions within any virtue or value based ethical approach – although what they have in common is an ethical approach that calls for attention to specificity and context. These range from complete postmodern relativism through to post-traditional positions (such as feminist, communitarian, new critical theory) that have a particular set of ethical values underlying their situated approach. Even with feminist or feminist-inspired value approaches to ethics there are significant debates around issues of care and power, focused around relationships with 'the Other', as we address below.

There are also debates about the extent to which justice-based ethical models and an ethics of care are in conflict, interrelated or can be reframed (see Porter, 1999; Ruddick, 1996; Sevenhuijsen, 1998). Eva Feder Kittay (2001) summarizes the main elements of an ethics of care in contrast with an ethics of justice, which we have adapted from a medical/health environment to a research context (see Table 1.1).

In contrast, Selma Sevenhuijsen (1998) has gone further to argue for a reformulation of the concept of justice so that it is no longer opposed to or separate from, and thus does not require reconciling with, an ethic of care. Feminist criticisms of justice from care perspectives, she says, have been directed towards a specific variety: that of liberal, rational, distributive models of justice. In her view, discussion about the compatibility of care and justice can usefully be freed from these parameters. There is a need to have concepts of justice that are not framed exclusively in distributive, sameness or universal terms, but which take into account situations and consequences. Thus Sevenhuijsen fundamentally reframes justice to see it as a process rather than

Table 1.1 Ethical models

Kittay's discussion, however, poses the two ethics as if they were in opposition to one another. Sarah Ruddick (1996) has taken a similar position, arguing that ethics of care and justice cannot be subsumed under each other and that they cannot be integrated, because in her view justice depends on a notion of the individual as a detached rather than relational being. Nevertheless, Ruddick also argues that justice as well as care applies to the moral domain. Others regard justice and care as complementary, and argue that they need to be integrated in thinking about moral issues (see review in Porter, 1999). This proposition retains the integrity of each ethical framework, as laid out in the Table 1.1, but sees them each as providing enabling conditions of moral adequacy for the other ethic.

Care	Justice
Self as self-in-relation	Autonomous self
Characteristic of informal contexts	Characteristic of formal contexts
Emphasis on contextual reasoning	Emphasis on principles
• Situations as defining moral problems and resolutions	• Hierarchy of values
• Use of narrative	• Calculation of moral rights and wrongs
Emphasis on responsibilities to others and ourselves	Emphasis on rights and equality
Acceptance of inevitable dependencies	Emphasis and valuing of independence
Moral importance of personal connections	Impartiality valued
Values and attempts to maintain connections among individuals	Protects against or adjudicates conflict between individuals
Temptations:	Temptations:
• Sacrifice or loss of self	• Failure to be merciful
• Failure to recognize autonomy of other	• Over-reliance on impersonal institutions
• Over-identification with other	• Overly rule-bound
Harm when connections are broken	Harm when there is a clash between individuals

rules: a process involving an ethics of care in a situated way based on values of reconciliation, reciprocity, diversity and responsibility, and with an awareness of power. Justice thus does not stand alone but is simultaneously incorporated into, and informed by, care. It is within this understanding of justice as part of care that we proceed to examine care-based ethical debates and then generate our own guidelines for ethical research practice.

Care-based ethical debates

Kittay (2001) refers to care and caring as a labour, an attitude and a 'virtue' (or value in our terms). A central catalyst to writings on a feminist ethics of care was the work of Carol Gilligan. She first used the concept in her work on gender differences in moral reasoning between boys and girls (Gilligan, 1983), in which she argued that girls and women deliberate in a 'different [ethical] voice' to boys/men because they find themselves dealing with dilemmas over their own desires and the needs of others, and the responsibilities that they feel for those within their web of connections in ways that are gendered. Other feminist work addressing a feminist ethics of care includes Nel Noddings' (1984) discussion of the central places of responsibility and relationships as an empathetic way of responding to others in an ethical manner; and Joan Tronto's (1993) analysis of the way that the practical, relational, caring work primarily undertaken by women is excluded from mainstream moral and political philosophy and theorizing because it is regarded as instinctual practice rather than willed action based on rules.

The work of these and other feminist theorizers in the field, however, has rarely been applied to a consideration of ethics in social research. Norman Denzin (1997) provides a notable exception here. He has put forward a strong argument for feminist theorizing to inform ethical research, expressly in relation to ethnography and specifically addressing the writing of it. As part of his critique of traditional voyeuristic and utilitarian knowledge-making protocol, Denzin takes issue with those who, such as Martyn Hammersley, want a focus on 'better' techniques, and who pose the 'turn' to postmodernism as if it is a choice or an option (see also Denzin and Lincoln, 2011). Rather, for Denzin, we inhabit and *live* in just such a cultural moment, and one in which morality and ethics are central issues:

> The ethnographic culture has changed because the world that ethnography confronts has changed. Disjuncture and difference define this global, postmodern cultural economy we all live in ... Global and local legal processes have problematicized and erased the personal and institutional distance between the ethnographer and those he or she writes about ... We do not own the field notes we make about those we study. We do not have an undisputed warrant to study anyone or anything ... The writer can no longer presume to be able to present an objective, noncontested account of the other's experiences ... ethnography is a moral, allegorical, and therapeutic project. Ethnography is more than the record of human experience. The ethnographer writes tiny moral tales. (Denzin, 1997: xii–xiv)

Denzin castigates modernist ethical models as resting 'on a cognitive model that privileges rational solutions to ethical dilemmas (the rationalist fallacy), and it presumes that humanity is a single subject (the distributive fallacy) ... This rights-, justice-, and acts-based system ignores the relational dialogical nature of human interaction' (1997: 271, 273). The universalist ethical models of duty and of utilitarianism are rejected and replaced by a personally involved care-based ethical system, based on a body of work Denzin refers to as the 'feminist, communitarian ethical model'. He sees this work as defined by its contention that:

> ... community is ontologically and morally prior to persons, and that dialogical communication is the basis of the moral community ... A personally involved, politically committed ethnographer is presumed and not the morally neutral observer of positivism ... In this framework every moral act is a contingent accomplishment measured against the ideals of a feminist, interactive, and moral universalism. (Denzin, 1997: 274)

Denzin explicitly draws on the work of feminist political theorists and philosophers such as Patricia Hill Collins (1991) and Syela Benhabib (1992). From a Black feminist position, Hill Collins critiques the traditional, positivist, masculinist and Euro-centric knowledge-making enterprise. She offers four criteria for interpreting truth and knowledge claims of social science: the first focuses on the primacy of concrete lived experience; the second on the use of dialogue in assessing knowledge claims; the third on the ethic of caring; and the fourth on the ethic of personal accountability. Hill Collins' ethical system for knowledge validation is concerned with ethics of care and accountability that are rooted in values of personal expressiveness, emotions and empathy. These are made accountable through an interactive 'call-and-response' dialogue. In such a mode, there is no need to 'de-centre' others in order to centre our own 'expert' voice and arguments adversarially. Rather, the centre of discussion is constantly and appropriately pivoted, so that participants can all exchange wisdoms, and acknowledge that experience and knowledge are partial at the same time as they are valid. Benhabib reworks Habermas' ideas around discourse ethics (including through her notion of 'open-ended moral conversations' which Maxine Birch and Tina Miller refer to in Chapter 6), to reject traditional liberal, abstract, autonomous and rights-based justice reasoning as the basis for moral deliberation. She argues that ethics is about concrete rather than generalized situations, in which relations of care belong at the centre rather than the margins. What is moral and ethical is arrived at through an active and situationally contingent exchange of experiences, perspectives and ideas across differences (particularly around gender, but also in terms of other social divisions). She puts forward 'moral respect' as 'symmetrical reciprocity', comprising a relation of symmetry between self and other that involves looking at issues from the point of view of others or putting ourselves in the place of others.

As Denzin (1997) conceives it, the personally involved care-based ethical system for social research that he derives from feminist communitarianism, privileges emotionality in the ethical decision-making process. It presumes a dialogic rather than autonomous view of self, and asks the researcher 'to step into the shoes of the persons being studied' (Denzin, 1997: 273) and build connected and transformative, participatory and empowering relationships with those studied. Researchers need to be what is often termed 'with and for the Other'. Ethnographic writing should be 'a vehicle for readers to discover moral truths about themselves' (Denzin, 1997: 284) and should be judged for its ability to 'provoke transformations and changes in the public and private spheres of everyday life' (Denzin, 1997: 275).

This view necessarily is a simplification of the complex and valuable arguments that Denzin makes, as well as those of the 'feminist communitarian' thinkers upon whom he draws. Parts of them, however, may be subject to the sorts of questions Sue Wise (1987) directed at previous feminist work (see earlier). What if one research group's empowerment is another's disempowerment, especially where both are considered oppressed groups? What happens if, as Donna Luff (1999) experienced in her study of women in the moral lobby, we find ourselves researching individuals or groups whom we dislike and/or consider socially damaging even if oppressed? And what if what is beneficial at one moment turns out to be the opposite in the long-run? Indeed, Denzin seems to imply that research following the feminist communitarian ethical model will not face these sorts of ethical questions:

> This framework presumes a researcher who builds collaborative, reciprocal, trusting, and friendly relations with those studied. This individual would not work in a situation in which the need for compensation from injury could be created. (1997: 275)

Other feminist theorists have criticized the approaches on which Denzin's work is based. Iris Young (1997), for example, challenges feminist and other ethical frameworks that imply a relation of symmetry between self and other, which involve looking at issues from the point of view of others or putting ourselves in the place of others (including Benhabib's notion of symmetrical reciprocity). The 'stepping into each other's shoes' that Denzin recommends assumes an easy reversibility of positions that is neither possible nor desirable according to Young. This is because individuals have particular histories and occupy social positions that make their relations asymmetrical. Young points out the difficulties of imagining another's point of view or seeing the world from their standpoint when we lack their personal and group history. Instead, Young argues for 'asymmetrical reciprocity', which means accepting that there are aspects of another person's position that we do not understand, yet are open to asking about and listening to. Asymmetrical reciprocity involves dialogue that enables each subject to understand each other across differences without reversing perspectives or identifying with each other. In other words, rather than ignoring or blurring power positions, ethical practice needs to pay attention to them. (See also Maxine Birch and Tina Miller, Chapter 6, for a further critique of attempting open-ended moral conversations.)

Selma Sevenhuijsen's (1998) work on an ethics of care also raises shortcomings in Denzin's particular feminist-derived position on ethics in social research. Like Denzin, she also regards postmodernism as a social condition based on diversity, ambiguity and ambivalence, which brings moral and ethical issues to the fore. Like Young, however, she does not accept 'being with and for the Other' as a sufficient basis for formulating ethics. For her, though, this is because this stance does not capture the concrete relations of dependency and connection that are central to an ethics of care.

> First of all, the ethics of care involves different moral concepts: responsibilities and relationships rather than rules and rights. Secondly, it is bound to concrete situations rather than being formal and abstract. And thirdly, the ethics of care can be described as a moral activity, the 'activity of caring', rather than as a set of principles which can simply be followed. The central question in the ethics of care, how to deal with dependency and responsibility, differs radically from that of rights ethics: what are the highest normative principles and rights in situations of moral conflict? (Sevenhuijsen, 1998: 107)

So, while Denzin calls for a care-based ethical system to shape the research process, he slips away from fully recognizing its implications back towards the autonomous separateness he rejects.

Furthermore, while Denzin seems similar to Sevenhuijsen in seeing emotionality and empathy as central to ethical judgement, unlike her he does not also stress the need for caring and '*care*ful' judgement to be based on practical knowledge and attention to detail in the context of time and place. Within Sevenhuijsen's version of an ethics of care, ethics thus needs to be interpreted and judged in specific contexts of action – it is fundamentally contingent practice-based.

Feminist ethics of care and practical guidelines

Feminist political theorists, who advocate an ethic of care perspective on issues, argue that a feminist approach to ethics should not seek to formulate moral principles that stand above power and context. Ethics is about *how* to deal with conflict, disagreement and ambivalence rather than attempting to eliminate it. A feminist ethics of care can help researchers think about how they do this by 'illuminating more fully the sources of moral dilemmas and formulating meaningful epistemological strategies in order to deal with these dilemmas, even if only on a temporary basis' (Sevenhuijsen, 1998: 16). The importance and centrality of attention to specificity and context means that ethics cannot be expected to be a source of absolute norms. It has to connect to concrete practices and dilemmas, as the chapters in the rest of this book illustrate. It is attention to these issues that can provide the guidelines for ethical action.

Thus we conclude with a – contingent – attempt to generate some guidelines for ethical research practice arising out of a feminist ethics of care, indicating where they are elaborated empirically in following chapters by our co-contributors. Importantly, it should be noted that when we refer to 'the people involved' below, we include the researcher as well as participants, funders, gate-keepers and others. We suggest that these guidelines framed as questions can be useful for researchers to consider in deliberating dilemmas, choosing from alternative courses of action, and being accountable for the course of action that they ultimately decide to pursue.

- Who are the people involved in and affected by the ethical dilemma raised in the research?

  Maxine Birch and Tina Miller address these issues in their chapter on participation in the research process (Chapter 6).
- What is the context for the dilemma in terms of the specific topic of the research and the issues it raises personally and socially for those involved?

  Andrea Doucet and Natasha Mauthner consider this in their chapter on how we come to produce ethical knowledge (Chapter 8).
- What are the specific social and personal locations of the people involved in relation to each other?

  Linda Bell and Linda Nutt explore these elements in their discussion of professional and research loyalties (Chapter 5), as do Andrea Doucet and Natasha S. Mauthner in the context of analysing data (Chapter 8).
- What are the needs of those involved and how are they interrelated?

  Jean Duncombe and Julie Jessop delve into this issue in their examination of emotions and 'rapport' in interviews (Chapter 7).
- Who am I identifying with, who am I posing as other, and why?

  Linda Bell and Linda Nutt tackle this question in their chapter on divided loyalties to professional considerations and research etiquette (Chapter 5). Pam Alldred and Val Gillies' chapter on the implicit notion of the modernist subject that researchers work with in interview-based research also touches on some of these issues (Chapter 9).
- What is the balance of personal and social power between those involved?

  Val Gillies and Pam Alldred address this question explicitly in their chapter about research as a political tool (Chapter 3), as does Tina Miller in her chapter on reconfiguring research relationships (Chapter 2). This question is also addressed by Linda Bell and Linda Nutt in their chapter which focuses on conflicting expectations when researchers are also working professionals in other spheres – health, welfare and social work in particular (Chapter 5).
- How will those involved understand our actions and are these in balance with our judgement about our own practice?

  Both Val Gillies and Pam Alldred (Chapter 3), and Jean Duncombe and Julie Jessop (Chapter 7) write about these issues in their chapters in relation to the intentions researchers espouse for their research on the one hand, and regarding the intimacy between researcher and respondent that can resemble friendship on the other.
- How can we best communicate the ethical dilemmas to those involved, give them room to raise their views, and negotiate with and between them?

  Both Tina Miller and Linda Bell (Chapter 4), and Maxine Birch and Tina Miller (Chapter 6) consider these issues in the context of seeking access to participants and gaining their consent to taking part in research projects.
- How will our actions affect relationships between the people involved?

  Both Linda Bell and Linda Nutt (Chapter 5), and Jean Duncombe and Julie Jessop (Chapter 7) address this question in their respective chapters: in relation to professional and research motivations, and to forms of friendship that are created in the research process.

We hope that other researchers will find these guidelines useful for consideration in deliberating ethical dilemmas in their research practice. We are not claiming that this list of guidelines for working with a feminist ethics of care in social research constitutes a definitive model. Rather, we see it as work in progress. We offer it here in the spirit of working towards a means of implementing a feminist ethics of care as a guide for how ethical dilemmas in empirical research may be practically resolved.

References

Alderson, P. and Morrow, V. (2004) *Ethics, Social Research and Consulting with Children and Young People.* Barkingside: Barnardos.

Benhabib, S. (1992) *Situating the Self: Gender, Community and Postmodernism in Contemporary Ethics.* New York: Routledge.

Blaxter, L., Hughes, C. and Tight, M. (2010) *How to Research.* Buckingham: The Open University Press.

Calvey, D. (2008) 'The art and politics of convert research: doing "situated ethics" in the field', *Sociology*, 42 (5): 905–18.

David, M., Edwards, R. and Alldred, P. (2001) 'Children and school-based research: "informed consent" or "educated consent"?', *British Educational Research Journal*, 27 (3): 347–65.

Davidson, J.O. and Layder, D. (1994) *Methods, Sex and Madness.* London: Routledge.

Denzin, N.K. (1997) *Interpretive Ethnography: Ethnographic Practices for the 21st Century.* London: Sage.

Denzin, N.K. and Lincoln, Y.S. (2011) 'Introduction: the discipline and practice of qualitative research', in N.K. Denzin and Y.S. Lincoln (eds), *The Sage Handbook of Qualitative Research*, 4th edn. London: Sage. pp. 1–33.

Edwards, R. and Glover, J. (2001) 'Risk, citizenship and welfare: an introduction', in R. Edwards and J. Glover (eds), *Risk and Citizenship: Key Issues in Welfare.* London: Routledge. pp. 1–18.

Edwards, R. and Weller, S. (2012, forthcoming) 'The death of a participant: moral obligation, consent and care in qualitative longitudinal research', in K. ti Riele and R. Brookes (eds), *Negotiating Ethical Challenges in Youth Research.* Abingdon: Routledge.

Feenan, D. (2002) 'Researching paramilitary violence in Northern Ireland', *International Journal of Social Research Methodology: Theory and Practice*, 5 (2): 147–63.

Gilligan, C. (1983) *In A Different Voice: Psychological Theory and Women's Development.* Cambridge, MA: Harvard University Press.

Hammersley, M. (1999) 'Some reflections on the current state of qualitative research', *Research Intelligence*, 70: 16–18.

Hammersley, M. (2004) *Educational Research: Policy-Making and Practice.* London: Paul Chapman.

Hammersley, M. and Traianou, A. (2012) *Ethics in Qualitative Research: Controversies and Contexts.* London: Sage.

Hill Collins, R. (1991) *Black Feminist Thought.* London: Routledge.

Jaggar, A. (1991) 'Feminist ethics: projects, problems, prospects', in C. Card (ed.), *Feminist Ethics.* Lawrence, KS: University Press of Kansas. pp. 78–104.

Kittay, E.F. (2001) 'Ethics of care workshop: tools and methods in bioethics', EURESCO Biomedicine Within the Limits of Human Existence Conference, Davos, Switzerland, 8–13 September.

Kvale, S. (1996) *Interviews: An Introduction to Qualitative Research Interviewing.* London: Sage.

Kvale, S. (2008) *Interviews: Learning the Craft of Qualitative Research Interviewing.* London: Sage.

Luff, D. (1999) 'Dialogue across the divides: "moments of rapport" and power in feminist research with anti-feminist women', *Sociology*, 33 (4): 687–703.

Mason, J. (1996) *Qualitative Researching.* London: Sage.

Maynard, M. (1994) 'Methods, practice and epistemology: the debate about feminism and research', in M. Maynard and J. Purvis (eds), *Researching Women's Lives From a Feminist Perspective.* London: Taylor & Francis. pp. 10–26.

Noddings, N. (1984) *Caring: A Feminine Approach to Ethics and Moral Education.* Berkeley, CA: University of California Press.

Oakley, A. (1992) *Social Support and Motherhood.* Oxford: Blackwell.

Parry, O. and Mauthner, N. (2008) 'Whose data are they anyway? Practical, legal and ethical issues in archiving qualitative data', *Sociology*, 38 (1): 139–52.

Porter, E. (1999) *Feminist Perspectives on Ethics.* Harlow: Pearson Education.

Punch, M. (1986) *Politics and Ethics of Fieldwork.* London: Sage.

Rose, H. (1994) *Love, Power and Knowledge: Towards a Feminist Transformation of the Sciences.* Cambridge: Polity Press.

Ruddick, S. (1996) *Maternal Thinking: Towards a Politics of Peace.* Boston, MA: Beacon Press.

Sevenhuijsen, S. (1998) *Citizenship and the Ethics of Care: Feminist Considerations on Justice, Morality and Politics.* London: Routledge.

Simons, H. (1995) 'The politics and ethics of educational research in England: contemporary issues', *British Journal of Educational Research*, 21 (4): 435–49.

Spicker, P. (2011) 'Ethical covert research', *Sociology,* 45 (1): 118–33.

Tronto, J. (1993) *Moral Boundaries: A Political Argument for an Ethic of Care.* London: Routledge.

Wise, S. (1987) 'A framework for discussing ethical issues in feminist research: a review of the literature', in V. Griffiths, M. Humm, R. O'Rourke, et al. (eds), *Writing Feminist Biography 2: Using Life Histories, Studies in Sexual Politics No. 19.* Manchester: University of Manchester Press.

Young, I.M. (1997) *Intersecting Voices: Dilemmas of Gender, Political Philosophy and Policy.* Princeton, NJ: Princeton University Press.

2

Reconfiguring research relationships: regulation, new technologies and doing ethical research

TINA MILLER

Introduction

This chapter examines the changing environment that researchers increasingly encounter as they plan, design and undertake qualitative research. This changing environment emerges as a consequence of the growth of ethical review and regulation alongside new technological and computer–mediated research advancements. In combination, these developments have reconfigured in significant ways aspects of the research enterprise in the 10 years since publication of the first edition of this book. The spread of ethical regulation has attracted critical attention and raised concerns among research communities, while developments in technologies have redrawn the contours of research relationships and practices in innovative and often beneficial ways: but also in ways which pose new ethical questions in relation to our understandings of researcher-participant responsibilities and issues around participation, power and public and private domains. These parallel developments will be explored in this chapter by reflecting on two (companion) research projects which used the same qualitative longitudinal research design, but were conducted 10 years apart. In the years which elapsed between the first (Transition to Motherhood) study and second (Transition to Fatherhood) study, ethical governance and regulation of social science research increased and new information technologies changed research practices and possibilities, which will be demonstrated through examples from the studies. Strategies to manage some of these new ethical issues will be discussed as well as critical consideration given to the parts of the research process which fall under the gaze of the ethics committee and those emergent, context specific and often more problematic aspects, which do not. Paradoxes are encountered as consideration is given to what should and should not, and what can and cannot, be regulated in rapidly changing offline and online research worlds.

As outlined earlier (see the Introduction), a major development in social science research in recent years has been a growth in ethics frameworks, review, regulation and governance, described by Haggerty (2004) as 'ethics creep'. This has been accompanied by debate about what this all signals in terms of support, 'surveillance' or 'censorship' of researchers and knowledge production more generally (Dingwall, 2006; Haggerty, 2004; Stanley and Wise, 2010). In the debates that have ensued no one seems to be arguing that thinking and behaving ethically is not a fundamental tenet of good research practice: but questions of how far this should be/can be enforced, mandatory and regulated, and by whom and at what point in the research cycle remain. One of the key issues raised in relation to the development, role and constitution of research ethics committees hinges on the fact that 'ethical questions have a particular character of "unknowability"' and that ethics review has been based on a model of 'anticipatory' and 'pre-study review', which sits at odds with qualitative research (Dixon-Woods et al., 2007: 801; Richardson and McMullan, 2007). Anticipatory review of research proposals – before a study can commence – has long been critiqued on a number of grounds including the time taken to negotiate the process (get ethics approval), the 'expertise' of the review committee, and the potential for this anticipatory approach to foster a tick-box mentality, such that gaining ethics approval becomes a curiously disconnected facet of a research project's life. The more recent recognition in research frameworks that ethical issues can arise as research proposals are operationalized (ESRC, 2010: 16) raises further questions about the regulatory nature of the ethics committee and its power and reach in any proposed ongoing role. However, regardless of the changes which might unfold, it is the power invested in ethics committees to determine at the pre-study stage what is ethically (in)appropriate, which is initially discussed below. This is in the light of the longer term (ethical) consequences which can unfold from pre-study ethics approval conditions, in contexts where research endeavours and researcher-participant encounters have become more technically complex, and distinctions and understandings of public and private reframed.

The ways in which power operates in and through research ethics regulation and then how it patterns research practice and relationships, has been an enduring focus of critical debate in the social sciences research literature initiated by feminist researchers (Edwards and Ribbens, 1998; Oakley, 1981; Ribbens, 1989). In the earlier edition of this book we described our interests in ethics and qualitative research as being 'rooted in a genuine and legitimate concern with issues of power', acknowledging 'that research is a political, rather than neutral process' (Edwards and Mauthner, 2002: 18; see also Aldred, 2008). And it is clear that issues of power and the political continue to mediate ethics debates: but contexts have changed significantly. The growth of a range of new technologies and computer mediated online research sites for example, weblogs ('blogs'), discussion forums, Facebook, emails, mobile phones, Twitter and new digital recording mediums, together with digital data storage and sharing (see Natasha S. Mauthner, Chapter 10) have significantly changed research practices and encounters. But while social scientists have become increasingly interested in the ways in which 'cyberspace can expand the social researcher's toolkit' these tools have presented new ethical concerns (Hookway, 2008: 92; see also Ess and the AoIR ethics working committee, 2002; Eynon et al., 2008; Rundall, forthcoming). These concerns include how power (of the researcher *and* participant) operates in these new, sometimes virtual and ethereal research relationships, which increasingly involve indelible data trails; how protection of the participant *and* researcher is understood and managed and confidentiality/anonymity maintained; where participation begins and ends and who is consenting to what in these more fluid research encounters.

Encouragingly research tool innovations, facilitated by new technologies, have created new research spaces (for example, anonymous web-based interactions), which have helped to overcome some of the ethical concerns explored in the earlier edition of this book. The emergence and integration into research design and practice of new, everyday technologies have changed research possibilities and created opportunities for wider (and more diverse) participation in research (Rundall, forthcoming). The increased dialogue and democratization of social science research signalled by these changes fit closely with ideals of feminist research, but clearly there are ethical consequences too. In the sections that follow the implications for qualitative research practice of increased ethics regulation alongside computer-mediated and other technological advances are explored through two studies; the Transition to Motherhood study (Miller, 2005) and Transition to Fatherhood study (Miller, 2011a). By revisiting issues around access, consent and the parameters of participation examined through examples from the Motherhood study used in the first edition of this book (Miller and Bell, Chapter 4; Birch and Miller, Chapter 6), and setting these alongside the more recent Fatherhood study, which shares the same research design, the ways in which research boundaries and ethical responsibilities have become reconfigured will be illuminated. Strategies to manage old and new ethical dilemmas in new research contexts are also discussed.

The two studies

Transition to Motherhood study

The data collection phase of this qualitative longitudinal project ran from 1995 to 1998 and commenced without ethics approval and before university research ethics committees (URECs) were commonplace. This UK study explored women's experiences of transition to first time motherhood, focusing on identity work and narratives (Miller, 2005, 2007; see also Birch and Miller, Chapter 6). Potential participants were identified using snowballing techniques through gate-keepers (recruited via social networks at a local primary school) and asked to contact me by letter or telephone (landline) if they were interested in participating in the study. Eventually 17 women were recruited and verbally agreed by telephone to take part in the study which involved three interviews (one preceding, and two following, the birth) over approximately one year in which they became a mother for the first time. In 1995 at the start of this project there was no university research ethics committee although local research ethics committees (LRECs) had been established to review medical research (Department of Health, 1994, 1997). However a decision was taken *not* to access a potential sample via antenatal clinics (which could have been a fruitful and potentially speedier strategy) in order to avoid having to obtain ethics approval from the LREC which at the time involved a lengthy approval process alongside a sense that medical/health ethics committees did not understand or were not predisposed towards qualitative research. Once recruited, participant's 'consent' was assumed at the first interview (which was usually conducted in the participant's home) and discussed in relation to willingness to take part in subsequent interviews. Information about the project was delivered verbally.

Transition to Fatherhood study

In its original research design this UK study followed that of the earlier transition to motherhood study, however as the project progressed a fourth interview was conducted with some of the participants so that the data collection phase was extended to two years. As in the earlier study, this project also explored men's experiences of transition to first-time fatherhood focusing on identity work and narratives (Miller, 2011a, 2011b). Unlike the earlier study, ethics approval from the UREC was required before the research could commence. The committee gave approval for the study on the basis that any potential participants must opt into the research and so posters and/or leaflets were distributed to shops, work and leisure premises advertising the project and inviting men (who were about to become fathers for the first time) to volunteer to take part. Eventually 17 men were recruited via this opt in method, each making contact either by telephone or email or via a stamped addressed postcard enclosed in the advertising leaflets. The recruitment strategy set by the UREC resulted in a lengthy recruitment phase and a less diverse sample than the study design had intended.[1] Subsequently, email became the main means of communication throughout the study. For example obtaining written, 'informed' consent was a requirement set by the ethics committee and this was initially negotiated through email, project information sheets – another requirement set by the ethics committee – were also sent by email and email was used regularly during the project to set up subsequent interviews and send other project information. In turn email and mobile phones (texts and voicemail) were used by the participants to confirm interview arrangements and also to share birth announcements, baby photographs and other communications. At the first antenatal interview the longitudinal study was again explained and participants were asked to sign a consent form at that time effectively consenting to all three (initially planned) interviews.

Although the shifts in university ethics requirements and technologies do not appear particularly dramatic when outlined in the two studies above, their impact on the research process, and repercussions for research relationships and knowledge production, are much more profound. Although one study had formal ethics approval and the other did not, it is the more recent 'ethics approved' Fatherhood study in which more perplexing ethical issues have been encountered.[2] These have emerged as a consequence of the new (now familiar and so perceived as unproblematic) technologies that have become available since completion of the first study and have been employed in the second study. In particular the use of various technologies – email, mobile phones, digital photos and blogs – have created new and rich 'data' sources and trails, which were unforeseen and unknowable at the outset of the fatherhood study. These technologies have also facilitated retaining the sample and extending the life of the longitudinal fatherhood study as contact with the sample has been readily achieved via email and text messaging so that further (initially unplanned) interviews could be conducted: but technologies can be used by our participants too in ways not possible in the past as documented below. It is these developments, set within a much wider array of computer based/Internet-mediated research tools and possibilities, which are reconfiguring research relationships. These shifts require us to think anew, ethically, beyond a researcher's 'moral deliberation, choice and accountability', which was a concern in the first edition of this book (see Edwards and Mauthner, 2002: 14) to whether we can expect 'moral deliberation' on the part of our participants too. The reconfiguring of research boundaries and research possibilities raise new questions about how (and whose) power operates across these domains. These areas are now examined further through a focus on aspects of the research process – collecting qualitative (longitudinal) data – and researcher-participant relationships.

Collecting qualitative data

Once ethics approval has been obtained and a sample accessed (through routes often prescribed by the UREC) and informed about the study (through receipt of an information sheet as required and approved by the ethics committee) and provided their 'informed' consent (usually a signature on an UREC approved consent form) data collection can commence. But what constitutes 'the data' in this technologically rich age and when does data collection begin and end? In the two studies outlined above the face-to-face interviews were designed as the data collection phase of the research projects. Yet while this was largely the case in the earlier motherhood study (interactions between the interviews only involving landline telephone calls to arrange subsequent interviews), in the fatherhood study the regular use of emails and mobile phones soon began to blur the boundaries around what these interactions ('email conversations') constituted: were they data? Historically 'door knob disclosures' have been a recognized feature of qualitative interviewing as interview recording ends and participants relax. In the Motherhood study I would sometimes ask if I could turn the tape recorder back on when such a situation arose (Miller, 2005, see ch. 7) but 'the data' was still captured on a (traditional) recording device. In the Fatherhood study I found that I was amassing information from the participants via emails and text messages which could contain information which was highly relevant to the study focus, but which fell outside the data-collecting interviews. I had pre-study UREC approval for data collection through the face-to-face interviews and the participants had consented to this: but what was emerging around the interviews could not be 'unknown' and indeed left an indelible (literally) trail of other data on the individual's experiences of becoming fathers, which provided a different perspective if compared to the data generated in the interviews.

The mismatch between formal, pre-study ethics-committee-approval and what can unfold as projects commence is highlighted here: but so too is the importance of ethical training for the researcher so that she/he is able to think and act ethically in unforeseen/unknowable circumstances. The need for ethical training and thinking has become heightened as ever more complex ways of collecting qualitative data are available and employed alongside research strategies that combine multiple data collection tools as well as participants who are known/related to one another. The indelibility of some of the data collected through research approaches leave trails, which in turn raise new ethical questions about anonymity and confidentiality and *whose* is being maintained/protected. In the Fatherhood study the information collected around the face-to-face interviews, for example through emails, text messages and voicemails was not used as data to be analysed or included as extracts, but it will have influenced in some ways my engagement with the recorded and transcribed (ethics committee approved) data and its analysis and interpretation. Is the lesson to be taken from this that in designing future research projects I should think of data collection much more broadly as encompassing all types of (virtual and physical) interactions? Certainly this would overcome my ethical concern with what constituted 'the data' in this study. But would the UREC give approval for such a wide-ranging research application and would potential participants be comfortable consenting to something along the lines of 'anything you may say or do could be used as data'?

Questions of what is and is not data – and who has the power to say – are further tested through the increasing use of Internet posted 'blogs' and other Internet communications, which are providing relatively new data sources and global research forums (Hookway, 2008; Snee, 2010). There are then a range of ethical issues (as well as research benefits) associated with using publicly available online data sources, and the merits and possibilities of online ethical regulation premised on offline modes of research, has been a focus of recent debate (Eynon et al., 2008). But what does consent and protection mean in these *public* Internet spaces, which also have global reach[3] as well as potential implications for private lives? Developments in research possibilities (for example, modes of data collection) can reconfigure the boundaries between public and private spheres (see Edwards and Ribbens, 1998) as well as cultural traditions and practices. Indeed the global reach of online research possibilities now requires that our 'efforts to respond to ethical concerns and resolve ethical conflicts … take into account diverse national and cultural frameworks' (Ess, 2002). The timeliness then of discussions around (cultural) meanings of consent, anonymity, legal protections and power in both (global) online and offline research communities is clearly evident. This timeliness is further underscored by the growing interest in, and practice of, data sharing, digital archiving and data re-use (see Natasha S. Mauthner, Chapter 10, this volume; Neale et al., 2012).

Research relationships

Examining aspects of the researcher–participant relationship was a particular concern in the first edition of this book: in particular how the researcher and participant are positioned (for example, in relation to the ways in which power might operate) and the presumptions that mediate the interview encounter. In their chapter in the first edition (reproduced as Chapter 3, this edition) Gillies and Alldred reflected upon the 'presumptions about research that both interviewee and researcher bring to the interview' and the 'space constructed for an interviewee to occupy', both of which facilitate 'conventional modes of self-expression' and elicit accounts of the 'modernist subject'. But while the questions posed in their chapter remain highly pertinent, their reach has been extended as interview spaces have become multiplied through new online and offline interview techniques and possibilities. New data collection spaces have prompted questions not only concerning the changed nature of the 'presumptions' held about interviews, interviewees and data collection, but also about how researchers – and power – are constructed and employed in these new research spaces. These shifts prompt a re-examination of the presumptions which have underpinned the ethical principle of protection.

A key focus in ethics frameworks and professional guidelines for research has been the researcher-participant relationship and the requirement that research is designed to protect participants and avoid or minimize coercion, harm and 'risk' to them. Even though it has been argued that these concerns are exaggerated and that 'social scientists cannot … harm human subjects in any comparable way' to the possibilities which exist in biomedical sciences, these principles continue to guide ethics governance and review (Dingwall, 2006: 52). More recently it has been recognized that the principles of protection and avoidance of harm and risk should include 'research staff' too (ESRC Framework, 2005). In the Fatherhood study, a condition of receiving ethics approval was that my mobile phone number and the address to which I was going when interviewing must be left with a colleague (most interviews were carried out in the home of the participant). This requirement, which emanated from UREC concerns with both my safety and potential litigation should something go wrong, was a practical strategy which could be easily accommodated into my research practise. However other facets of the researcher–participant relationship may not be so easily or neatly contained (Aldred, 2008; Coy, 2006; Melrose, 2002; Rowe, 2007). The proliferation of qualitative research strategies facilitated by online and offline research tools have led to questions about what the *researcher* is consenting to, how researcher–participant relationships are managed and the extent to which ethics frameworks and governance can, or should, reach across all these parts of the research process.

As noted above, in qualitative research and especially longitudinal qualitative research, email can provide a quick and effective way (provided participants have ready access which is not of course always the case) of setting up interviews and maintaining contact over the life of a project (Ison, 2008; Meho, 2006). But it can also redraw in subtle ways research boundaries and researcher-participant relationships, enhancing rapport (or facilitating 'faking friendship' see Duncombe and Jessop, Chapter 7, this volume) while making anonymity and confidentiality much harder to maintain or ensure. For example in the fatherhood study my personal email details (provided for contact purposes by me) were regularly added by participants to block email birth announcements. Although I took such actions as signalling a commitment to the study, as a practical strategy I would in future make sure I had a dedicated project email address and mobile phone and number as a means of protecting my own privacy. Yet such practical strategies can only go so far as will be outlined below. Internet communication in all types and guises can equally well be used by participants to, if they choose, 'answer back' and publicly respond to our research findings. In many ways this could be seen as the ultimate indication of a democratized research environment, in which long-held feminist concerns with unequal power in the research relationship are (finally) resolved: in practice however old ethical concerns with power and the potential for exploitation must now be refocused to include the researcher as potential subject.

An unexpected example of democratization of qualitative research processes was recently, powerfully, brought home to me. I was searching the Internet for links to my recently published book on the Fatherhood study (Miller, 2011a) and came across a link to my book on a 'blog' written by one of the study participants. In this posting – which is included below – the participant (an academic) eloquently reflects on the process of being in the longitudinal research study and comments on my interpretation of the interview data. I take his comments to be insightful and positive, but it could have been a very different story – and I would probably not have included it had that been the case. My ethical decision making in whether to include the blog was based on an understanding among blog researchers that blogs are 'public data', which do not require 'authorial permission' (because of their public availability) and so are 'academic fair game' (Hookway, 2008: 105; Snee, 2010). The inclusion of the participant's blog[4] helps to illuminate some of the shifts identified and consequent ethical questions that have been raised across this chapter so far. For example, questions posed in the first edition of this book (see Miller and Bell, Chapter 4, and Birch and Miller, Chapter 6) focused on what participants were consenting to and how their participation in a research project was understood and experienced. But while the participant's blog (below) illuminates his experiences of participation, and so could be seen to resolve an earlier ethical concern, others are raised. If we return to the ethical principle of protection and ensuring that our research practices do not cause harm or 'risk' to our participants we might now ask what protection is afforded to the researcher when participants respond in public (unregulated) forums?

The global reach, together with the (near) indelibility of information logged in cyberspace forums are well documented and have been a cause of broader, popular and media concern (for example concerns with social networking and especially facebook). Clearly there are potential costs associated with democratized research practices which occupy a virtual space beyond the reach of ethics frameworks, professional ethics guidelines and (pre-study) ethics review and governance. Getting used to our research participants 'answering back' once a project is over may just be something we will get used to – perhaps even come to seek as a measure of the validity of our analysis and interpretations of the data. But in the meantime this action could feel troubling because while researchers are bound by professional codes of ethical practice and their work (publications in a variety of genres) regulated and subject to professional scrutiny (journals increasingly seek confirmation that research had ethics approval) and peer review, the blogger is not subject to any of these processes. Yet a defamatory blog could be professionally and personally ruinous. And so, the blurring of conventional understandings of public and private boundaries, researcher power in relation to the definitive (published) account of the study findings and the unravelling of taken-for-granted research endings, look set to alter research–participant relationships in new and unchartered ways.

Did I really say that?

I have been meaning to say something about Tina Miller's book *Making Sense of Fatherhood*, about the experience of being a first time dad, but I have been too busy being a *second time dad*, although I did read it before Baby 2 was born. I really enjoyed it, not least for reminding me of episodes and feelings I had forgotten about; it also provided the occasion for an odd parlour game at Christmas, in which friends/partners tried to guess which of the anonymous interview subjects was me. The thing that was most interesting about reading a book in which you are one of the research subjects is, of course, being confronted with your own words inflected by the social scientist. Reading a short chunk of your own words inevitably generates a desire to clarify, elaborate, or revise – at no point did I find myself thinking that Tina had misrepresented me at all, but it made me realize something obvious – a very long extract of me talking at length doesn't count as evidence, whereas a short extract of me talking along the same lines as other men saying similar things does. I was forced to think quite hard about what you can and cannot say about the things people say to you in interviews on a *research project* I was working on during the same period I was being interviewed by Tina, and we ended up going for a modest interpretative strategy in which one assumes that people are able to reflect coherently on their own practices, and that this sort of talk provides some insight into their own evaluative practices. Tina does something similar with the stories that me and other dads told her, so I do not have any complaints. But reading her book has reminded me of the inevitability of a disjuncture between the concerns animating those who provide elicited talk, and the purposes for which this talk is being solicited by the social scientist. Which might be obvious. And I don't think this is quite as ethically problematic as might be supposed – the other thing that reading my own words, some of them at least, written back at me made me think is that participants in research projects like this might be best thought of as *gifting* their words to the researcher, in a sense, providing them with raw material upon which to do analysis and interpretation. Which does raise some questions of what is owed back in return for this sort of gift – I think, at a minimum, some commitment to not thinking of your research subjects as moral fools, hypocrites, or dupes (the basic models for a lot of critical social science, after all).

It is clear then that new technologies have had a profound effect on conceptualizations and understandings of qualitative research, where it begins, where and when data is being collected and how and when research projects end – and who determines this. Increasingly there is a need to think about ethical issues both within and *beyond* the intended (ethics approved) research design and process together with how areas of ethical concern might be managed.

Managing ethics in qualitative research: some strategies for researchers

Debates about the role and spread of ethics committees and ethics regulation have been noted above. Among criticisms of the move to a culture of ethical governance there has been a concern with how useful pre-study review of research proposals can be, given the unknowable quality of qualitative data collected using off line and online approaches. But this does not mean that further scrutiny of research practise and process across the life of a study is what is being argued for – indeed the regulatory nature of current practices of ethics review is found by many to be unhelpful and arbitrary in where it falls. But being able to discuss ethical concerns as they arise is a necessary and ethical way of conducting research – outside of a regulatory framework. A recent call for guidance in social science research ethics, 'rather than a model of regulation drawn from the NHS' (Stanley and Wise, 2010) echoes an earlier appeal for a shift 'from the static audit and accountability model which currently characterises many ethics committees to a democratic, process-sensitive, support forum' (Miller and Boulton, 2007: 2209). Guidance and support for researchers and discussion of ethical concerns as they are encountered, can be provided by colleagues and supervisors (see Miller and Bell, pages 70–1, this volume) but training of researchers to be able to feel comfortable and confident in making ethical decisions is also key. Currently many undergraduate and postgraduate research methods courses have solitary, apparently disconnected, lectures on ethics, rather than weaving ethics through the course and so encouraging ethical thinking across research areas. There are also practical steps which can be taken to reduce the possibility of (some) ethical issues arising, but of course we can never know exactly how our research will unfold. Below are some examples of strategies I have either used or would now use, based on the Motherhood and Fatherhood studies. Although these studies were longitudinal, and used face-to-face interviews for data collection purposes, contact with participants in the Fatherhood study was maintained via online communications and so the suggestions below have relevance for a range of qualitative approaches.

- Use a designated project email address – helps to maintain privacy of the researcher/to reduce blurring of public and private boundaries.
- Use a designated project mobile phone and number – helps to maintain privacy of the researcher/to reduce blurring of public and private boundaries. Mobile phones can also

be usefully used to maintain contact with participants (and/or to collect data). Although in a pilot study with teenage fathers, which ran alongside part of the Fatherhood study, mobile phones were beneficial in accessing the younger participants but these participants changed their mobile phones and numbers regularly and this method of contact was only partially successful.

- Show participants how you will use their data, for example what data extracts can look like in an article/book chapter. This can reduce any anxieties on the part of the participant and helps to foster trust and rapport between researcher and participant. It may also reduce the possibility (or temper the content) of public responses (for example, blogs) from participants to our research projects. Or as noted above, perhaps this is something we should embrace as evidence of the democratization of the research process?
- Explain to participant's that your analysis and interpretations of the data should (usually) mean that they will be able to recognize themselves in your data (they will know who they are) – but that others will not, as any other identifying features (geographical location, etc.) will have been changed.
- Using a short end-of-study postal 'questionnaire' (hard copy, email copy, or web-based) can be a very useful tool in collecting information (data?) on 'how participation in the project has been for you?'. This technique was used in both the Motherhood and Fatherhood studies (Miller 2005, 2011a, see ch. 7 in both books for further discussion) and provided an opportunity for the participant's to reflect (privately) on their side of the research process.
- Identify someone/a forum you trust, for example, supervisor, colleagues, other web based forum where you can feel comfortable discussing ethical concerns as they are encountered.

Conclusion

An underlying intention running throughout this chapter has been to explore what parts of the qualitative research process are routinely subject to ethics review (with the potential for regulation) and what elements of the research process are not, set against a backdrop of increasing research spaces and possibilities. Taking this perspective it becomes clear that ethical review and governance as currently configured do not and cannot, reach elements of unfolding research projects, however much they may regulate at the pre-study stage. This is not to argue that being asked to consider potential ethical issues in advance of a study is a redundant exercise – clearly it is not, even if the forum in which it is done, and the power given to regulatory bodies is questionable. But having ethical guidance from other researchers available across a research project's life seems a much more appropriate way to support and guide researchers in this rapidly changing context.

The growth of online research practices and other technologies, which reconfigure off line research possibilities, have changed, in quite dramatic ways, research opportunities and relationships and as has been shown, there are benefits and costs. Ethical principles and concerns around protection harm and 'risk' need to be rethought as the boundaries between public and professionally regulated spheres and private and unregulated spheres become less clearly demarcated. University ethics approval and professional guidelines and accountability cannot protect the researcher from public online spaces: ethical regulation then in both directions can only go so far. In some ways the changes outlined across this chapter lead to an increased sense of vulnerability on the part of the researcher rather than as has conventionally been the case (examined in the earlier edition of this book), the participant. But at the same time this must be tempered with the increased democratization of the research process evidenced through an array of new 'bottom-up', more inclusive data collection technologies. Our feminist research principles and ethical concerns of wanting to redress power imbalances in research relationships and increase reciprocity and participation in and through our research, seems to have been addressed – but ironically in ways which prompt new ethical questions and challenge in new ways our thinking about qualitative research relationships.

Notes

1 Requiring that men must actively opt into the study was unlikely to result in accessing individuals for whom the pregnancy was not a happily anticipated event or who did not feel relatively confident about talking about themselves – having a story to tell. Although the resulting longitudinal data on their experiences of transition was varied, complex and profound, I am aware that the voices of those who may have felt initially more ambivalent, reluctant or fearful as they anticipated the birth of their child are not represented.

2 An obvious difference between the two studies is that of the researcher's and participant's gender. While it is acknowledged that all face-to-face interviews are a social interaction and as such gender differences will be one facet of this interaction, the longitudinal design of the fatherhood study helped the process of rapport building across the Fatherhood study diminishing elements of gendered difference which might otherwise have inhibited/influenced the data collection process. Gendered differences were not a reason for more ethical issues being encountered in this particular project. (For further reflections on aspects of the research process see Miller, 2011a: ch. 7.)

3 It is of course acknowledged that access to Internet and other technical mediums is patterned unequally globally.

4 I have not included the blog address but given the ease and virtual indelibility of posts on the Internet, I recognize it will be easy enough to trace.

References

Aldred, R. (2008) 'Ethical and political issues in contemporary research relationships. *Sociology*, 42: 887–902.

Coy, M. (2006) 'This morning I'm a researcher, this afternoon I'm an outreach worker: ethical dilemmas in practitioner research', *International Journal of Social Research Methodology*, 9 (5): 419–31.

Department of Health. (1994) *Standards for Local Research Ethics Committees: A Framework for Ethical Review*. London: Department of Health.

Department of Health. (1997) *Ethics Committee Review of Multi-Centre Research: Establishment of Multi-centre Research Ethics Committees. HSG (97) 23*. London: Department of Health.

Dingwall, R. (2006) 'Confronting the anti-democrats: the unethical nature of ethical regulation in social science', *Medical Sociology Online*, 1: 51–8.

Dixon-Woods, M., Angell, E., Ashcroft, R.E., et al. (2007) 'Written work: the social functions of research ethics committee letters', *Social Science and Medicine*, 65: 792–802.

Edwards, R. and Mauthner, M. (2002) 'Ethics and feminist research: theory and practice', in M. Mauthner, M. Birch, J. Jessop., et al. (eds), *Ethics in Qualitative Research*. London: Sage. pp. 14–31.

Edwards, R. and Ribbens, J. (1998) *Feminist Dilemmas in Qualitative Research*. London: Sage.

ESRC (2005) *Research Ethics Framework*. Swindon: ESRC. Available at: http://www.esrcsociety today.ac.uk/ESRCInfoCentre/Images/ESRC_Re_Ethics_Frame_tcm6–11291.pdf (accessed August 2011).

ESRC (2010) *Framework For Research Ethics*. Swindon: ESRC. Available at: http://www.esrcsocietytoday.ac.uk/ESRCInfoCentre/Images/Framework%20for%20Research%20Ethics%202010_tcm6–35811.pdf (accessed August 2011).

Ess, C. and the AoIR ethics working committee (2002) Ethical decision-making and Internet Research: Recommendations from the AoIR Ethics Working Committee. Available at: http://aoir.org/reports/ethics.pdf (accessed August 2011).

Eynon, R., Fry, J. and Schroeder, R. (2008) 'The ethics of internet research', in N. Fielding, R.M. Lee and G. Blank (eds), *Handbook of Online Research Methods*. London: Sage. pp. 23–41.

Haggerty, K.D. (2004) 'Ethics creep: governing social science research in the name of ethics', *Qualitative Sociology*, 27 (4): 391–414.

Hookway, N. (2008) '"Entering the blogosphere": some strategies for using blogs in social research', *Qualitative Research*, 8 (1): 91–113.

Ison, N.L. (2008) 'Having their say: email interviews for research data collection with people who have verbal communication impairment', *International Journal of Social Research Methodology*, 12 (2): 161–72.

Meho, L. (2006) 'Email interviewing in qualitative research: a methodological discussion', *Journal of the American Society for Information Science and Technology*, 57 (10): 1284–95.

Melrose, M. (2002) 'Labour pains: some considerations on the difficulties of researching juvenile prostitution', *International Journal of Social Research Methodology*, 5 (4): 333–51.

Miller, T. (2005) *Making Sense of Motherhood: A Narrative Approach*. Cambridge: Cambridge University Press.

Miller, T. (2007) '"Is this what motherhood is all about?" Weaving experiences and discourse through transition to first-time motherhood', *Gender & Society,* 21: 337–58.

Miller, T. (2011a) *Making Sense of Fatherhood: Gender, Caring and Work.* Cambridge: Cambridge University Press.

Miller, T. (2011b) 'Falling back into gender? Men's narratives and practices around first-time fatherhood', *Sociology,* 45 (6): 1094–109.

Miller, T. and Boulton, M. (2007) 'Changing constructions of informed consent: qualitative research and complex social worlds', *Social Science & Medicine,* 65 (11): 2199–211.

Neale, B., Henwood, K. and Holland, J. (2012) 'An introduction to the timescapes approach: researching lives through time', *Qualitative Research,* special issue, January.

Oakley, A. (1981*) Interviewing Women: A Contradiction in Terms? In Doing Feminist Research,* ed. H. Roberts. London: Routledge and Kegan Paul.

Ribbens, J. (1989) 'Interviewing-an "Unnatural Situation"?', *Women's Studies International Forum,* 12: 579–92.

Richardson, S. and McMullan, M. (2007) 'Research ethics in the UK: what can sociology learn from health?', *Sociology,* 41 (6): 1115–32.

Rowe, M. (2007) 'Tripping over molehills: ethics and the ethnography of police work', *International Journal of Social Research Methodology,* 10 (1): 37–48.

Rundall, E. (2012) 'Ethics in the field: key ethical considerations which inform the use of anonymous asynchronous websurveys in "sensitive" research', in J. MacClancy and A. Fuentes (eds), *Ethics in the Field.* Oxford: Berghahn. In press.

Snee, H. (2010) Using blog analysis, realities toolkit #10. Available at: http://eprints.ncrm.ac.uk/1321/2/10-toolkit-blog-analysis.pdf (accessed October 2011).

Stanley, L. and Wise, S. (2010) 'The ESRC's 2010 framework for research ethics: fit for research purpose?', *Sociological Research Online,* 15 (4): 12.

3

The ethics of intention: research as a political tool

VAL GILLIES AND PAM ALLDRED

Introduction

Many feminists have criticized the traditional approach of Western scientific research, questioning in particular the premise that facts can be gathered objectively. This chapter argues that the epistemological shift from a reliance on the positivist paradigm of scientific truth necessitates a new scrutiny of the intentions underlying feminist research. While feminists take up a range of positions in relation to the implications of the critique of positivism for their research – which means that our aims can range from the production of more inclusive or less biased research to the rejection of this type of knowledge claim altogether – the questions raised about the politics or ethics of research can usefully inform feminist research of whatever hue. Once our faith in objective positivism is shaken, the goals of feminist research tend to be transformed from attempting to better understand or represent women's experiences, to the explicitly political aim of challenging gender oppression and improving women's lives. Research therefore becomes an explicitly political tool to be used strategically to make political interventions. But how do we address issues of intention for research when feminist aims themselves have also been subject to the same questioning as has 'Truth'?

Within a modernist research paradigm, ethics have been seen as abstract, transferable principles. Moreover, they are concerned with the research process itself: the rights and wrongs of how knowledge (as objective fact) is collected. Research ethics have therefore focused on how well participants are treated, but has not been extended to encompass broader questions about the ethics of knowledge itself, for instance, the political role played by research findings or by the relations set up by the knowledge claims (Burman, 1992). We argue for the need to broaden our conception of ethics to include the political objectives or intentions for research, as well as such questions about the ethics of knowledge relations. That is, who claims to know, and how, and the power relationship produced by this. Once research is acknowledged to be a political activity (for example, Mayall, 1999), questions of ethics cannot be separated from political aims and intentions. Judgements of ethical practice therefore become situation specific, with criteria tied to politically informed intentions, which is why ethics can no longer be abstracted into codes of practice (as Rosalind Edwards and Melanie Mauthner argue in Chapter 1, this volume). This redefining of ethics to encompass knowledge relations as well as the relations set up within the practices of research, collapses established boundaries between political activism and ethical feminist research.

The political and personal perspectives of researchers inform the intentions we have for the research. They are also the means by which we evaluate the impact and the indirect implications of our research. Although all feminist research may be regarded as 'transformative' (Harding, 1987), precise political aims are rarely discussed or critically evaluated. While most feminist researchers rely on some basic abstractions and universal categories for good reasons, few of us explicate our motivation beyond the aim of generating 'feminist knowledge' or 'doing feminist research'. Taken-for-granted notions of what is progressive in research can therefore be left unquestioned, with good intention seemingly adequate justification. This might be partly because of the difficulty of warranting 'feminist' interventions as the terms of feminist politics have been queried, but perhaps it is also partly a legacy of the depoliticization of research in positivist empiricism. It forecloses the space we wish to open up for discussion of our, and others', intentions for research. Questioning the intentions that lie behind someone's research must not be interpreted as questioning their feminist commitment, but rather as trying to help clarify political aims and means. In some situations, such as when negotiating hostile audiences, we might not fully expose our political intentions in order to keep our place on the platform, as chapters in *Feminist Dilemmas* argued (Alldred, 1998; Standing, 1998). Strategic silences, such as when we present our research 'findings' without our account of the political role we hope they will play, may be seen as politically and ethically legitimate, but in contexts of feminist debate and reflexivity we argue for making explicit the links between research, politics and ethics.

This chapter focuses on three main areas of feminist research, which might be positioned differently along the epistemological continuum in terms of the political aims and intentions they embody. First, we examine feminist efforts to represent women in order that their voices and experiences are heard. Second, we focus on feminist attempts to initiate personal change through action research. Third, we look at feminist post-structuralist aims to deconstruct and thereby undermine oppressive knowledge structures. We aim to highlight the assumptions that underpin each approach, and the potential ethical dilemmas raised by them. We begin by exploring how knowledge has been conceptualized in recent Western feminist thought because these epistemological debates are crucial to the (re)definition of ethics. We argue that if knowledge is understood as essentially political, then ethical principles must also be understood in terms of political practice.

Epistemological debates

Having identified positivism as oppressive and as failing in its own terms to be truly objective, some feminists have attempted to produce knowledge that is closer to the 'truth' about women. For some, the identification of bias and androcentricism in traditional scientific research pointed to male scientists' failure to live up to the principles of good science. An approach that Sandra Harding (1990) termed 'feminist empiricism' suggested increasing the numbers of female scientists to help eliminate distortion, ignorance and prejudice, and thereby reform the otherwise inadequate practices of positivist research. As many feminists, including Harding herself, pointed out, this aim left untouched the gendered assumptions that underlie the very project of science itself, and merely incorporated female scientists within a male defined framework. As an alternative to this positivist approach, Harding called for a scientific epistemology to encompass a 'feminist standpoint', suggesting that research grounded in women's experiences could produce a more complete picture and less distorted knowledge claims.

Feminist research has provided a critique not only of the findings of positivist research, but also of the aims, assumptions and methods that underpin the empiricist approach to knowing. Feminists have questioned the notions of neutrality and objectivity, arguing that reason cannot be separated from emotion or subjective interest. The universal validity of knowledge produced by a male-dominated elite was also challenged, revealing the way this ignored or marginalized women's perspectives and experiences (Harding, 1991). By highlighting the way claims of objectivism naturalize particular embedded perspectives, issues of gender and power were implicated in the process of creating 'scientific knowledge' and therefore also its 'findings'. Critics thereby exposed the essentially political nature of claims to truth, and feminists in particular showed how women's subjectivities come to be defined through masculinist knowledge structures.

According to Harding (1990), epistemologies are 'justificatory strategies', necessary both to defend the value of feminist 'knowledge' and to guide theory, practice and politics. In this sense, justificatory strategies are regarded as tools to develop and validate alternative truth claims made by feminists, enabling and justifying feminist action to effect change. However, for many other feminists, any claim to objective truth raises a number of problematic issues about knowledge and power (Burman, 1996; Hollway, 1989; Weedon, 1987). Although Harding's endorsement of the feminist standpoint approach as a 'successor science' has been influential, it has also been widely criticized for its reification of a single, universal feminist standpoint, which allows the continued marginalization of, for example, black, lesbian, working-class or post-colonial women's perspectives (Burman, 1996; hooks, 1990; Stanley and Wise, 1993).

A rigid reliance on supposedly universal categories, such as women, excludes and manipulates by policing legitimate 'insides' and constructing ineligible 'outsides'. As Diane Elam argues 'a feminism that believes it knows what a woman is and what she can do both forecloses the limitless possibilities of women and misrepresents the various forms that social injustice can take' (1994: 32). Yet without access to basic generalizations, feminism struggles to preserve its moral and political role in challenging the oppression(s) of women. Many feminists are wary of attempts to effect social change by unqualified universal appeals to 'women' and 'women's interests' (Riley, 1988; Spelman, 1988), but some have gone further and, drawing on postmodernist work, reject altogether universalizing classifications such as gender or identity (Butler, 1990, 1993; Fraser and Nicholson, 1990). Many feminists saw how postmodernist and post-structuralist[1] critiques resonated with long-standing feminist critiques of 'whose truth' counts. They question the essentializing implications of some feminist theory and are suspicious of any reliance on a unitary system of justification (Elam, 1994; McNay, 1992). Instead they highlight the pluralistic, complex social identities that individuals draw on, and recast 'knowledge' as a situation-dependent resource. The resulting focus on difference and multiplicity has led many to consider the implications of the postmodern approach for feminist research and politics. While methodologies which emphasize the contingent and situated nature of knowledge and subjectivity have been broadly taken up among feminist researchers, the accompanying challenges to assertions of feminist knowledge or perspectives have provoked intense debate. Concerns have been voiced over the value or dangers that such an approach generates for feminist politics, and the ethical dilemmas it raises in terms of research (Jackson, 1992; Ramazanoglu with Holland, 2002; Soper, 1991).

In particular, there is a concern that a focus on the heterogeneity of women's experience dissolves many of the assumed commonalities that feminism was built on. Without a central, definable notion of the female subject, established theoretical and political distinctions seem to become redundant. As Janet Ransom points out 'what threatens to disappear is the hook on which to hang our feminism' (1993: 166). There is also concern that the rejection of theoretical abstractions or generalizations, in favour of an exclusive focus on plurality and cultural diversity, obscures the existence of broad and systematic structures of inequality and oppression. The understandable concern is that with no recourse to legitimation through claims of justice or truth, feminism becomes merely one of many equally valid perspectives.

While most feminists recognize the risk that gender generalizations may be made at the expense of individual, contextual experience, many also oppose an exclusive focus on difference. Although the debates about 'difference' among Western feminists during the 1980s and early 1990s have been crucial in identifying the exclusionary potential of universalizing any single feminist perspective, important subsequent arguments have highlighted the risks that a sole focus on 'difference' can present to feminist political analyses. As critiques of multiculturalism have revealed, 'respect for difference' sometimes conceals a vacuum in the critique of injustice and of the existing power relations. Postmodern critiques of the concepts of truth and justice have therefore been accused of paralysing practical efforts towards social progress, by levelling the ground on which moral judgements are made. At the extreme or theoretically pure end of postmodernist approaches is a relativism which is regarded by many as delegitimizing feminist (or any other political) action. Relinquishing the warrant of truth may be seen as kicking the platform that feminists and others have recently had (some) access to, out from under our feet (Burman, 1990). Furthermore, such an epistemologically orientated focus, can reduce feminist struggle to a mere theoretical exercise which can conceal and leave unchallenged the embedded structures of privilege. The promotion of epistemological theory over political practice and physical experience has been criticized on theoretical as well as ethical grounds. Susan Bordo (1990) has argued that a postmodern approach exchanges a positivist preoccupation with objectivity and neutrality ('a view from nowhere') for an equally problematic fantasy of protean dislocation characterized by constantly shifting viewpoints ('a dream of everywhere'). Bordo also draws attention to the inescapable physical and material locatedness that works to shape and limit human thought and action:

> we are standing in concrete bodies, in a particular time and place in the 'middle' of things, always. The most sophisticated theory cannot alter this limitation on our knowledge, while too-rigid adherence to theory can make us too inflexible, too attached to a set of ideas, to freshly assess what is going on around us. (1998: 96)

Confronted with the problematic consequences and ethical dilemmas associated with modernist and postmodernist epistemologies, some feminists have argued for a progressive synthesis of the two approaches. For instance, Nancy Fraser and Linda Nicholson have suggested that each perspective illuminates significant shortcomings of the other, claiming that a 'postmodernist reflection on feminist theory reveals disabling vestiges of essentialism, while a feminist reflection on postmodernism reveals androcentricism and political naivete' (Fraser and Nicholson, 1990: 20). Some feminists informed by post-structuralism or postmodernism have sought to move beyond the essentializing tendencies of some approaches to feminist epistemology, but claim to avoid relativizing by demonstrating how individual women's lives are shaped by multiple influences and experiences that interweave to produce intricate power relations. Fraser and Nicholson view gendered experience as fragmented, diverse and situated, but attempt to link such analyses to wider social theory to construct a practical politics of emancipation. Similarly, Erica Burman claims that local analyses in which the researcher does not claim to have privileged access to the truth or to be presenting the only possible interpretation of events can still guard against relativism by attending to both the micro- and the macro-politics of the situation (Burman, 1992, 1993). Nevertheless, some feel there are intractable contradictions between postmodernism and feminism (McNay, 1992), and have expressed unease at the incorporation of such a radically undermining critique of traditional emancipatory objectives. These theoretical and epistemological debates have important implications for feminist research and ethics in terms of political practice.

Feminist intentions: why research is political

By questioning the way that we justify our political statements about women's lives, a whole league of questions are raised about the nature of current feminist research. The ethical dilemmas posed include, for example, how do we know such a thing to be true, and that a particular response will be in (even specific) women's interests? Most feminist researchers tread an uneasy path between retaining certain abstractions and general categories (such as gender or ethnicity), while also recognizing diversity and critiquing essentialism. We suggest that a consequence of this struggle to reconcile aspects of foundationalism with post-structuralist critiques should be a magnified spotlight on intention and political praxis. Feminist researchers need recourse to concepts of justice and morality in order to make claims about (how we see) the world, and as Fraser and Nicholson argue, we need access to 'the large scale theoretical tools needed to address large political problems' (1990: 34). But to ensure sensitivity to the heterogeneity of experience and power, there is a responsibility to place ourselves in the picture that we are 'describing', thereby revealing the partiality of our own perspective. This involves locating research in terms of its objectives and outcomes, by fully articulating the motivating political intentions.

Within modernist accounts, the intent is to find 'truth', and while a political intent may be recognized, it is believed that knowledge itself will prove emancipatory. It is this very aspect of modernism, the myth of progress towards 'enlightenment' that produces the corollary presumption that Western (modernist) knowledge practices represent the furthering of 'civilization'. It was the West's presumed purchase on superior knowledge which has underpinned and justified the colonization of 'less civilized nations' and the neo-imperial relations still maintained. Critiques of such modernist tropes first made postmodernist, post-colonial and post-structuralist approaches of interest to feminists. First-wave Western feminism emerged as a modernist movement believing emancipation would follow from the discovery of 'truth', whereas contemporary feminists have differing views about the role 'truth' might play in achieving emancipatory aims. For some feminist researchers abandoning theoretical purity has lead to a more practical focus on challenging inequality and improving women's lives. According to Liz Stanley (1990), feminists should be transcending the theory/research divide, and recognizing the symbiotic relationship between manual and intellectual activities. This is one approach to re-valuing knowledge for its pragmatic use to feminists, rather than valuing its status as truth in the conventional modernist paradigm. From this perspective, it is not simply knowledge of women's lives, but knowledge that *works for* women that counts. In which case it is necessary to discuss what knowledge is for, in terms of what we want it to do or achieve with it.

Although we may make certain compromises in the light of hinders' or other practical concerns, as researchers we are broadly guided in our choices by what we believe is 'for the best'. But despite good intentions, feminists cannot transcend the personal accountability and partial nature of knowledge production. As such, both our intentions for our research and the political assumptions underpinning these, need to be personally recognized and publicly acknowledged. This is not to suggest that we are incapable of promoting causes outside of our own experience or personal involvement, but it is to reassert that such interventions are conducted from our own particular frames of reference. While particular concepts of morality and justice are vital, they are actively constructed, deconstructed or maintained through particular political struggles and perspectives. As Susan Bordo points out 'we always "see" from points of view that are invested with our social, political, and personal interests, inescapably "centric" in one way or another, even in the desire to do justice to heterogeneity' (1990: 140).

Knowledge and empowerment: three key strands in feminist research

While the will to make a difference is understood as a basic feminist principle, it is generally recognized that there are multiple, contested 'feminist' readings of what needs to change. It is this disconnection from abstract notions of 'truth' for a broad acceptance of multiple 'feminisms' that brings the ethics of intention more sharply into view. We will now examine three distinct strands within feminist research in order to draw out the implicit political/ethical issues associated with each approach.

Representing women

A fundamental objective of much feminist research is to represent the views and experiences of women, in order to challenge their marginalized status. This was a key strategy for second-wave Western feminists. Many regarded themselves as conduits, channelling perspectives and voices which would otherwise remain silent, muted or invisible. Asserting that knowledge always embodies a perspective means that the researcher's own role in constructing 'knowledge' about other women needs to be recognized as an active and particular one, as opposed to being a neutral, 'objective' research instrument. Recognition of the researcher's role in constructing 'knowledge' about women has generated numerous debates about the ethics and politics of 'representing the other' (see for instance, Wise and Stanley, 2003, and Wilkinson and Kitzinger, 1996). In this section we consider the dilemmas which characterize these debates before moving on to emphasize the central significance the ethics of intention assumes in relation to feminist attempts to represent women other than ourselves.

A central issue for feminist research is whether individuals can, or should attempt to represent groups that they do not belong to, especially groups with less power and influence, as many of the chapters in *Feminist Dilemmas* discussed (for example, Alldred, 1998; Ribbens and Edwards, 1998; Standing, 1998). Although feminist researchers often emphasize the commonalities between themselves and the participants of their research as a validation of their right to represent other women, structural and individual differences sometimes conflict with similarities (for example, Maxine Birch and Tina Miller in Chapter 6, this volume). As bell hooks has argued, efforts by dominant groups to represent those who are oppressed can amount to a form of colonization, reinterpreting and thereby erasing the 'Voice' of the speaking subject (hooks, 1990). Similarly, Daphne Patai (1991) argues forcefully that the intractability of the power relation between Western academic feminists and 'Third World' women means that research by the former on the latter is never ethically justifiable. Like hooks and Patai, many feminists are uneasy about over-attribution to the concept of gender as a universal experience across 'race', class and other social distinctions.

Even when specific experiences or identities are shared by the researcher and researched, affinity in itself cannot be regarded as an authoritative basis for representative research. Paradoxically, when an emphasis is placed on sameness, power differences are highlighted in terms of whose version of the account is eventually told, even if the research is presented as a co-construction. Fore-grounding commonality at the expense of difference risks generating a falsely homogenized view of particular experiences, and may result in an over representation of issues that resonate with White, middle-class researchers. Thus, although sharing an experience or standpoint may generate empathy and a desire to speak on behalf of others, it can compromise critical reflexivity by encouraging a reliance on unchallenged assumptions and inferences (Hurd and McIntyre, 1996; Reay, 1996). In particular, political intentions might remain unexplicated behind assumed shared political perspectives. As critiques of identity politics have shown (Butler, 1990), even if we do share identities, we cannot assume that common identities produce common political perspectives.

In response to these ethical/political concerns, some feminists have argued against speaking for others, suggesting that a researcher's warrant extends only to representations of themselves and their immediate communities. Inevitably, this proposal has generated much debate and dispute, not least over what constitutes a common identity. Many writers point to the highly specific experience of being an academic feminist (Kitzinger and Wilkinson, 1996), while others stress the multifaceted nature of an individual's identity and subjective positioning in order to highlight the unfeasible basis of this idea (Bhavnani and Phoenix, 1994; Stanley and Wise, 1993). Taken to its logical conclusion, the call to 'only speak for ourselves' would preclude all discussion other than solipsistic reflections on personal experience, given that no two individuals will share exactly the same standpoints. Clearly, we would not want to draw this conclusion because it forecloses possible political alliances including acts of solidarity which fully recognize difference and the power relations that the act is embedded in.

While valid ethical concerns have been expressed about the practice of speaking for others, equally valid questions have been raised about the morality of not speaking for them. As Rosalind Edwards states:

> Can, or should, white middle-class women academics, such as myself, research and represent in writing the voices of black, mainly working-class women? For me, the question has always been another way around: can I possibly be justified in leaving them out? (1996: 83)

The argument that researchers should avoid representing individuals or groups who inhabit less powerful social positions is a difficult one to sustain morally, never mind epistemologically. Feminist researchers cannot begin to challenge women's oppression without addressing wider social hierarchies and divisions, and this requires that women use any power and influence that they have on behalf of others. Not to speak about, or for 'others' encourages silences and gaps, which marginalize and exclude, while cementing the privilege of those with the more powerful voices. As Christine Griffin (1996) points out, when we speak for others we cannot become them, we can only tell our story about their lives. What we can do, however, is make explicit our intentions for telling our story of their lives, and our intentions for the processes of participation, interpretation and writing/representation.

One way that feminists have responded to the issue of representing others has been for researchers to 'put themselves in the picture', so that the research account is not a disembodied 'view from nowhere' (Fraser and Nicholson, 1990) or reveal the contingent nature of their analysis (Gillies and Robinson, 2010; Burman, 1992). This then raises questions about how such 'stories of life-stories' (research accounts) can be judged as more or less appropriate. If notions of authenticity and 'truth' are problematized, we are left to evaluate the legitimacy of particular representations, not in terms of accuracy, but according to what we reveal about the basis of our interpretation or on the grounds of an account's effects. In some situations, members of an oppressed group may be better placed to represent other members of the same group because they are likely to have a situated (personally invested) understanding of what needs to change. For example, Black feminists pushed the issue of 'race' onto feminist agendas, highlighting previously neglected issues of White power and privilege. However, this does not proscribe 'less'/differently oppressed others from speaking against injustice. Nor does it excuse those who do not.

The choice feminist researchers face between remaining 'respectfully silent' for fear of appropriating the experiences of 'others', and speaking out on their behalf, must be seen as an instrumental, political choice, rather than an abstract, theoretical ethical dilemma. It requires reflection on a number of questions concerning the research, the researcher and the researched. First, the overall intention of specific representational research needs to be acknowledged and clarified in terms of what might be achieved by speaking for or about 'others'. Second, the researcher's position in relation to those whom she is representing needs to be thoroughly explored, in terms of her own social, political and personal interests, and the assumptions she brings to her understanding of those she is researching. As Caroline Ramazanoglu and Janet Holland argue 'In connecting theory, experience and judgement, the knowing feminist should be accountable for the sense she makes of her own and other people's accounts, and how her judgements are made' (1999: 386). Third, there needs to be careful consideration of the likely impact of the 'knowledge' produced, to ensure that it could not work against the interests of those it seeks to represent, or against another group. This includes trying to imagine the different political contexts into which the research account might play, and the deployment of the material in ways that are contradictory to the researcher's politics or intentions. As Christine Griffin notes 'Researchers are always speaking for others. This is not something to be denied or avoided: it is a (potential) power and a responsibility' (1996: 100).

Initiating personal change through action research

Another key strand of feminist research focused on initiating a more direct form of change through a politicization of those taking part in the research. Sharing a similar rationale to the 'consciousness raising' associated with the late 1960s and 1970s women's liberation movement in the West, 'action research' aims to generate insight, confidence and mutual support for research participants. Indeed, action research today has a precedent in Paulo Friere's (1972) concept of 'conscientization' – a process by which people 'deep[en] awareness of [their own] sociocultural identity and their capacity to transform their lives' (Taylor, 1994: 109). 'Empowering' the women who take part is a primary aim of this kind of research, with fully participatory research involving participants in all stages of the research process, including the identification of the initial question or problem to be studied. The focus of the research intervention is on those who experience the research personally, rather than on how the research represents participants or their social group generally in the broad political arena.

The notion of empowering women through the research process is appealing to many feminists. However, the associated ethical dimensions are complex. By definition, action research is intervening in people's lives and so entails a use, and potential abuse of power. Maye Taylor argues that because of this the 'ethical guidelines for research have to be stringently applied' and there must be 'respect for the whole life of the person, not just as a research subject' (1994: 112). However participant-led the research may be, the researcher plays a crucial role in initiating, facilitating and constructing meanings – a point that is often played down in the emphasis on democratic rapport and participant empowerment. Simplistic ideas of participation and empowerment can obscure other aspects of the researcher's power and responsibility: 'It is we who have the time, resources and skills to conduct methodological work, to make sense of experience and locate individuals in historical and social contexts' (Kelly et al., 1994: 37; Birch and Miller, see Chapter 6, this volume). While participants may engage with the research and exercise a high degree of autonomy in organizing and reflecting on the topic, the researcher herself remains central to the process. Valuable as they were at the time, second wave feminist attempts to develop egalitarian research relationships (as well as therapeutic and pedagogic ones), have been criticized (along with the whole framework of liberal humanist political narratives) by later feminist and post-structuralist work for being naively optimistic and theoretically weak regarding its analysis of power (Fraser, 1989; Probyn, 1993; Ticeneto Clough, 1992). In particular, the democratized research ideal is shown to rest on the fantasy that power can be shared and the differing positions occupied by researcher and researched neutralized (Burman, 1992; Marks, 1996, see also Gillies and Lucey, 2007). Not only does this fail to recognize the power the researcher may retain in the research interaction despite attempts to allow participants to set the agenda (Burman, 1992), the preoccupation with relations in the interview itself distracts from the relations of power set up within the academy (Probyn, 1993). Applying the same reflexivity to the institutionalized power relations of researcher–researched highlights the dynamic of representation where one party has little or no say and the other has full authorial power: the researcher is not merely author, but interpreter, editor and political editor/ambassador (Burman, 1992).

At a fundamental level, a feminist researcher brings to the research her judgement or assumption that there is a need for social change – a principle that lies at the root of feminism. In models of participatory research in which the end goal is not fixed at the outset, specific notions of what, where and how this change should be affected are supposed to emerge during the course of the project. However, the researcher and perhaps each of the participants will have particular understandings and interpretations of the process of change being studied in action research, and may attach different values to the dynamics identified. The enabling of participants to reflect differently on their experiences is an intention that directly connects to a political agenda. Affecting participants' understandings is clearly a political impact, and while participants in action research may themselves identify problems, research questions and be encouraged to develop their own solutions, the parameters of 'enlightenment' are likely to be drawn by the researcher and funder. For example, in the context of action research, few feminist researchers would be prepared to 'facilitate' the interpretation of racist or homophobic discourse as empowering to participants. If a women's group identified asylum seekers as the source of their housing problem and decided to picket a local hostel, would the researcher be justified in challenging this construction? Again this question could be reversed: would the researcher be justified in not challenging this construction?

This illustrates the political nature of the researcher's role and the need for reflexive thinking about research ethics to be extended to what are sometimes set aside as 'political issues'. The example above shows how an ethical researcher necessarily makes political decisions, and the political role of a researcher is more complex than simply to accept and represent participants' perspectives. Even those working within an empirical realist perspective would probably share the view that they are responsible for considering the impact of the views that by publishing they are re-presenting or 'giving voice' to. For some of us, this would limit even the 'voice-as-empowerment' approach to research, so that where 'giving voice' to individual participants conflicted with our broader political judgements, the latter would be more decisive. However, the dilemma presented might be far more complex than this. If ethical research means taking responsibility for the political consequences of the accounts we produce, it entails trying to imagine unintended consequences, how the crudest versions of our accounts might function, how the findings might function when stripped of our qualifiers. It is hard to see how far one ought to take this responsibility, but by tying our research to an explicitly political agenda we might block extreme readings of our accounts and retain some control over the political uses to which the 'knowledge' we produce might be put. The political judgements that inform such decisions about representation contribute to the reflexivity 'in the academy' that Probyn (1993) urges, and analysis of the personal interpretive resources drawn on would enter into reflexive discussions about the micro-politics of research that Burman (1992) highlights. Both strands inform the politics/ethics of research and produce the relations of power between researcher and researched.

Although the emphasis may be on participants' own negotiation of change, action research projects are inevitably structured around particular definitions of empowerment and politicization. Without an exposition of these politically informed intentions, the value of such projects is difficult to measure either empirically or ethically. Furthermore, vague notions of empowerment can obscure the limitations of research as well as any potentially negative consequences. Where the aim is to raise consciousness, many feminists have agonized over whether politicizing participants is necessarily helpful, when it makes apparent the limitations on their autonomy or resources without actually challenging these limitations themselves (see Birch, 1998, chapter in *Feminist Dilemmas*). Similarly, Kelly et al. highlight the more 'grandiose' claims made for the emancipatory impact of some projects, and reassert the constraints of feminist research, drawing our attention to the level at which change is prompted:

> Participating in a research project is unlikely, in the vast majority of cases, to transform the conditions of women's lives. We cannot for example, provide access to alternative housing options, childcare places or a reasonable income. Nor are the women's services to which we may refer women, especially in the resource-starved voluntary sector, always able to meet their needs. (1994: 37)

If these limitations are not acknowledged and understood, there is a risk that participants may feel further disempowered by the research because of their perceived inability to live up to raised expectations to effect meaningful change in their lives. More significantly, participants living with oppression are likely to have constructed vital defence mechanisms and coping strategies to enable them to survive.

Approaching a research project with the aim of encouraging participants to 'enlighten' themselves, may at times be simplistic and patronizing, particularly given the amount of feminist research that is conducted by middle-class academics on or 'for' working-class women. Despite the critique of the notion of false consciousness, middle-class intellectuals might still implicitly construct working class or other disadvantaged people as victims of distorted perceptions unable to recognize and address their oppression. As Valerie Walkerdine asks:

> The idea of a true as opposed to a false consciousness simply assumes a seeing or a not seeing [yet] what if a working-class person sees and yet has myriad conscious and unconscious ways of dealing with or defending against the pains and contradictions produced out of her/his social and historical location? (1996: 149)

Awareness and sensitivity to an individual's social, cultural and historical location is crucial in facilitating any meaningful, constructive reflection on experiences. Certain interpretations or strategies regarded as counterproductive by the researcher may make perfect sense from the participant's point of view. If these constructions are challenged or disrupted during the course of the research, it is important that realistic, practical alternatives are actually available. Otherwise, well-intentioned action research which aims to raise women's consciousness of the injustices of their situation could leave individual women feeling more vulnerable.

Deconstructing and undermining 'knowledge' structures

In another distinct approach to research, feminists have sought to challenge and destabilize the knowledge structures through which power is exercised and oppression maintained. Feminists informed by post-structuralism have drawn attention to the productive function of language, highlighting the relationship between knowledge and power and effectively problematizing gendered truth claims. The resulting social critiques can be seen as offering a focus for resistance, demonstrating how language or 'discourse' may constrain women, and shape their experiences and subjectivities (Hollway, 1989; Radtke and Stam, 1994; Wilkinson and Kitzinger, 1995). A major aim of this work is to identify and undermine dominant, coercive networks of 'knowledge', thereby opening up discursive space for manoeuvre and resistance (Burman, 1990; Burman et al., 1996; Probyn, 1993).

However, the principle of deconstruction concerns many feminists who are critical of the relativistic tendencies of some analyses. Theorists engaged in deconstruction may produce analyses that lack an ethical and political context, leaving them open to charges of nihilism (Seidman, 1995). Debates concerning the ethics of post-structuralist feminism often centre on the consequences of deconstructing the category of women and of undermining the guarantors of truth. While some feminist theorists, such as Elam (1994), stress the potential benefits of renegotiating feminism's gains to generate a more radical, non essentialist, non-identity-based approach to politics, others, such as Jackson (1992), emphasize the responsibilities of feminists to preserve and build on what has already been achieved through a collective notion of womanhood. Concern about abstract theory also focuses on the extent to which postmodern deconstruction promotes academic hegemony at the expense of practical, realizable politics. Those engaged in feminist theory and research are orientated towards a political aim of critiquing and changing the social world, yet in order to pursue this goal personal investments must be made in the academic mode of production (Stanley, 1990). As Beverley Skeggs (1995) also notes, feminists in academia are locked into a paradox, in which ensuring the survival of feminist departments within universities may clash with basic feminist principles.

Most academic feminist research is conducted to obtain a research degree or publications, and while a basic intention of the work may be to understand and transform, there is also the more immediate incentive of furthering individual careers. These two functions of feminist research, abstract social change and more instrumental personal gain, can conflict, particularly when feminist work is located in an exclusively academic context, as several of the chapters in *Feminist Dilemmas in Qualitative Research* (Ribbens and Edwards, 1998) explored. While the discourse of women's studies created feminist spaces and jobs within universities, the pressure now to 'sell' material under the title of 'gender' raises dilemmas about incorporation, regulation and de-radicalization for feminist research.

Deconstructive research, informed by postmodernist approaches, may seek to expose assumptions that may be damaging to women, but without careful consideration of the impact of such deconstruction, the act of exposure itself may become the primary goal, and the particular impacts it has in specific local contexts not fully considered. Applying the critique of knowledge to one's own practice involves reflecting fully on the research intervention to question what social relations and 'facts' it corroborates and bolsters, and what meanings it blocks, undermines implicitly or questions directly. The production of theory, explanation and criticism can work to sustain, reify and legitimize some forms of social action, while excluding, deterring or problema-tizing others. By seeking to identify the politics of 'knowledge', post-structuralist informed feminists themselves produce political 'knowledge', which reflects their own grounded, partial interpretations of the world. Encouraging and enabling resist-ance to oppressive discourses and practices through a destabilization of the 'truths' which underpin them, necessarily requires a consciously motivated, political stance. Feminists use deconstruction as a device to make way for more empowering con-structions, but the struggle to produce 'better' 'knowledge' will always be fought in the context of complex, shifting political debates, and local effects as well as potentially historically shifting conditions.

Reflexivity: thinking forwards as well as back

The conclusion that the research we produce and the values we promote are inevitably grounded in partial, invested viewpoints does not detract from the crucial role that feminism, and other social criticism must play in defining or struggling towards a bet-ter world. It does, however, undermine any notion that feminism necessarily represents the universal interests of women. The recognition that women are oppressed in contra-dictory ways highlights the importance for feminists of thoroughly deconstructing any assumed commonalities with other women before reconstructing a contingent basis for progressive research, theory and or practice. This process involves an open evaluation of the specific political intentions underpinning feminist-inspired work, and an observ-ant consideration of the ethical dimensions in terms of who may be marginalized or excluded as a result. In other words, this involves a shift of emphasis from the justifica-tion of feminist claims on the grounds of moral absolutes, to a more specific, situated warranting of particular representations or actions.

The practice of reflexivity is generally regarded as an acknowledgement of the researcher's constitutive role, but emphasis feminists have traditionally placed on the research process itself, can, in some cases, actively draw attention away from the wider political context it is situated in. Focusing on methods and the interaction between researcher and researched has become so important within feminist research that, at times, it seems to substitute for feminist practice, as if the research was the political action in itself. Miriam Glucksmann (1994), among others, has pointed to the angst-ridden efforts of feminists to foster egalitarian relationships with the women they are researching, and she suggests that reflexivity and reciprocity is potentially confused with actual feminist politics:

> Nobody imagines that we could transform the various relations between women: we do not and could not overcome the structured inequalities between women *within the research process*. Yet the creation of a transparent and equal relation between researcher and researched where each is equally involved and each gets something from the process does sometimes appear to become the objective of the research ... We find a quasi solution for frustration in the current political climate by focusing down onto the research process, perhaps the one situation in which we can have an active role, and over which we do have some control. (Glucksmann, 1994: 151, emphasis added)

While conducting research constitutes a political activity, in that knowledge produced is knowledge subsequently lived, there are limits to what can be achieved through the process of feminist research. Paying careful attention to the 'internal' dynamics of a particular project reveals the messy, complex and subjective nature of research, but does not generate 'knowledge' that is somehow more authentic, or necessarily more progressive. Neither does it alter the very real, and sometimes institutionalized differences that exist between researchers and those being researched. This form of reflexivity is limited, providing a localized, bounded account of a researcher's subjectivity and research subjects' active participation. 'Silences' remain despite efforts to acknowledge the contradictions, complexities and dilemmas of doing research (Kelly et al., 1994).

Within feminist research the principles of self-reflection and transparency that have been developed and applied to the research dynamic are rarely extended to include the overarching political intentions or commitments inspiring specific projects. We argue that without the guarantees of 'a feminist politics' or 'feminist perspectives' to fall back upon, we are obliged to reflexively explore the ethics of our intentions for research, a process that could be described as forward reflexivity. Voicing the hopes that lie behind research interventions is novel in mainstream methodology discussions because it contrasts starkly with the positivist assumption that the social relations being researched are left unaltered by the research process, and that findings merely represent or reflect the world neutrally. However, a careful consideration of the possible impacts of a research project both on immediate and broader relations highlights many of the pitfalls and ethical dilemmas raised by feminist research. Without linking specific research to a wider commitment to social change, that is, discussing our intentions for research in the light of our political hopes, we miss the opportunity to develop more effective, ethically responsible, research interventions. In addition, when we produce information that is disconnected from our political aims, we might be risking our findings being invoked to back analyses we would not support politically. Exposing the political project we as researchers are engaged in clarifies our objectives, attempts to account for personal understandings and assumptions, and ultimately provides the only justification we can for our judgements about the representations or interventions we make.

Note

1 In particular, we are identifying the theoretical strands that postmodernism and post-structuralism share in terms of their critiques of modernity and 'truth'.

References

Alldred, P. (1998) 'Ethnography and discourse analysis: dilemmas in representing the voices of children', in J. Ribbens and R. Edwards (eds), *Feminist Dilemmas in Qualitative Research: Public Knowledge and Private Lives*. London: Sage. pp. 147–70.

Bhavnani, K.-K. and Phoenix, A. (1994) *Shifting Identities, Shifting Racisms: A 'Feminism and Psychology' Reader*. London: Sage.

Birch, M. (1998) 'Re/constructing research narratives: self and sociological identity in alternative settings', in J. Ribbens and R. Edwards (eds), *Feminist Dilemmas in Qualitative Research*. London: Sage. pp. 171–85.

Bordo, S. (1990) 'Feminist, postmodernism, and genderscepticism', in L.J. Nicholson (ed.), *Feminism/Postmodernism*. New York: Routledge.

Bordo, S. (1998) 'Bringing body to theory', in D. Welton (ed.), *Body and Flesh: A Philosophical Reader*. Oxford: Blackwells.

Burman, E. (1990) 'Differing with deconstruction: a feminist critique', in I. Parker and J. Shotter (eds), *Deconstructing Social Psychology*. London: Routledge.

Burman, E. (1992) 'Feminism and discourse in developmental psychology: power, subjectivity and interpretation', *Feminism and Psychology*, 2 (1): 45–60.

Burman, E. (1993) 'Beyond discursive relativism: power and subjectivity in developmental psychology', in H. Tam, L. Mos, W. Thorngate, et al. (eds), *Recent Trends in Theoretical Psychology* (Vol. III). New York: Springer Verlag. pp. 208–20.

Burman, E. (1996) 'Introduction', in E. Burman, P. Alldred, C. Bewley, et al. (eds), *Challenging Women: Psychology's Exclusions, Feminist Possibilities*. Buckingham: Open University Press.

Burman, E., Alldred, P., Bewley, C., et al. (1996) *Challenging Women: Psychology's Exclusions, Feminist Possibilities*. Buckingham: Open University Press.

Butler, J. (1990) *Gender Trouble: Feminism and the Subversion of Identity*. New York: Routledge.

Butler, J. (1993) *Bodies that Matter*. New York: Routledge.

Edwards, R. (1996) 'White woman researcher – black women subjects', in S. Wilkinson and C. Kitzinger (eds), *Representing the Other*. London: Sage.

Elam, D. (1994) *Feminism and Deconstruction: Ms en Abyme*. London: Routledge.

Fraser, N. (1989) *Unruly Practices: Power, Discourse and Gender in Contemporary Social Theory*. Cambridge: Polity Press.

Fraser, N. and Nicholson, L. (1990) 'Social criticism without philosophy', in L. Nicholson (ed.), *Feminism/Postmodernism*. New York: Routledge.

Friere, P. (1972) *Cultural Action for Freedom*. Harmondsworth: Penguin.

Gillies, V. and Robinson Y. (2010) 'Managing emotions in research with challenging pupils', *Ethnography in Education*, 5 (1): 97–110.

Gillies, V. and Lucey H. (eds) (2007) *Women Power and the Academy: The Personal Is Political*. London: Palgrave.

Glucksmann, M. (1994) 'The work of knowledge and the knowledge of women's work', in M. Maynard and J. Purvis (eds), *Researching Women's Lives from a Feminist Perspective.* London: Taylor & Francis.

Griffin, C. (1996) '"See whose face it wears": difference, otherness and power', in S. Wilkinson and C. Kitzinger (eds), *Representing the Other.* London: Sage.

Harding, S. (1987) *Feminism and Methodology.* Milton Keynes: Open University Press.

Harding, S. (1990) 'Feminism, science, and the anti-enlightenment critiques', in L. Nicholson (ed.), *Feminism/Postmodernism.* New York: Routledge.

Harding, S. (1991) *Whose Science? Whose Knowledge? Thinking from Women's Lives.* Milton Keynes: Open University Press.

Hollway, W. (1989) *Subjectivity and Method in Psychology: Gender, Meaning and Science.* London: SAGE Publications.

hooks, b. (1990) *Yearning: Race, Gender and Cultural Politics.* Boston, MA: South End Press.

Hurd, T. and McIntyre, A. (1996) 'The seduction of sameness: similarity and representing the other', in S. Wilkinson and C. Kitzinger (eds), *Representing the Other.* London: Sage.

Jackson, S. (1992) 'The amazing deconstructing woman', *Trouble and Strife,* 25: 25–31.

Kelly, L., Burton, S. and Reagan, L. (1994) 'Researching women's lives or studying women's oppression? Reflections on what constitutes feminist research', in M. Maynard and J. Purvis (eds), *Researching Women's Lives from a Feminist Perspective.* London: Taylor & Francis.

Kitzinger, C. and Wilkinson, S. (1996) 'Theorizing representing the other', in S. Wilkinson and C. Kitzinger (eds), *Representing the Other.* London: Sage.

Marks, D. (1996) 'Constructing a narrative: moral discourse and young people's experience of exclusion', in E. Burman, G. Aitken, P. Alldred, et al. (eds), *Psychology, Discourse, Practice: From Regulation to Resistance.* London: Taylor & Francis.

Mayall, B. (1999) 'Children and childhood', in S. Hood, B. Mayall and S. Oliver (eds), *Critical Issues in Social Research: Power and Prejudice.* Buckingham: Open University Press.

McNay, L. (1992) *Foucault and Feminism: Power, Gender and the Self.* Cambridge: Polity Press.

Patai, D. (1991) 'US academics and third world women: is ethical research possible?', in S. Berger Gluck and D. Patai (eds), *Women's Words: The Feminist Practice of Oral History.* London: Routledge.

Probyn, E. (1993) *Sexing The Self: Gendered Positions in Cultural Studies.* London: Routledge.

Radtke, H. and Stam, H.J. (eds) (1994) *Powerl Gender: Social Relations in Theory and Practice.* London: Sage.

Ramazanoglu, C. and Holland, J. (1999) 'Tripping over experience: some problems in feminist epistemology', *Discourse: Studies in the Cultural Politics of Education,* 20 (3): 381–92.

Ramazanoglu, C. with Holland, J. (2002) *Feminist Methodology: Challenges and Choices.* London: Sage.

Ransom, J. (1993) 'Identity, difference and power', in C. Ramazanoglu (ed.), *Up Against Foucault, Explorations of Some Tensions Between Foucault and Feminism.* London: Routledge.

Reay, D. (1996) 'Insider perspectives or stealing the words out of women's mouths', *Feminist Review,* 53 (Summer): 57–73.

Ribbens, J. and Edwards, R. (eds) (1998) *Feminist Dilemmas in Qualitative Research: Public Knowledge and Private Lives.* London: Sage.

Riley, D. (1988) *'Am I That Name?' Feminism and the Category of 'Women' In History.* London: Macmillan.

Seidman, S. (1995) 'Deconstructing queer theory', in L. Nicholson and S. Seidman (eds), *Social Postmodernism: Beyond Identity Politics.* Cambridge: Cambridge University Press.

Skeggs, B. (1995) 'Women's studies in Britain in the 1990's', *Women's Studies International Forum,* 18 (4): 475–85.

Soper, K. (1991) 'Postmodernism and its discontents', *Feminist Review,* 39: 97–108.

Spelman, E.V. (1988) *Inessentially Speaking: Problems of Exclusion in Feminist Thought.* London: Women's Press.

Standing, K. (1998) 'Writing the voices of the less powerful: research on lone mothers', in J. Ribbens and R. Edwards (eds), *Feminist Dilemmas in Qualitative Research: Public Knowledge and Private Lives.* London: Sage.

Stanley, L. (1990) 'An editorial introduction', in L. Stanley (ed.), *Feminist Praxis.* London: Routledge.

Stanley, L. and Wise, S. (1993) *Breaking Out Again: Feminist Ontology and Epistemology.* London: Routledge.

Taylor, M. (1994) 'Action research', in P. Banister, E. Burman, I. Parker, et al. (eds), *Qualitative Methods in Psychology: A Research Guide.* Buckingham: Open University Press.

Ticeneto Clough, P. (1992) *The End(s) of Ethnography: From Realism to Social Criticism.* London: Sage.

Walkerdine, V. (1996) 'Psychological and social aspects of survival', in S. Wilkinson (ed.), *Feminist Social Psychologies: International Perspectives.* Buckingham: Open University Press.

Weedon, C. (1987) *Feminist Practice and Poststructuralist Theory.* Oxford: Blackwell.

Wilkinson, S. and Kitzinger, C. (eds) (1995) *Feminism and Discourse: Psychological Perspectives.* London: Sage.

Wilkinson, S. and Kitzinger, C. (eds) (1996) *Representing the Other.* London: Sage.

Wise, S. and Stanley L. (2003) 'Review article: "Looking back and looking forward: some recent feminist sociology reviewed"', *Sociological Research Online,* 8 (3).

4

Consenting to what? Issues of access, gate-keeping and 'informed' consent

TINA MILLER AND LINDA BELL

Introduction

This chapter examines ethical issues that arise in the course of accessing potential participants. Gaining 'informed' consent is problematic if it is not clear what the participant is consenting to and where 'participation' begins and ends. We argue that 'consent' should be ongoing and renegotiated between researcher and researched throughout the research process. We also argue that satisfactorily completing an ethics form at the beginning of a study and/or obtaining ethics approval does not mean that ethical issues can be forgotten, rather ethical considerations should form an ongoing part of the research. In this chapter we explore the ongoing ethical dilemmas around gate-keeping, access, re-access and consent through examples from three projects, two employing single interviews and another with a longitudinal component. A further key concern involves the ways in which the researcher and any 'gate-keepers' (Miller, 1995, 1998, 2005; Reeves, 2010) influence who eventually become research participants.

The first of these research projects involved a woman researcher (Linda) accessing and interviewing partners of 'violent men'. These men were attending a therapy centre that was being evaluated by Linda's male colleagues. The issues involved in this project will be discussed later. The second study involved accessing and interviewing Bangladeshi women living in a town in southern England, about antenatal practices. The final project was a longitudinal study exploring women's experiences of first-time transition to motherhood. The ethical issues that we address in this chapter are enmeshed, in the context of these particular projects, with the important issues of gender and ethnicity

The shift towards a focus on subjective experience and the meanings individuals give to their actions has led to a concern with the research process itself and the ways in which qualitative data are gathered. Feminist researchers have influenced debates around the research process, reflecting upon their own roles in the co-production of research data and questioning the power relationships that are produced and underpin data gathering (Edwards and Ribbens, 1998; Oakley, 1981; Ribbens and Edwards, 1995; Stanley and Wise, 1990, 1993). In turn this has led to a questioning of the ongoing ethical dimensions of the research process. In the UK there is no law requiring the submission of research proposals to ethical committees. However, professional and academic research guidelines and committee structures have been available to researchers for many years and are widely used to guide the early stages of the research process (BSA, 1993, 2002). Yet, while initial guidance is welcomed it is argued that this can obscure the need to continually reflect on the ethical implications of researching people's lives. Ethics committee requirements that the research relationship must be formalized through written consent at the outset also has implications for those trying to research hidden groups or those who are difficult to access (Renzetti and Lee, 1993). Individuals who identify themselves as socially excluded or belonging to a marginalized group, are unlikely to formally consent in writing to participation in a study (Miller and Boulton, 2007).

As feminist researchers we identify knowledge production as being grounded in individual and collective experiences and this means that the course of a project may only be guessed at initially. While informing participants about the research aims at the outset of a project is vital, final research findings may not resonate with those aims. The precise nature of 'consent' for the participants might only become clear eventually, at the end of a study, when the researchers' impact on shaping the study is visible. This raises questions about what is it that the participant is consenting to. Just 'participation', in the sense of being interviewed? (For a further discussion of dimensions of participation see Maxine Birch and Tina Miller in Chapter 6, this volume). However, if we are to enable/empower participants to share in this construction of more than the interview data, suggesting an 'egalitarian' or participatory focus to the research, might we tacitly expect interviewees also to be interested in reading their own interview transcripts, or to contribute in other ways to the analysis or to the final written product? Is this 'egalitarian' focus somehow ethically 'more acceptable' although, at the same time, it requires a greater contribution from participants than they may have thought they were consenting to? (These issues are developed further in Chapters 2 and 6.)

Accessing potential participants not only requires providing information about the research, but also that individuals are in a position to exercise choice around whether or not to give their consent to participate. Yet much qualitative research relies upon gate-keepers as a route of initial access to participants. The notion of 'gate-keeper' has frequently been used in sociological and anthropological research[1] (Burgess, 1982; Liebow, 1967; Reeves, 2010; Whyte, 1955), referring to those who are in a position to 'permit' access to others for the purpose of interviewing. This is important from an ethical perspective because it suggests the potential exercising of power by some individuals over others. Some research projects may consider a representative of a particular group as a gate-keeper (with all the methodological implications this may imply – see Wallman [1984] on 'resource keepers' in households). In the research examples below we discuss how gate-keepers' power was exerted in differing ways in relation to those individuals we wished to access for interview purposes. Controls the gate-keepers exercised varied, for example from the cultural and hierarchical (Bangladeshi women study) to the therapeutic and paternalistic ('male therapy centre' study). We argue that issues around access and gate-keeping and notions of what constitutes 'informed' consent have clear ethical implications for feminist research.

In the following sections we use examples from three research projects to explore the ethical dilemmas that can surface in gaining access and re-access to research participants. Interplay between notions of access, 'coercion' and motive and/or motivation provides a recurrent theme across these discussions in which issues of gender, power and ethnicity are implicit. Our concerns lead us to reflect upon the ethical dilemmas raised by notions of 'informed' consent and the sometimes tenuous link between research aims and research outcomes. Finally, we consider practical ways in which feminist ethical guidelines can be used to alert researchers to the ongoing ethical considerations that can arise in qualitative research.

Ethical dilemmas encountered in gaining access to research participants

Decisions taken around access are closely bound up with questions of ethics and may be increasingly influenced by ethics committee requirements (see Chapter 2, this volume). Similarly, the differences between gaining access and consent are not always clear. Access to research participants is both a crucial aspect of the research process and one that is often dealt with as relatively unproblematic in mainstream – offline – research methods textbooks (see Robson, 2008[2]). The potential dilemmas encountered around access can become subsumed within discussions about 'sampling' and 'populations' (see Mason, 1996). As noted above, other issues, for example around 'gate-keepers', may also be significant. An overriding concern within professional research guidelines is often that 'coercion' has not been exerted and participation in any research project is 'voluntary' (Miller and Boulton, 2007; Wiles et al., 2005; see also Linda Bell and Linda Nutt in Chapter 5, this volume).

Implicit within such guidelines is the assumption that providing consent is 'voluntary', 'coercion' is deemed not to have occurred. Yet such an assumption ignores the potentially complex power dynamics that can operate around access and consent especially where issues of gender and/or ethnicity are manifest. Nor do such guidelines take account of ethnographic research (Calvey, 2008; Mattingly, 2005; Miller, forthcoming). So, in the process of moving from the written research proposal to operationalizing the research plan – which will increasingly have been subject to review by an ethics committee – the researcher can experience problems around access and encounter ethical dilemmas. Having decided *who* is to be accessed the problem of *how* arises. Even supposing that this is straight-forward, the researcher must continually reflect on the ways in which decisions around *routes* of access can affect the data collected.

Access to potential research participants can be achieved through employing a range of strategies. Participants can be recruited via highly structured and selective strategies, for example, quota sampling or through much less formal channels such as snowballing using the researcher's own social networks. Whichever approach is adopted, the *motives* around why some people become participants and others resist should concern the researcher and be documented in a research diary. Clearly some potential participants may find resistance more difficult. The control of gate-keepers has been noted in previous research (Miller, 1998) but not specifically in relation to their power to sanction access to less powerful individuals and groups such as Bangladeshi women for example. So, although feminist researchers have recognized and increasingly documented the need to reflect on the relationship between the ways in which participants are accessed and the data collected (Edwards and Ribbens, 1998; Mauthner, 2000), the ways in which decisions taken around access can be closely bound up with questions of ethics are less well explored (but see Emmel et al., 2007; Reeves, 2010). Our initial concern is with the ways in which judgements are made about who might be 'suitable' interviewees and the lengths that might be gone to in order to access those identified as such. Moreover, does the researcher feel that s/he can be more tacitly 'coercive' of potential participants, as in the case of the 'male therapy centre' research, if s/he perceives that the research is underpinned by a good ethical motive? Or if interviewees view their participation as minimal, a single interview for example rather than a longer-term commitment as in a longitudinal study? We explore these questions in the following sections through a focus on different research projects we have been involved in individually.

Accessing women respondents for single interviews via male gate-keepers

The first of these studies, the 'male therapy centre' project was commissioned to evaluate the work of a therapy centre concerned with male violence. This example illustrates protracted, and ethically fraught dimensions of accessing hard to reach participants perceived (though not necessarily self-defined) as potentially vulnerable.[3] The role of gate-keepers in this project is particularly relevant to feminist research ethics, since two 'layers' of male gate-keepers controlled access, in different ways, to women whose partners used the therapy centre. Interviews with these particular women emerged as a key feature of the overall evaluative study. Potentially, gate-keeping issues had serious implications for being able to work confidentially with these women partners. The sensitive nature of the topic of investigation also meant that the research eventually had to be based on single rather than repeat interviews with women. This avoided some other ethical dilemmas noted initially but also precluded any attempts to involve interviewees more closely in interpreting research findings over a longer period. However, the sensitive topic of male violence also raises a question as to whether the female interviewees or the funders of the research, in this case the therapy centre, were the main beneficiaries of the project's findings, especially given the small number of women eventually accessed.

In this project Linda's male academic colleagues initially planned to interview men using the therapy programme in order to examine whether there were any changes over time to their perceptions or violent behaviour as a result of the therapy. However, the (male) researchers and therapists felt that this 'before' and 'after' data available from interviews with men would only give a partial indication of 'success' or 'failure' of the centre's programme. They decided that what was called an 'independent check' was needed on the validity of the men's accounts, so it was planned to ask women partners of men attending the centre whether they 'really had improved' following therapy. After the project had started, Linda was therefore asked if she would join the research team and interview women partners on that basis. She rejected this original plan since, as a feminist, she objected to the idea that women were just there to confirm or deny someone else's 'reality'. Her first reaction was that it was no use trying to 'link' women in to the men's versions or accounts of their 'realities' in this way, but that taking a feminist perspective meant that women should be asked to give their own accounts of their experiences.

Beyond this initial objection, however, it soon became clear that questions of accessing 'women partners' for interview were going to be the key issue (see Hoff, 1990: 148, 249, on 'the problem of access'). Linda felt it was unlikely that women would be willing to come forward to be interviewed if contact with them stemmed from a men's centre. The therapists and male researchers had designed a project into which the women were then 'fitted' and for whom they acted as gate-keepers. A second 'layer' of gate-keeping involved the 'violent men' themselves and, as discussed below, it was not clear initially how to gain access specifically to women whose partners used the centre *without* involving their male partners in some way.[4]

Reactions from women's groups to Linda's developing work were sometimes negative (see also Hoff, 1990: 249–50, on feminist activist concerns). This underlined that a significant emerging feature of this research was that the centre could be having a profound impact on women, but was primarily set up to assist men. Owing to the nature of the whole project, including evaluation of the therapy programme with individual men by male colleagues, Linda felt that ethically it was essential that these women partners' voices should be heard in relation to the centre and its programme.[5] Linda made a judgement that, due to the nature of the research, it was *these* women (whose partners were currently using the centre) that she should interview, despite the difficulties of access, rather than any other women who had been subjected to violence.

Linda and her colleagues realized that she would have to take *active* steps in order to reach these particular women. This suggests persuasion, even tacit coercion, would be needed in order to access and interview what she might consider 'a reasonable number of women partners'. Two further gendered aspects of the project emerged. The first was the tacit assumption on the part of Linda's colleagues that partners of men using the centre would actually be women. Linda acknowledged that this might not be the case, and offered to interview any partners, male or female. However, she also felt that due to the frequently gendered nature of violence, and especially if she were working with a small sample of interviewees, that accessing a small mixed group could seriously affect the nature of the research in terms of the 'representativeness' being sought by the therapists. At this stage Linda therefore began to think in terms of a sample of 'all women' or 'all gay men'.

At the outset Linda deliberately avoided contact with men using the centre. She took this decision to help ensure future confidentiality for any partners who might agree to be interviewed. Nevertheless, Linda had not realized initially, that some of her potential 'sample' of women partners were well known to the centre therapists. Some partners had been in direct contact with the centre by telephone or in person (as she was to discover during the research) and a majority of these partners were women. Colleagues suggested that Linda should simply telephone these partners and ask them to talk about their partner's violence towards them. However, Linda felt that this was again a potential breach of confidentiality and felt unease at the prospect of raising the issue of violence directly with these women. By this stage women's centres and other organizations had contacted Linda concerned in particular with the ethics of doing research with male abusers. Linda explained that she was doing research that was intended to give the partners of 'violent' men more of a 'voice' in relation to the male therapy centre. However their fears highlighted Linda's own intentions to behave in ways that would not be, inadvertently or otherwise, damaging to women partners.

This process of accessing and interviewing women partners illustrates a number of ethical issues, for example the difficulties of access via (male) gate-keepers. Furthermore Linda decided to 'distance' her interviewees from the therapy centre and male partners by using her own university connections to further ensure the confidentiality of women's participation and of their interview accounts. Linda and her colleagues agreed that she would 'reach' these women partners by letter (Box 4.1) in which the 'serious' nature of the research would be conveyed. By adopting an 'impersonal' stance and linking herself specifically to her university, Linda hoped that women might not feel 'intruded' upon personally, and would feel able to come forward to be interviewed.

BOX 4.1

RESEARCH STUDY

An independent research project run through the University of Y is investigating women's experiences of violence, particularly in a domestic setting. We are contacting you to ask whether you would be willing to take part in this research.

The research will involve talking to a woman researcher working at University of Y in confidence, and completing an anonymous questionnaire. We are keen to talk to as many women as possible, and to give them the opportunity to discuss their concerns with us. This project is part of a wider study being run in association with the Z Centre, but the woman researcher will have no contact with men using the Centre, and interviews will be arranged confidentially and in places agreed between her and women taking part in the study.

Information on services and projects that aim to help women experiencing violence will be available from the researcher.

If you would like any further information about the study, or wish to take part, please contact Linda Bell on the following numbers:

Please leave a telephone number and name for us to contact if you wish, but you do not need to leave your surname, or address.

Thank you

Linda Bell.

After designing the letter Linda became dependent on the centre for distributing it. The only way seemed to be to give copies to men attending for therapy, asking them to pass it on to their partners. As noted earlier, these 'gate-keeping' activities yielded one interviewee whose partner was currently having therapy. Linda also asked the centre to make the letter available to any partners who contacted them. Through this latter route two more interviewees were recruited. Another woman who had heard about the research contacted Linda and offered to be interviewed. However, she rang back some days later to cancel the proposed meeting, as her partner had attacked her and broken her arm. It was never clear to Linda whether or not this was as a result of her attempt to participate in the research.

Each of the three women who gave full interviews perceived herself as a 'survivor' from the circumstances around the violence, and all had suggestions as to how women's perspectives could be taken on board more effectively by the centre in its work with 'violent' men. The interviewees all used their interviews to 'sound off' about the centre and the effects its work was having on them. For example, one interviewee complained her ex-partner 'hassled' her, using his attendance at the centre to suggest he was 'cured' of violent behaviour.[6] She contacted the centre, asking them to tell him to stop hassling her. One woman was hopeful that the therapy would be effective (she was still living with her partner), while the others had separated from their partners and were also more pessimistic that the man would stop being violent. Although Linda suggested repeat interviews and offered to keep in contact, no interviewees actually maintained contact with her. However, once the effects of the centre's work on these women had been revealed, re-interviewing them was felt to be unnecessary by all the researchers. Despite the limited sample, the interviews had thus served a useful purpose from a policy perspective. Specifically, a woman counsellor was recruited to work with centre partners and closer links were also developed with supportive women's centres.

A further dilemma remained. With only three interviewees Linda decided to try a different approach to boost the response. She had by now come into contact with a women's group who actively supported the work of the therapy centre and arranged with them to meet a potential interviewee on their premises (although she did not turn up in the event). The women's group suggested holding a meeting with their members and an 'open letter' was written inviting them to meet. Interestingly, despite (or perhaps because of) its much more 'direct' approach, this letter was not effective and the proposed meeting had to be abandoned due to lack of response. The letter had a very different tone to the earlier one; Linda was much more up-front about her own intentions, saying for example – 'my way of doing this research is to *listen to everything women want to tell me,* in confidence ...'. With such a sensitive topic, perhaps with hindsight this personalized the issue too much. Although no more interviews were arranged, Linda developed a short questionnaire that was posted to some members of this women's group, whose partners used the therapy centre and this provided further background material for the research.

By now Linda had also reported to colleagues that she herself was feeling intimidated by demands to increase the sample. This made her realize the *similarities* between herself and her interviewees, in their experiences of power, control or even, coercion by men.

Ethically, Linda felt that despite the small number of women accessed, these accounts did justify the time and effort spent on obtaining them. For the women who came forward with a story to tell, the interviews provided a sort of catharsis, which they acknowledged. For the therapy centre and male researchers, the research findings had revealed women (including Linda herself) describing their perceived lack of power and effective involvement with the centre. The political and therapeutic implications of this were subsequently acknowledged by the therapists and acted upon, particularly by recruiting a female counsellor. The research process therefore raised ethical dilemmas relating not only to issues of access and confidentiality, but also to male power in relation to women.

Using gate-keepers in accessing those who may be less powerful

The need to rethink routes and modes of access both at the outset *and* once a study is underway is clearly necessary in research that explores groups who may be difficult to access for a whole range of reasons. Modes of access may also increasingly be stipulated by ethics committees (see Chapter 2, this volume). The question of *who* is actually giving consent and to what must be considered throughout. However, control over decision making around access is not always in the hands of the interviewer and even when this appears to be so, can still be problematic when gate-keepers are used. The role of the gate-keeper in accessing those who may be less powerful and therefore less able to resist voluntary participation became a concern in Tina's research on Bangladeshi women (Miller, 1995). The small-scale pilot study was set up to explore Bangladeshi women's experiences of maternity services in a town in southern Britain. Tina had lived and worked in Bangladesh and was sensitive to the religious beliefs and cultural traditions of the women she hoped to interview. She also recognized that in order to access this largely hidden group she would have to find a gate-keeper. This proved to be more difficult than anticipated.

Initially, Tina hoped to access potential participants through a health visitor contact. Although Tina realized that this might result in a 'biased' sample (that is, women who were regular users of maternity services) she anticipated that snowballing could then be used to access other women. The health visitor who was approached felt unable to act as a potential gate-keeper as she was concerned about being perceived as coercive and mis-using her professional role. She suggested that Tina contact her colleague who was Bangladeshi and a community worker. When contact was finally made, Tina was surprised and dismayed to find that this colleague was not in fact Bangladeshi but Indian and therefore unable to act as a gate-keeper. Tina's dismay arose from the apparent cultural insensitivity demonstrated by the health visitor. However this contact was able to provide Tina with the name of a Bangladeshi woman who worked in the community assisting in language classes for members of the local Bangladeshi population. Contact was eventually made with J and she agreed to meet Tina and discuss her research. Fortunately she was interested in the research and agreed to let Tina 'join' a recently formed Bangladeshi women's group. Yet while the difficulty of accessing a gate-keeper was an initial and protracted problem it is the power that the gate-keeper was then able to assert in *volunteering* women that is of particular importance to this discussion.

The Bangladeshi women who came to the group – where among other activities, English-language classes were offered – were both vulnerable and largely powerless. The context in which they experienced and exercised agency was regulated by religious and cultural practices that encompassed all aspects of their lives. When, at the next meeting, Tina was introduced to the women she realized that in effect *wholesale access* had been provided by the gate-keeper. These women would find it difficult not to agree to participate in the study as it was J who had 'let her in'. J was not only responsible for setting up the women's group but she also occupied a respected position in the local community; she was more powerful than the other women in terms of her perceived social class and status. However, although the women had been volunteered and access given to a hard-to-reach group, the interviews themselves provided an opportunity for the women to exercise some agency and to resist talking about certain aspects of their lives. But in situations where those in more powerful positions, for example line managers, are asked to act as gate-keepers to potential respondents, how feasible is it for them subsequently to resist taking part? Similarly, when powerful gate-keepers are used notions around access, coercion and, more importantly, consent can become very difficult for the researcher – and researched – to disentangle. Who is actually giving consent and to what?

Access and longitudinal research

Further ethical dilemmas can arise for the researcher in longitudinal research. Here access clearly needs to be renegotiated prior to each interview (Miller, 1998). Ethical concerns can emerge when renegotiation of access is clouded by advice from others and when participants may be feeling particularly vulnerable. The point made earlier about whether researchers should ever be more 'coercive' when they perceive their research to be underpinned by good ethical motives is revisited here. In her research on first-time transition to motherhood (Miller, 2000, 2005), Tina planned to interview the 17 women who had agreed to participate in her study, on three separate occasions – once at seven to eight months antenatally, then at six to eight weeks postnatally and finally at around nine months postnatally. She had accessed all the women through snowballing and they were verbally willing at the outset to participate over the course of the study. The first round of interviewing took place antenatally with the women consenting to be contacted once their baby had been born so that a further interview could be arranged. All the women reiterated their 'consent' at this first interview although they had no way of knowing how they might be feeling in the early weeks following the birth of their baby and whether they would want to talk about their experiences.

For one participant the early postnatal period was much more difficult to cope with than she had anticipated and she initially 'chose' not to be interviewed when the first postnatal interview was due. It was this action that raised particular ethical concerns for Tina. These concerns arose because the participant had commented during telephone conversations with Tina that she had been diagnosed as having postnatal depression (a label she rejected) and that her husband and health visitor felt that she should not be interviewed. The lengthy telephone conversations with Tina suggested that she really did want someone to talk to and that she was clearly feeling lonely and isolated. Tina felt uneasy that her research should in some way be seen as a possible catalyst for reflection leading to unhappiness – or at least not helpful – by her health visitor and that this participant was, it seemed, being silenced by others. Tina was at the same time frustrated that this participant's experiences of early mothering might not be voiced thereby helping to perpetuate the myths that surround mothering being 'natural' and therefore easy. Was this a 'good enough' ethical motive for Tina to pursue this participant further, to be 'coercive'? In the extracts in Box 4.2 taken from Tina's fieldwork diary she contemplates what course of action to take.

BOX 4.2

[24/1/96] Spoke to respondent 4 again (having phoned her last week). We spoke for 15–20 minutes – apparently both the respondent's husband and her health visitor don't think she should progress with the interviews – but I feel she wants to, if only to have someone to talk to. I said I did not want to put any pressure on her, especially as others thought she should not proceed. She was unhappy that the health visitor had asked her to fill out a depression scoring questionnaire – she had scored 16 points and then 17 on the next occasion and so had been 'labelled'/ diagnosed as suffering from postnatal depression and prescribed anti-depressants. She was angry that she had been labelled in this way and treated with drugs (the implication was that she was not taking the drugs). She spoke of being lonely and 'stuck out here', isolated. After a long talk – with me telling her that not all women found becoming a mother easy – she arranged to meet me next Tuesday at her house for a [first] postnatal interview. I gave her my home number and said to phone me on Tuesday morning if she didn't feel up to being interviewed — although I sense that she will be relieved once she has been interviewed (fulfilled her obligations to me?). I am also aware of my position/role as researcher and not professional counsellor, but as a mother I empathise and realise I may find it difficult to disentangle/keep my various roles separate.

[30/1/96] I have just been telephoned by respondent 4 who sounded cheerful – hysterical almost – but said that she was phoning from her parents and therefore could not be interviewed today. She apologised but said she was cooking lunch for her dad. She said she would phone me (I suggested Thursday) at the office, or at home to arrange another time. I feel frustrated as I had my coat on ready to leave and had prepared to 'do' the interview after what had already been a frustratingly long build up. Will she contact me??

[15/2/96] Respondent 4 hasn't phoned, I wonder if I should send my interview prompt sheet in the form of a self-administered questionnaire? I will talk to (supervisor) about this (Ethics?!).

After discussions with her supervisor Tina decided to write to the participant and request that she contact her if she wanted to re-enter the study for the final interview. Tina was surprised, and pleased, when she did contact her once her child had reached nine months of age and her decision not to pressure the particpant eventually yielded a positive result.

'Informed' consent – to what?

The research studies above relied upon obtaining verbal consent. The requirement that researchers increasingly obtain written consent from participants poses new ethical considerations. The differences between access and consent are not always clear. As we noted in our earlier discussion, gate-keepers may in effect (unknowingly) imply and authorize consent where they provide access to less powerful groups. Similarly, researchers may choose to take 'consent' as given once a potential participant agrees to be interviewed and to participate in the research. While ethics committees increasingly require researchers to produce consent forms for them to vet and for research participants to sign, the formality of such procedures will certainly alienate some groups and individuals. This shift in academic social research mirrors concerns around coercion and safety that have existed for some time in health services research. It also resonates with growing concerns around risk and consumerism in research (Annandale, 1998). The practice of research is increasingly regarded as a risky enterprise in which the 'protection' of parties involved and issues of accountability come to the fore in written guidelines and contracts (Crow et al., 2006; Miller and Boulton, 2007). Yet, in research focusing on less visible aspects of the social world, for example domestic violence, access to research participants may be tenuous, based on notions of trust in the individual researcher. Any formal requirement to obtain written consent could fundamentally challenge such relationships.

Even more problematic than written consent are notions that consent is 'informed'. Research handbooks and ethical guides emphasize that consent must be obtained prior to any research commencing. Yet, what is it that participants are consenting to when they agree to join a study? If the focus of the research is to explore a period of transition, how can the outcome of the research be known? Feminist principles of research – reciprocity and empowerment – may be embraced by the researcher at the outset of research, yet goals may shift, prompting a more instrumental approach, for example assembling a viable sample or meeting deadlines (see Duncombe and Jessop in Chapter 7, this volume). While the dynamic nature of the research process is increasingly acknowledged in social research literature, the ethical dilemmas that this presents for feminist researchers and their research participants are less well explored (although see Luff, 1999, and Mauthner, 2000, for contributions to this area).

Obtaining 'informed consent' at the start of a project should not mean that it does not have to be thought about again. Researchers need to decide what they are inviting participants to consent to. Is consent just about participation in the research in terms of being interviewed or does it go further, involving reading and commenting on transcripts and the analysis of data? Even if the terms of participation are clearly agreed and consented to at the beginning of a study these can change. In her research on transition to motherhood (Miller, 2000, 2005) Tina offered to provide a summary of the research findings at the end of the study to the women who had participated. Yet by the end of the longitudinal research. Tina recognized that her findings would not in some cases resonate with the participants own expectations. While the women had all consented to participate by allowing themselves to be accessed, Tina admits to feeling some trepidation in returning to the participants at the end of the study with her findings. Her anxiety arose because she felt certain the women in the study had anticipated a different 'product', a more practical 'how to' guide to first-time mothering, when they agreed to join the research. Their overriding interest had been with how other women in the study had experienced and coped with becoming mothers. In contrast Tina's interpretation of the data led her to focus on the episte-mological and ontological shifts discernible in the stories that were constructed at different times through the women's transition. While participants were informed prior to the first interview that the research was about 'transition to motherhood' the findings could not be known before the research was carried out. Yet the women in the study had their own ideas about the research and its possible outcomes as noted in the extract below taken from one end-of-study questionnaire:

> I would hope being a participant in the research would help other women ... Tina is making a great achievement for women. I hope in enlightening us all, that we are allowed to feel the way we do. Well done Tina and thank you!

Tina was aware, retrospectively, that although some of the women had experienced their participation in the research as 'therapeutic' (see Birch and Miller, 2000) the research could only ever make a small contribution (if any) to changing societal atti-tudes to motherhood. Tina's research would almost certainly not be 'enlightening' everyone, as one participant clearly hoped in the extract above. However it may also be the case that as feminist researchers we are overly sensitive to the potential (ethi-cal?) impact of our research on those involved. This was demonstrated in one response Tina received when she wrote to confirm participants' addresses before returning their tape-recorded interviews to them at the end of the study. Abigail replied to the letter and, as well as confirming her address details, wrote '... it seems so long ago, that to be honest I'd forgotten about it'.

Some thoughts on practical guidelines around ethical issues in relation to access and consent

We have argued that decisions taken around access, re-access and gaining consent can be closely bound up with questions of ethics. Moreover, the differences between gaining access and consent are not always clear. From our examples, it is clear that researchers must continually reflect upon access routes in order to address complex issues around representation of individual voices; ethical concerns over 'consent' to participating in a research study; and activities of those acting as 'gate-keepers' who may perceive some potential interviewees as 'vulnerable', or otherwise be in a position of some power over them. Researchers should examine how far those 'volunteered' by such gate-keepers can resist participation, or alternatively whether some potential participants are being effectively excluded. Researchers should also examine the ways in which gender and ethnicity can affect who is accessed and by whom. Does apparent or tacit 'coercion' invalidate our notions of 'informed' consent? Furthermore, may there be a danger of excluding those groups who are difficult to access by using inflexible and – increasingly required by ethics committees – more formal methods of gaining consent (for example, written consent). Judging by our own experiences 'consent' needs to be ongoing and renegotiated between researcher and researched – not just at the time of access but possibly as transcripts are analysed and findings are published. Using a research diary to document access routes and decisions made throughout the research process is one practical way of developing an ethics checklist. This practice of regular reflection helps ensure that ethical and methodological considerations are continually reassessed.

Notes

1 This notion of 'gate-keeper' is related to that of the 'key informant' (Tremblay, 1957; Whyte, 1955). Unlike key informants, however, we would also define a 'gate-keeper' as someone who gives access to other interviewees but who would not necessarily actually take part in a study by being interviewed themselves (which was the position in the studies discussed in this chapter).

2 Robson does acknowledge, however, that different research designs imply different problems: If you are clear about your [research] intentions, perhaps with a pretty tight, pre-structured, design then the task [getting access] is probably easier initially, in that you can give them a good indication of what they are letting themselves in for. With a looser, more emergent design, there may be more difficulties ... as it is impossible to specify in advance exactly what you will do' (1993: 295).

3 However genuine issues of 'partner safety' should not be underestimated here. See Bell (1998).

4 As Dobash et al. note: 'Increasingly, evaluators [of programmes for violent men] have proposed the use of self-reports of victims. Unfortunately existing evaluations do not routinely include self-reports of women who have been victimised by the men receiving whatever form of intervention is being evaluated' (1999: 210).

5 There were concerns about the 'representativeness' of women's accounts in relation to the centre, and Linda was specifically urged to interview as many women as possible.

6 Recent research suggests male abusers may attempt to neutralize or eradicate women's experiences of abuse, including using their own participation in therapy to present themselves as non-violent (Anderson and Umberson, 2001; Cavanagh et al., 2001).

References

Anderson, K. and Umberson, D. (2001) 'Gendering violence: masculinity and power in men's accounts of domestic violence', *Gender and Society,* 15 (3): 358–80.

Annandale, E. (1998) 'Working on the front line: risk culture and nursing in the new NHS', in M. Allott and M. Robb (eds), *Understanding Health and Social Care.* London: Sage. pp. 297–86.

Bell, C. (1998) 'Counselling intervention with men who batter: partner safety and the duty to warn', *Counselling,* August.

Birch, M. and Miller, T. (2000) 'Inviting intimacy: the interview as therapeutic opportunity', *International Journal of Social Research Methodology,* 3 (3): 189–202.

British Sociological Association (BSA) (1993) *Statement of Ethical Practice.* Durham: Mountjoy Research Centre.

British Sociological Association (BSA) (2002) *Statement of Ethical Practice.* Durham: Mountjoy Research Centre.

Burgess, R. (1982) 'Early field experiences', in R. Burgess (ed.), *Field Research: A Sourcebook and Field Manual.* London: Allen and Unwin.

Calvey, D. (2008) 'The art and politics of covert research: doing "situated ethics" in the field', *Sociology,* 42 (5): 905–18.

Cavanagh, K., Dobash, R.E. and Dobash, R.P. (2001) '"Remedial work": men's strategic responses to their violence against intimate female partners', *Sociology,* 35 (3): 695–714.

Crow, G., Wiles, R., Heath, S., et al. (2006) 'Research ethics and data quality: the implications of informed consent', *International Journal of Social Research Methodology,* 9 (2): 83–95.

Dobash, R. et al. (1999) 'A research evaluation of British programmes for violent men', *Journal of Social Policy,* 28 (2): 205–33.

Edwards, R. and Ribbens, J. (eds) (1998) *Feminist Dilemmas in Qualitative Research.* London: Sage.

Emmel, N., Hughes, K., Greenhalgh, J., et al. (2007) 'Accessing socially excluded people – trust and the gatekeeper in the researcher-participant relationship. *Sociological Research Online,* 12 (2).

Hoff, L.A. (1990) *Nattered Women as Survivors.* London: Routledge.

Liebow, E. (1967) *Tally's Corner: A Study of Negro Street Corner Men.* Boston: Little Brown.

Luff, D. (1999) 'Dialogue across the divides: "moments of rapport" and power in feminist research with anti-feminist women', *Sociology,* 33 (4): 687–703.

Mason, J. (1996) *Qualitative Researching.* London: Sage.

Mattingly, C. (2005) 'Towards a vulnerable ethics of research practice', *Health,* 9 (4): 453–471.

Mauthner, M. (2000) 'Snippets and silences: ethics and reflexivity in narratives of sistering', *International Journal of Social Research Methodology,* 3 (4): 287–306.

Miller, T. (1995) 'Shifting boundaries: exploring the influence of cultural traditions and religious beliefs of Bangladeshi women on antenatal interactions', *Women's Studies International Forum,* 18 (3): 299–309.

ETHICS IN QUALITATIVE RESEARCH

Miller, T. (1998) 'Shifting layers of professional, lay and personal narratives: longitudinal childbirth research', in R. Edwards and J. Ribbens (eds), *Feminist Dilemmas in Qualitative Research.* London: Sage. pp 58-71.

Miller, T. (2000) 'An exploration of first-time motherhood: narratives of transition', PhD dissertation, University of Warwick.

Miller, T. (2005) *Making Sense of Motherhood: A Narrative Approach.* Cambridge: Cambridge University Press.

Miller, T. (forthcoming) 'Messy ethics: negotiating the terrain between ethics approval and ethical practice', in J. McClancy and A. Fuentes (eds), *Ethics in the Field: Contemporary Challenges.* London: Berghahn Books.

Miller, T. and Boulton, M. (2007) 'Changing constructions of informed consent: qualitative research and complex social worlds', *Social Sciences and Medicine,* 65 (11): 2199–11.

Oakley, A. (1981) 'Interviewing women: a contradiction in terms', in H. Roberts (ed.), *Doing Feminist Research.* London: Routledge and Kegan Paul.

Reeves, C.L. (2010) 'A difficult negotiation: fieldwork relations with gatekeepers', *Qualitative Research,* 10 (3): 315–31.

Renzetti, C.M. and Lee, R.M. (eds) (1993) *Researching Sensitive Topics.* London: Sage.

Ribbens, J. and Edwards, R. (1995) 'Introducing qualitative research on women in families and households', *Women's Studies International Forum,* 18 (3): 247–58.

Robson, C. (1993) *Real World Research.* Oxford: Blackwell.

Stanley, L. and Wise, S. (1990) 'Method, methodology and epistemology in feminist research processes', in L. Stanley (ed.), *Feminist Praxis: Research Theory and Epistemology in Feminist Sociology.* London: Routledge.

Stanley, L. and Wise, S. (1993) *Breaking Out Again. Feminist Ontology and Epistemology.* London: Routledge.

Tremblay, M.A. (1957) 'The key informant technique: a non-ethnographic application', *American Anthropologist,* 59 (4): 688–701.

Wallman, S. (1984) *Eight London Households.* London: Tavistock.

Whyte, W. (1955) *Street Corner Society.* Chicago: Chicago University Press.

Wiles, R., Heath, S., Crow, G., et al. (2005) 'Informed consent in social research. A literature review'. ESRC National Centre for Research Methods. NCRM methods paper series.

5

Divided loyalties, divided expectations: research ethics, professional and occupational responsibilities

LINDA BELL AND LINDA NUTT

Introduction

This chapter examines how professional and occupational responsibilities 'translate' into actual research situations, and the ethical dilemmas that accompany 'divided loyalties' towards research and employment, in the fields of health and social care. We define 'practitioner-researchers' here as those who have responsibilities as health/ social care practitioners (including trainee practitioners) and who are also conducting research (see Fox et al., 2007; Fuller and Petch, 1995; Robson, 2002). We explore two examples suggesting ethical dilemmas and potentially divided loyalties. The first focuses on social research that overlaps with paid professional employment as a social worker involved in foster care in the voluntary sector. The second involves the construction of a set of ethical guidelines for university student-practitioners embarking on research projects related to professional education. We suggest that despite the efforts of a number of different professional bodies, to ethically regulate the activities of their practitioners (and thus practitioner-researchers), ethical dilemmas will still arise in research practice. In this context, dilemmas are especially likely to occur when researchers who are also practitioners recognize the need to acknowledge relevant multiple responsibilities and sensitivities. These will include perceived responsibilities towards clients/service users, fellow practitioners and organizational bodies, other researchers, and (in the case of students) meeting academic/university agendas relating to student assessment, or complying with regulations or 'competences'[1] specified by agencies controlling professional education (see also Bell and Hafford-Letchfield, forthcoming).

One key concern for practitioner-researchers is therefore how to 'manage' all these responsibilities in practice, in ways that all parties would consider 'ethical'. Such 'self-regulatory' research processes (in which these responsibilities need to be actively managed) will have their counterpart, we would suggest, in the rhetoric of 'reflexive'/ 'reflective' professional practice that is currently found in much professional education relating to health and social care (Ashford et al., 1998; Reed and Proctor, 1993; Schon, 1987; Tsang, 1998). We also suggest that such reflexivity connects with other more 'individualized' forms of researcher reflexivity, as found for example in feminist research (Mauthner, 2000). However, it is partly the reflexive positioning of different professional practitioners (for example, social workers and nurses vis-a-vis each other) as well as those following different research or professional paradigms within the same profession (Holland, 1999) which encourages such 'self-regulation'[2] in both professional practice and in research practice.

In this chapter we will explore issues of 'confidentiality' and 'negotiation' within the research process. We will also consider issues around 'access' and seeking 'informed voluntary consent' from participants. These areas will be illustrated through our substantive examples, in which we show how a focus on all these issues ties together research and professional practice in ways that we think may be different from other researchers' concerns. One of us (Linda Nutt) has worked as a practitioner-researcher while the other (Linda Bell) has been closely involved in practitioner-education including research supervision. In attempting to 'stand outside' practitioner-research in order to reflect on and discuss research ethics concerns, we are aware of the difficulties involved in speaking simultaneously to professional and 'other' researcher audiences, such as sociologists. Even the languages used by these varied kinds of researchers about research and research ethics may differ; however, we are attempting here to present practitioner-research and the ethical dilemmas it raises in ways which would be recognizable to practitioner-researchers as well as to a wider audience.

We suggest that the necessary 'self-regulation' of the practitioner-researcher means s/he may also have to choose whether or not to emphasize the role of 'practitioner' when carrying out research. This involves making professional as well as research judgements within specific research settings, and our examples will show that potential conflict or tensions between these roles needs to be acknowledged. For example, the practitioner-researcher may make initial decisions about separating or connecting these roles, which may then be difficult to achieve in practice. In addition, some professional guidance may recommend a particular course of action when practitioners are dealing with a research role and with professional (clinical) obligations (Royal College of Nursing [RCN], 1998: 19, see below).

While ethics are clearly bound up closely with research as well as with professional practice, we suggest further that these elements cannot be unravelled in a simplistic way rendering one kind of methodological research approach 'ethical' and another not. However, some of the literature emanating from 'practitioner research' suggests that particular methodological approaches to research should be more ethically acceptable to practitioners, because they either take a participatory and inclusive stance towards research participants (Everitt et al., 1992), or provide more reliable 'evidence' on which to base professional practice (Macdonald and Macdonald, 1995). We end the chapter by exploring some of these debates, since clearly these claims are based in different epistemological positions.

Approaches to practitioner research ethics

Many professional bodies issue guidelines for their practitioners relating to professional conduct and in some cases to appropriate research practice. As Wise points out:

> most professional groups whose jobs bring them into contact with members of society tend to have a set of guidelines, which carry varying degrees of authority, to guide their practice: social workers and doctors are two examples that come immediately to mind ... (1987: 187; see also BASW, 1996, 2011; National Institute of Medical Herbalists, n.d.; UKCC, 1992)

Nursing with its focus on holistic care and management of 'risk' for patients (Reed and Proctor, 1993) also produces research guidelines for practitioners that emphasize safety and the carrying out of acceptable procedures (see RCN, 2009). Nurses carrying out research are expected to be appropriately qualified, and also to be willing to publish and thus share their findings with other practitioners. In an earlier version of their research ethics guidelines, there is also acknowledgement by the RCN of potential tensions between clinical (professional) and research roles. Nurses were specifically advised that 'nurses who have a research role in a clinical area should seek clarification about the division between their research role and their professional obligations' (RCN, 1998: 19). It is necessary to consider, however, how easy or difficult this clarification might be to accomplish in practice. These nursing research ethics guidelines effectively 'meshed' with the concurrent nursing UKCC 'Code of professional conduct' (UKCC, 1992) to which all nurses should adhere. This Code similarly emphasized 'the interests, condition or safety of patients and clients' while instructing nurses to protect all confidential information concerning patients and clients obtained through professional practice. The UKCC Code also required that nurses should report to an 'appropriate person or authority' any circumstances under which safe and appropriate patient care could not be provided.

The most recent nursing research ethics guidelines available on the RCN's website (RCN, 2009) illustrate how much this whole field of practitioner (research) ethics has become formalized since 2001. Following the introduction of the Department of Health Research Governance Framework for Health and Social Care, professional nurses are now expected to participate in 'good quality' research while following strict ethics procedures; the nursing research ethics guidelines now include advice on research governance in global contexts, internet ethics and responsibilities under the Human Tissue Act 2004.

This professional example surely raises a first, key dilemma for practitioner-researchers from all professions/occupations. While all approaches to research ethics may emphasize 'confidentiality' as an important element, for a health or social care practitioner-researcher there may be circumstances in which this assurance does not preclude reporting something discovered in the course of research practice to an 'appropriate' recipient (as noted above, UKCC, 1992). 'Absolute' confidentiality within the research setting would therefore be precluded in certain risky situations. Some researchers who are not health or social care practitioners may feel that this compromise over confidentiality strikes at the heart of 'ethical research' itself. As discussed further below, this dilemma can run through the process of constructing ethical research guidelines for student-practitioners, and is also a theme picked up through the account below of research into foster care.

Like nursing, social work has had its own professional code of practice ethics, as distinct from research ethics, (BASW, 1996, 2011) with significant changes since 1996. The BASW Code is an interesting document due to the degree of 'reflexivity' used in explaining and discussing the reasons for inclusion of the different clauses making up the document. The most recent BASW code focuses around these key principles: 'human dignity and worth', 'social justice', 'service', 'integrity' (including 'confidentiality') and 'competence'. In 1996 the Code had a clear emphasis on a value-base of anti-discriminatory professional practice[4] and also discussed confidentiality in similar terms to the nursing practice code. It was suggested that confidential information should only be disclosed with the consent of the client, except where there is clear evidence of serious danger to the 'client, worker, other persons or the community', when it should be disclosed appropriately. This professional practice Code clearly has implications for social work practitioners who are also doing research.

When considering 'informed' voluntary consent and questions of access to participants from the point of view of practitioner-researchers, many of the same issues will be raised as in other kinds of research (see Miller and Bell in Chapter 4, this volume). However, there may be explicit recognition, which varies from one profession/occupation to another, that in working with clients/service users as research participants, the practitioner-researcher will need to clearly acknowledge specific aspects of the relationship between the practitioner and client/service user. The BASW (social work) code, for example, recognizes the idea of a power imbalance between social workers and their clients, and also recognizes the disadvantages suffered by social work 'clients' in society more generally. The theoretical implications of this recognition for research are explored, for example, by Boushel's discussion of 'race' in which she 'identifies some of the political, personal and technical challenges an anti-racist approach presents' for social welfare research (2000: 71). Similarly, feminist approaches to professional practice or practitioner research will need to acknowledge the same kind of issues as identified below in the foster care research example (see also Langan and Day, 1992).

In a broader sense, nursing and other 'health' research is usually acknowledged to be locked into a 'medical' model requiring the sanction of research ethics committees, whether in universities or in hospital trusts (see Miller and Bell in Chapter 4, this volume). It may be implied that, in this context, research usually involves pre-determined, outcome-based 'clinical' projects, and so importance may thus be attached to gaining 'informed consent' from participants in clinical procedures. This implies gaining access and obtaining consent at the initial stage of the research from clients/service users especially where these people are perceived as in any way 'vulnerable' (for example, people who are older, or who have mental health problems). In a methodological context, these ethics committee processes may thus have significant implications for practitioner-researchers conducting qualitative research who apply to such committees. For example, issues of 'negotiation' during the research process, including re-negotiation at different stages, have already been highlighted in this volume as an aspect of 'ethics' (Miller and Bell, see Chapter 4, this volume). However, continuing to renegotiate may not be considered acceptable by an ethics committee. 'Confidentiality' may also be addressed in a formal way at this early stage, through required production of consent forms or information sheets concerning the planned research, even though this may not always be appropriate (as noted by Miller and Bell).

In terms of re-negotiation during the research process, it may be that practitioner-researchers are thrown back onto their own guidelines for professional ethics; although in practice a degree of professional 'reflexivity' or 'reflective practice' would seem to be what is most useful in these circumstances (Ashford et al., 1998: 11) there may in fact be tensions between this reflective practice and the competence-based practice framework currently underpinning professional education in social work, nursing or other occupations. As both of our examples below reveal, effective negotiation may be considered a key aspect of 'ethics' in relation to qualitative practitioner-research, since it relates in complex ways to professional competence, reflective practice/reflexivity and to the multiple responsibilities and sensitivities indicated at the start of this chapter.

'Ethical' practitioner research in practice?

We now explore these key themes around confidentiality, access, informed consent and negotiation through our two substantive examples. These two examples illustrate situations in which different approaches to acknowledging the role of 'practitioner' are taken (whether by design or necessity) by practitioner-researchers themselves. We explore these ethical issues in relation to differing contexts of expectations and agendas surrounding practitioner-researchers. We illustrate these contexts by drawing on different parts of one practitioner-researcher 'spectrum', namely student social work practitioners doing research projects, and a fully experienced and qualified social work practitioner undertaking a research degree (doctorate).

Professional practice and doctoral research on foster care: separate or connected?

The research topic Linda Nutt (2006) has explored concerns foster care. Her research uses a broadly qualitative, feminist approach to investigate how foster carers make sense of their everyday lives in relation to their families and to the 'extra' children for whom they care. The study aims to understand the lives of foster carers in and on their own terms (see Nutt, forthcoming). Linda Nutt completed the study, outside her work time, as part of her doctorate when simultaneously employed by the Fostering Network (FN). Her paid post involved providing a social work consultancy service to foster carers registered with six local authorities – authorities from which she also drew her research sample. Here we examine the complexities of this situation, particularly in relation to the mix of professional and academic statuses of the researcher. We explore how Linda Nutt attempted to conceptualize her research and her work as separate entities within different worlds, and how the research journey exposed the practical problems of achieving this. She found there were too many crossovers, and eventually reflects that she could not avoid being the same person who wore both hats.

Linda's professional training was as a social worker; schooled in the use of the 'case work relationship', she expects to help clients understand their personal situations and take decisions as to what change, if any, they wish to effect in their lives (Biestek, 1961; Ferard and Hunnybun, 1962). Before commencing this research she decided that she would not be a 'social worker' in the research interviews as she wanted to conduct them in a very different manner. For her this was new, less sure ground and she wanted to keep separate the two experiences of 'doctoral researcher' and 'social work practitioner'. As a feminist researcher she addressed the power relations between herself and interviewees and planned that the foster carers she would interview should remain 'in control'. She did not want the foster carers to feel in any way 'subordinate' (as they might in a social worker–client relationship) but as a researcher she aimed for equality and an interview schedule that was sufficiently loose to allow the carers to explore their own agendas.

Linda naively believed that, if she interviewed foster carers who were not known to her, that they would not identify her as the worker employed by FN to provide a social work service in their area. In fact, her name was well known in foster care networks and the fact of her FN post must have affected the creative process of the interview. Interviews are interactional events, constructed as they happen (Hammersley and Atkinson, 1983: 15), they are the product of a particular time and place (Gubrium and Holstein, 1995), which means that Linda, as interviewer, was intimately involved in creating the data and, more importantly, in organizing the meanings via her analysis. For some carers this information would have provided a commonality of knowledge (Finch, 1984) and could therefore be viewed not so much as problematic but more as an additional resource. However, when interviewed, all the foster carers, even those who were so new that they awaited the placement of their first foster child, used a social services vocabulary. They used a professional discourse that provided a professional shorthand and which Linda recognized and found immediately seductive and impossible to ignore. Interviewer and interviewee were both immersed in the foster care world. Reflecting back on this situation, Linda now feels that too often she nodded in complicity – assuming that her understandings were their understandings when, in fact, 'shorthand' risks misunderstandings which could discredit the data and invite problematic, ethical implications on analysis. The following example is one carer's description of a baby's family visits to the foster carer's home:

With one baby I had contact three times a week. Here – sometimes more when Grandma came and you are, you know, trapped and the house is invaded but the, they say that it is best for the children but what about our children? But I suppose it is, for them you know. But they don't tell you or explain just say that her mum has – and it was better than the screams when they took her to the Family Centre and then I could give the guardian the detail of it all which I couldn't have if they took her off each time – you know.

Conversations depend upon cultural assumptions, and in this example there are a number of expressions and assumptions involving this shorthand – 'contact', what is 'better' and for whom, the 'guardian', 'family centre' and interpreting 'they'. Together with the foster carers, Linda was actively involved in constructing an understanding of foster care, but were interviewees responding to Linda as a researcher, or Linda Nutt as the FN social worker with official social services links?

This is relevant to how the carers felt about the interview, about her and about the material that they produced. This 'intrusion' was particularly clear in three interviews. Two male carers requested specific advice and information. Linda therefore turned off the tape, discussed their problem and once this formal business was completed, switched on the tape and resumed the study. In another interview with a female carer she instinctively commented on the social service process of dealing with allegations against foster carers in response to the carer's particular experience. Upon reflection she considers this inappropriate. She had commenced the study with particular judge-ments concerning what did and did not constitute 'research'. One of these judgements was that she would 'just listen' to the carers rather than actively contribute to the data. She had not thought through that this is untenable: that the interview is always a social interaction. These three interviews reveal some of the practical difficulties of keeping separate the identities of researcher and practitioner. For Linda the boundaries proved fragile.

Except for the many expressions of 'you know'[5] so as to involve Linda in the inter-action, none of the foster carers sought any personal information from her. If there was uncertainty about how to 'place' her (Edwards, 1993), foster carers did not appear to allow this to inhibit the stories they wished to tell. Did they see her position as an 'insider' or an 'outsider' – or perhaps as identified by Song and Parker (1995) as ambig-uous and therefore not readily definable? There was, apparently, no interest in her as a person but we do not believe, as posited by Edwards (1993), that a more equal exchange would have elicited more information – though it might have produced different data. Edwards argues that an exchange of information, particularly personal information, aids the informants to 'place' the researcher and this encourages disclosure. Perhaps, on some occasions, some of the foster carers were reassured that they could 'place' Linda within their foster care world.

Reflecting on the 'snowballing' sampling techniques used in this study, Linda believed that, if the contacts were made via the foster carers' own networks, this would ensure that carers had a choice not to participate. However, as she has no information about how she and the study were described by each contact foster carer, she cannot know if the added dimension of her official post (if known) acted as a pressure to ensure compli-ance with the request – one thing she sought to avoid. Perhaps the use of snowballing may have inadvertently exacerbated the dilemma, as she used the implicit power of her work position, so that the ethical intention of 'voluntary' consent was contaminated.

It is also possible that the way the research was conducted may have influenced some foster carers' use of the FN service Linda was paid to provide. For example, in several interviews, although she thought she understood what the carers were saying, because she wanted them to be more explicit, wanted their words on tape, she played the naive researcher requesting description and explanation. Did this undermine their confidence in her as a FN foster care 'expert' whom they could contact for advice and information? Moreover was this response, in fact, actual deception, as she was, in a sense, giving dishonest messages to the carers by feigning non-comprehension and how ethical was this practice (see also Punch, 1994)?

Due to the intimate nature of their interviews, it is also possible that some carers may have been inhibited from using her FN social work service. Brannen (1988) has suggested that it is safer for participants if they never again meet the researcher as this minimizes any gossip and maximizes the chances of secrecy and anonymity. It also frees them to speak with emotion. Over time, five of the 27 fostering households have contacted Linda Nutt in her FN capacity to seek social work advice and support about fostering problems. Four acknowledged her as also a researcher but one male carer seemed not to realize that he already knew her. He related the facts of his problem and described the foster children as though she had never visited his house. For him, the researcher and the FN worker were two separate people; he now sought the professional social worker.

Throughout the year that Linda Nutt was conducting her research interviews she was concerned to keep apart what she conceptualized as two 'separate' identities. She was aware that the information that the foster carers shared in their research interviews was frequently very intimate and given in the belief that she would not divulge it to their local authority – with whom her other identity worked. She also harboured ideas, probably irrationally, that researchers behaved differently from social workers. One way that she attempted to put boundaries around her 'separate' practitioner and researcher worlds was in her decisions about which note-paper she used. Initially she decided to send letters and notes to the carers on home-headed stationery (Linda as independent researcher), rather than FN business paper (Linda as social work practitioner). She also sent Christmas cards updating them on the progress of the research. This posed a problem one year when FN audited her role and sent questionnaires to random carers who had used her paid service. Three of the foster carers Linda had interviewed were also selected by FN for their sample and she then felt (ethically) unable to send them cards in case they interpreted her action as some sort of bribe to say that she had given them 'good' advice. On another occasion FN required volunteer foster carers who would be interviewed for the media. Linda decided to write to her study sample with the details. She then found it a dilemma as to whether this should go out on FN paper (as work) or on personal stationery (because her links with them were forged through the research). In the end she sent those carers who definitely knew about her FN post the letter on work stationery and used home paper for the others.

The ways in which issues around confidentiality, negotiation and professional competence are interwoven and complex are illustrated in the following example where professional social work responsibilities conflict with the demands of research. As noted above, Linda Nutt was a paid professional social worker bound by general social work codes of practice. This example illustrates not only the difficulties arising when social work dilemmas impact upon research, but the practical impossibility of separating the two worlds:

> As she was leaving the home of a new carer following the research interview Linda noticed an unambiguously sexually explicit picture in the hallway. For most researchers this would not be an issue: art is a matter of personal taste. But Linda wasn't just a researcher she was also a practitioner. Frequently when children are placed in foster homes little is known about their life experiences so new carers are instructed to assume that all children have been sexually abused unless specifically told otherwise. It is thus always considered essential not to give fostered children messages that could be interpreted as in any way sexual. As noted earlier, confidentiality is an absolute for researchers but cannot always be for practitioners. There is a statutory responsibility to disregard confidentiality where children are at risk. Nonetheless, because she wanted to keep the roles clear and separate – to act as a researcher (and be in receipt of information) and not as an employee of the FN (who would give them information), Linda chose not to tackle this issue with these new carers but spent several days considering this ethical dilemma. In the end the FN social worker practitioner identity overcame that of the researcher identity and Linda informed the local authority of her unease regarding the picture and its potential impact upon the foster children. Her reaction to its subject matter was guided by her professional training and the fact the painting was displayed in a house that offered refuge to children who could have been sexually abused. She did not mention this to the carers but left the social services department to make their own assessment.

Following this incident, Linda Nutt had felt obliged, as a practitioner-researcher, to recognize and act on her professional social work code of ethics which puts the safety of children above all confidentiality assurances. Linda Nutt, against her best endeavours, acted as 'research worker as helper' (Sainsbury et al., 1982), by contacting the local authority. We recognize that there may be divergent views about what, for her, was a dilemma. This would probably not have been an issue for an 'academic' researcher – people's art preferences being their own individual and private choices. Linda's action leaves her open to the criticism of, at the very least, making too many assumptions and, at worst, an abuse of power and an exploitation of the relationship between herself and her interviewees. Nonetheless, as a practitioner-researcher and therefore bound by social work practice ethics she could not deny her overriding responsibility towards the foster children. But in doing what she did, she breached any researcher (ethical) understandings of confidentiality and principles of anonymity. All the participants had been assured that their local authorities were not being formally notified as to which carers were participating in the study. In this case not only did she identify the carers but she raised cautions regarding their foster care practice leaving them with possible consequences.

This particular dilemma was symptomatic of a confusing situation caused by the insoluble problem of balancing transparency of action (and ensuring that all the carers who participated in the research study knew about Linda Nutt's professional post); and the knowledge that this risked the production of a more 'public' description of their lives-as-foster carers with the recognition of her official FN status. Full disclosure would have risked a changed, and more restricted and possibly less emotional set of data.

Although enabling people to behave in an emotional manner is familiar territory to a social worker or counsellor, Linda Nutt decided not to reflect back to carers in their interviews any statements in a way that might encourage them to examine strong and painful emotions concerned with their fostering. The way a story is told can reveal how the teller knows her/himself (Birch and Miller, 2000). Linda wanted interviewees to tell her about issues which were important to them; however, she chose not to demonstrate empathy that might encourage them to reveal more than they wished (see also Duncombe and Jessop in Chapter 7, this volume). She witnessed great pain in some foster carers as they talked about their experiences but, although acknowledging this, she remained intent not to encourage further painful disclosure: not to 'social work' them. Although some revealed their inner lives, there was no reciprocal exchange: there was, whatever the original intention, no equality of relationship. Linda is unsure how she would conduct herself if she were to start her research again, but she is aware that different social worker or feminist 'techniques' might have helped some of the carers live more peacefully with some very painful emotions. The retelling of past experiences can in itself help to make sense of the past and redefine elements more positively (Birch and Miller, 2000). One carer whose interview recounted a series of personally felt sad and frustrating events telephoned upon receiving her tape (after it had been transcribed), to thank Linda for the interview and 'memories of happier times'.

All researchers have to be self-regulating in their standards of ethical behaviour. It may be that, as illustrated above, the role of the social work practitioner-researcher is in some ways clearer than that of the 'academic researcher'. For practitioner-researchers, an important part of their ethical codes and of their concepts of ethics is to act 'responsibly'. In some cases, ethical commitment may go beyond the research participants to include significant others such as in this study, looked-after children. Linda Nutt began her study with a particular set of theoretical and 'ethical' research guidelines in mind, which attempted to separate practitioner and researcher; but despite this, she found that, in practice, qualitative practitioner research cannot be totally managed and controlled by taking this approach.

Production of ethical guidelines for university student-practitioners embarking on final projects and dissertations as part of the diploma in social work

The guidelines discussed below bring together ethical issues already raised, such as confidentiality and negotiation during the research process, with other perspectives relating to individual 'private' research, 'public' professional expectations and university assessment requirements that are all relevant to student-practitioners doing research. Crucially these different expectations relate to power and control both within, and over, the research setting. The student-practitioner is not therefore seen as a 'free agent' who can construct his or her own research agenda, and then carry it through without reference to others. Wise (1987) notes that since ethical guidelines acknowledge differential power relations within the research setting, they can help guard against potential exploitation and abuse of power. This point would apply to situations involving simply the 'researcher' and the 'researched'. However, in practitioner-research, the 'researched' may often be assumed to be a service user/client on the receiving end of professional practice of some kind. Where research is done between practitioners of different kinds, the power relations in the research encounter may be somewhat different.

Dilemmas about 'exploitation' relating to the above mentioned multiple responsibilities and sensitivities will, however, be magnified due to the complex nature of expectations encountered when carrying out, as in this example, a final-year project or dissertation as part of professional education and training. Such research projects relate to both professional and practice-based (placement) situations and to academic requirements. The student is considered to be 'responsible' as a trainee practitioner for adhering to and applying ethical practice guidance[6] and also any wider ethical framework of her/his profession and/or professional body (BASW, 1996, 2011).

There are also differing agendas relevant to ethical research practice with which the student may be expected to comply. Academically, the student will be expected to produce a piece of work that is 'academically sound' with the implication that this will mean it is 'ethically' acceptable, although the nature of this 'academic/ethical soundness' may be unclear except in so far as it successfully/ unsuccessfully meets criteria for assessment. We could ask, in this situation, who is being 'exploited'? Might the student find her/himself in an ethically and academically untenable position during project work if they were to mis-read others' agendas? In these circumstances the interests of the student-practitioner, as well as those of the service user research participant, the 'professional' participant, and all those with a 'stake' in the student's research project, need to be carefully balanced. Paradoxically, a set of ethical guidelines, though seemingly constraining, may also act to free student practitioners to carry out certain kinds of work and follow agendas that are significant to them (for example, feminist agendas).

In 1998, due to issues raised by students themselves as well as academic staff on a professional education programme in social work (Diploma in Social Work [DipSW]) in a higher education institution, it was decided to construct a set of guidelines[7] that would try to balance all the differing agendas referred to above. In the initial drafting, the first overriding principle was that students should adhere to the value principles taught as part of their professional training; these were outlined in the programme 'planner', a document issued to all the institution's DipSW students annually.

The BASW (1996) practice guidelines were also referred to specifically in the ethical guidelines. These were also common to all sets of students, who were at that time being trained in three 'strands': DipSW (two year); BA (Hons) with DipSW; Postgraduate

Diploma/MA with DipSW. The academic requirements for each set of students therefore differed, although all were expected to produce a final project related to their specialist social work 'pathway' (working with children and families; adults with specific needs; palliative care; criminal justice).

Other key issues raised in the initial draft guidelines included:

- seeking informed voluntary consent from participants (with a caveat that it is expected students will find greater difficulty in conducting research with their own clients/service users);
- not naming participating agencies or individuals in the student's final report;
- negotiating effectively both with participating agencies/ individuals outside the university and with academic tutors;
- confidentiality – with the previously noted dilemma concerning 'absolute' confidentiality highlighted;
- issues around the ownership and dissemination of research findings, which sought to balance the rights of student, the university and research participants (including individuals and organizations).

In revising this initial draft in consultation with colleagues, two key issues came to light, one concerning 'generalized' ethical research principles and the second methodological approaches to research. The previous draft guidelines had rightly emphasized the significance of professional ethics and professional practice in this context, and this emphasis was retained in the final guidelines. However, in the second draft we suggested a stronger connection with more generalized 'research ethics' and principles, such as 'beneficence', 'justice' and 'respect', were also listed in the revised guidelines. The possibility of needing to obtain the approval of a relevant research ethics committee was also raised. Ethics committees within higher education will vary in the way that they have been established, although as noted in Miller and Bell (see Chapter 4, this volume) many will take as a model the ethics committees established in hospital or health trusts (see also Tierney, 1995). We suggest that this model has broader implications for research in social care and the social sciences, since where 'evidence based' approaches to practice are emphasized specifically, this can raise methodological issues around the perceived status of 'qualitative' research approaches (see next section, below).

In this context, the intention of the revised guidelines was to set the work of student social work practitioners into a broader 'research' context as well as a 'professional' one, and so to balance these agendas in some way. However, some might argue that appeals to these 'broader ' principles, not strictly focused on professional concerns, might seem to be adding to the 'idealism' surrounding research practices noted earlier.

Of significant concern when constructing the guidelines, was that this 'idealism' might pre-suppose assumptions favouring particular methodological approaches to research. It was noted during consultation with colleagues that some people tended to favour specific models of research, including participatory approaches. These concerns were specifically related to 'ethics'; for example there was debate about the 'ethics' of participant observation and particularly about covert observation. It therefore seemed necessary to spell out to student-practitioners that while 'ethics' were indeed closely bound up with 'research' as well as with 'professional practice', this could not be unravelled in a simplistic way rendering one kind of research approach 'ethical' and another not. Again the intention was to ensure that while the agendas of the university, professional practitioners and their organizations, clients/service users and the students themselves were addressed (particularly with regard to adequate negotiation and reporting of findings), students were not going to be unnecessarily constrained in undertaking interesting and worthwhile research projects. Being able to take up approaches emphasizing anti-racism (as noted by Boushel, 2000), or feminism albeit in a professional context might depend upon the careful balancing of such constraints. We therefore advised:

> Remember that although some approaches to research specifically aim to involve service users (e.g. action research), this does not mean some kinds of research project are automatically more 'ethical' than others. You still need to pay attention to ethical principles whether you are doing an experiment, a survey or a piece of qualitative research.

While methodologically and sociologically these statements might still raise more questions than they answer (not least, what is meant here by 'ethical'?) the underlying message was conveyed: as a practitioner-researcher the student is not unduly restricted in the choice of methodology and methods despite any connections which may be drawn in the literature between professional practice and 'participatory' or 'evidence based' approaches to research (as discussed further below). However, they would be expected to negotiate fully with others and to act 'responsibly' in both professional practice and research activities. (The implication of this may be, de facto, to rule out such activities as 'covert' work.) To this extent, student-practitioners should then be in a position to actually 'do research' as 'self-regulating' practitioner-researchers; to acknowledge and grapple with at least some of the kinds of research dilemmas experienced by practitioner-researchers such as those discussed earlier by Linda Nutt.

Ethics and evidence: the significance of methodology as an aspect of practitioner research

Although there is little space here to discuss the broader implications of 'evidence-based practice', particularly in health (see, for example, Gomm and Davies, 2000; Kendall, 1997), we note below the broader idea that 'ethical' research can be perceived as 'justifiable' research, which produces clear and effective answers to questions about 'outcomes' (however these may be defined; see, for example, Macdonald and Macdonald, 1995). The application of 'evidence based' approaches to professional practice and therefore to the commissioning of 'appropriate' research have often been discussed elsewhere in health literature (Rosenberg and Donald, 1995; Sackett et al., 1996), including growing discussions in the field of complementary and alternative health care. As noted by other commentators (Jordan et al., 1998; Kendall, 1997) heavy emphasis is placed by 'evidence-based' adherents on research 'evidence' taken from specific kinds of research that are deemed more 'reliable' than others (especially randomized, controlled trials [RCTs]). This in itself raises important issues around the perceived status of qualitative research, although health researchers have also pointed out the difficulties of using RCTs to evaluate health care (Bowling, 1997: 200–1).

As we noted at the beginning, some literature emanating from 'practitioner research' does, conversely, suggest that particular methodological approaches to research should be more 'ethically acceptable' to practitioners. The implications of this are, therefore, that research methodology itself relates in complex ways to issues of research ethics, professional practice, and practitioner research. For example, an emphasis on the underpinning, 'enabling' 'value base' of social work research is developed in advice given to practitioner researchers by Everitt et al. (1992), who suggest, both methodo-logically and ethically, that 'participatory' forms of research are the most acceptable forms of research for social work practitioner-researchers. Although not necessarily made explicit, the emphasis in Everitt et al. (1992) seems to be on 'qualitative' research approaches.

Linda Bell's experience of working with student social work practitioners certainly suggests these students tend to favour 'qualitative' approaches to research. However they do not necessarily choose 'participatory' research that would fully involve research participants (although this is probably related more closely to professional and academic requirements than to any student views about the 'ethics' of particular research methodologies). Furthermore, research carried out with fellow practitioners rather than with social work clients may be preferred by students, partly as a way of avoiding 'ethical' research dilemmas. So perhaps 'participatory' research remains an 'ideal' rather than a reality for these students? As noted earlier by Linda Nutt, the power imbalance remains, de facto, between the social worker and the client; and will surely remain during research unless definite steps are taken to shift it.

Macdonald and Macdonald (1995) however seem to be taking a slightly different line and challenging any apparent 'ideal' emphasis on 'participatory' research by pointing out that social workers do actually need to find out 'what works' for their clients. They thus emphasize an approach to research which involves testing out interventions so as develop 'evidence based' practice. Their view is that finding 'what works' is almost impossible, without rejecting what they call a 'take your pick' approach to social work intervention. In practical research terms this could mean assigning clients randomly to different interventions, collecting the 'evidence' and comparing the results (in an RCT). Macdonald and Macdonald (1995) appear to take an essentially 'ends justifies the means' approach by pointing out that most current social work interventions are not 'tested' anyway, and that not all clients receive the same service either. They ask: 'how ethical is it to operate a programme, with little rationale, and no inbuilt attempt to make sure we are not doing more harm than good?' (1995: 48).[8]

Developing complementary and alternative medicine (CAM) professions, such as medical herbalism, whose practitioners are becoming increasingly involved in research, may also, like Macdonald and Macdonald, emphasize the ethical necessity of using 'appropriate' forms of research, methodologically speaking. For some, this may mean an emphasis on randomized controlled trials or other experimental designs (Ernst, 1996) rather than qualitative research approaches which could emphasize 'holistic' approaches to research participants. However this may be disputed between practitioners of different persuasions or regulating bodies (Bell et al., 1999; Stone, 2000). Stone's comments interestingly suggest an intertwining of issues around ethics and methodology in this CAM research context based on 'patient-centredness', in which 'the patient is an active participant in his or her healing process' (2000: 208):

> There is no reason to assume that the autonomy-focused ethics of Western, liberal democracies should automatically provide the theoretical underpinnings of CAM any more than assuming that the empirical, rational scientific mode is the most appropriate way of establishing the efficacy of CAM therapies. As with research methodologies, so a wider array of ethical theories (such as care-based ethics, feminist ethics and narrative ethics) might need to be invoked in order to adequately capture the subtleties of the CAM relationship. (Stone, 2000: 208)

'Evidence-based' approaches to practitioner research might suggest favouring a movement away from 'listening to people (clients)' when conducting research as a practitioner-researcher. However, as discussed above, Linda Nutt was very keen to continue to listen to research participants, although this led her in some senses to 'play down' her role as a practitioner (except in circumstances where she perceived that this practitioner role had to take precedence over that of 'researcher').

Conclusion

In this chapter we have used two examples from different parts of one practitioner-research 'spectrum', student practitioners and an experienced social worker taking a research degree, to explore various issues defined as relevant to practitioner research ethics: these include 'confidentiality', and 'negotiation' of the research process in 'professional' contexts. We have tried to demonstrate how these issues translated into actual research situations, including the issues around developing a set of ethical guidelines for student practitioner-researchers. We conclude that since practitioner-researchers have to negotiate a range of responsibilities, these in themselves could be seen to constitute an 'ethics of caring' (see Edwards and Mauthner in Chapter 1, this volume). Therefore decisions about emphasizing or 'playing down' the role of 'practitioner' may be an important part of such negotiation. As suggested in our final section, the broader methodological context of differing epistemological positions within practitioner-research is also relevant. For student-practitioners with multiple responsibilities towards academic, professional and client audiences, ethical guidelines can help to emphasize the 'practitioner' role while allowing practical decisions about research to be taken by 'self-regulating' individuals as they interpret both the guidance and the actual research situation. For experienced practitioners, decisions about the presentation of self may be an overriding element in allowing research to be conducted 'ethically'. Recent developments in research governance (as noted in endnote 6 below) do not alter (but, we would argue, strengthen) the need for practitioner-researchers to be self-regulating as they conduct research.

Notes

1 These competences will include aspects of professionally and theoretically based knowledge, skills (for example, in communication with clients/service users) and values (such as taking an anti-oppressive approach). Competences may be formally grouped into an overall framework relevant for professional education. For a discussion of tensions between 'competence' and 'reflection' see Ashford et al. (1998).

2 'Self regulation' may be considered an important concept underlying aspects of reflexive practice 'competence' *within* specific professions and is reflected in professional education, for example, the current degree in Social Work. It is a separate issue from official 'regulation' and registration of some practitioners. See also DOH Research Governance Framework for Health and Social Care (2001).

3 For example, in 1996 the BASW Code stated: '[Social workers] will not discriminate against clients, on the grounds of their origin, race, status, sex, sexual orientation, age, disability, beliefs, or contribution to society, they will not tolerate actions of colleagues or others which may be racist, sexist or otherwise discriminatory, nor will they deny those differences which will shape the nature of clients needs and will ensure any personal help is offered within an acceptable personal and cultural context'.

4 Implications of tacit knowledge, as Altheide and Johnson (1994) explain, may be significant but also problematic.

5 Student social workers must currently meet practice requirements set by the General Social Care Council (since 2001). This Council will be replaced by the Health Professions Council in 2012.

6 I (Linda Bell) produced the final set of guidelines during 1999 and acknowledge the support of colleagues Dr Oded Manor, who began the work, Ms Lesley Oppenheim and other colleagues working on the DipSW programmes at Middlesex University. Since that time there have been many changes to social work education and to research governance in the UK (including the development of local authority ethics committees and the Dept of Health's Research Governance framework for Health and Social Care). While the principles inherent in these guidelines remain important for social work students, in 2011 they also expect to have to meet external ethics requirements when conducting research projects.

8 'Empiricism does not provide an escape route from "theory" to "truth" – observation is never theory free, it cannot be. However it offers a way of making explicit the theoretical underpinnings of our conceptualizations, hypotheses or assumptions about problems (and solutions), and the possibility of controlling for some of these influences when seeking to test their relative usefulness' (Macdonald and Macdonald 1995: 48).

References

Altheide, D.L. and Johnson, J.M. (1994) 'Criteria for assessing interpretive validity in qualitative research', in N.K. Denzin and Y.S. Lincoln (eds), *Handbook of Qualitative Research.* London: Sage. pp. 485–99.

Ashford, D., Blake, D., Knott, C., et al. (1998) 'Changing conceptions of reflective practice in social work, health and education: an institutional case study', *Journal of Interprofessional Care,* 12 (1): 7–19.

Bell, L. and Hafford-Letchfield, T. (eds) (2012, forthcoming) *Ethics, Values and Social Work Practice.* Maidenhead: McGraw-Hill.

Bell, L., Bell, C., Chevallier, A., et al. (1999) 'Herbalism and osteoarthritis; a study investigating herbal treatment outcomes, patient and practitioner viewpoints'. Paper given at the British Sociological Association Medical Sociology Conference, York, September.

Biestek, F. (1961) *The Casework Relationship.* London: George Allen and Unwin.

Birch, M. and Miller, T. (2000) 'Inviting intimacy: the interview as therapeutic opportunity', *International Journey of Social Research Methodology,* 3 (3): 189–202.

Boushel, M. (2000) 'What kind of people are we? "Race", anti-racism and social welfare research', *British Journal of Social Work,* 30: 71–89.

Bowling, A. (1997) *Research Methods in Health: Investigating Health and Health Services.* Buckingham: Open University Press.

Brannen, J. (1988) 'The study of sensitive subjects', *Sociological Review,* 36 (3): 552–63.

British Association of Social Workers (BASW) (1996) *The Code of Ethics for Social Work.* Birmingham: BASW

British Association of Social Workers (BASW) (2011) *The Code of Ethics for Social Work.* Birmingham: BASW

Department of Health (UK) (2001) *Research Governance Framework for Health & Social Care.* London: DoH.

Edwards, R. (1993) *Mature Women Students: Separating or Connecting Family and Education.* London: Taylor & Francis.

Ernst, E. (1996) 'The ethics of complementary medicine', *Journal of Medical Ethics,* 22: 197–8.

Everitt, A., et al. (1992) *Applied Research for Better Practice.* British Association of Social Workers. London: Macmillan.

Ferard, M.L. and Hunnybun, N.K. (1962) *The Caseworker's Use of Relationships.* London: Tavistock.

Finch, J. (1984) '"It's great to have someone to talk to": the ethics and politics of interviewing women', in C. Bell and H. Roberts (eds), *Social Researching: Politics, Problems, Practice.* London: Routledge and Kegan Paul. pp. 166–80.

Fox, M., Green, G. and Martin, P. (2007) *Doing Practitioner Research.* London: Sage.

Fuller, R. and Petch, A. (1995) *Practitioner Research – The Reflexive Social Worker.* Buckingham: Open University Press.

Gomm, R. and Davies, C. (eds) (2000) *Using Evidence in Health and Social Care.* London: Sage and Open University.

Gubrium, J. and Holstein, J. (1995) *The Active Interview.* Thousand Oaks, CA: Sage.

Hammersley, M. and Atkinson, P. (1983) *Ethnography: Principles in Practice.* London: Tavistock.

Holland, R. (1999) 'Reflexivity', *Human Relations,* 52 (4): 463–84.

Jordan, L., Bell, L., Bryman, K., et al. (1998) 'Evaluating communicate: organisational issues and their relevance for clinical evaluation', *International Journal of Language and Communication Disorders,* 33: 60–5, Supplement.

Kendall, S. (1997) 'What do we mean by evidence? Implications for primary health care nursing', *Journal of Interprofessional Care,* 11 (1): 23–34.

Langan, M. and Day, L. (1992) *Women, Oppression and Social Work: Issues in Anti-Discriminatory Practice.* London: Routledge.

Macdonald, G. and Macdonald, K. (1995) 'Ethical issues in social work research', in R. Hugman, and D. Smith (eds), *Ethical Issues in Social Work.* London: Routledge. pp. 46–61.

Mauthner, M. (2000) 'Snippets and silences: ethics and reflexivity in narratives of sistering', *International Journal of Social Research Methodology,* 3 (4): 287–306.

National Institute of Medical Herbalists (n.d.) *Code of Ethics. Code of Professional Practice.*

Nutt, L. (2006) *The Lives of Foster Carers. Private Sacrifices, Public Restrictions.* London: Routledge.

Nutt, L. (2012, forthcoming) 'Foster care in ambiguous contexts: competing understandings of care', in C. Rogers and S. Weller (eds), *Critical Approaches to Care: Understanding Care Relations, Identities and Cultures.* London: Routledge.

Punch, M. (1994) 'Politics and ethics in qualitative research', in N.K. Denzin and Y.S. Lincoln (eds), *Handbook of Qualitative Research.* London: Sage. pp. 83–97.

Reed, J. and Proctor, S. (1993) *Nurse Education: A Reflective Approach.* London: Edward Arnold.

Robson, C. (2002) *Real World Research: A Resource for Social Scientists and Practitioner Researchers,* 2nd edn. Oxford: Blackwell.

Rosenberg, W. and Donald, A. (1995) 'Evidence based medicine: an approach to clinical problem-solving', *British Medical Journal,* 310 (April): 1122–6.

Royal College of Nursing of the United Kingdom (RCN) (1998) *Research Ethics: RCN Guidance for Nurses.* London: RCN

Royal College of Nursing of the United Kingdom (RCN) (2009) *Research Ethics: RCN Guidance for Nurses.* London: RCN

Sackett, D., Rosenberg, W., Muir Gray, J., et al. (eds) (1996) 'Evidence-based medicine: what it is and what it isn't', *British Medical Journal,* 312: 71–2.

Sainsbury, E., Nixon, S. and Phillips, D. (1982) *Social Work in Focus: Clients' and Social Workers' Perceptions in Long-Term Social Work.* London: Routledge and Kegan Paul.

Schon, D. (1987) *Educating the Reflexive Practitioner: Towards a New Design for Teaching and Learning in the Professions.* San Francisco, CA: Jossey Bass.

Song, M. and Parker, D. (1995) 'Commonality, difference and the dynamics of disclosure in in-depth interviewing', *Sociology,* 29 (2): 241–56.

Stone, J. (2000) 'Ethical issues in complementary and alternative medicine', *Complementary Therapies in Medicine,* 8: 207–13.

Tierney, A. (1995) 'The role of research ethics committees', *Nurse Researcher,* 3 (1): 43–52.

Tsang, N.M. (1998) 'Re-examining reflection – a common issue of concern in social work, teacher and nursing education', *Journal of Inter Professional Care,* 12 (1): 21–31.

UKCC for Nursing, Midwifery & Health Visiting (1992) *Code of Professional Conduct.* London: UKCC.

Wise, S. (1987) 'A framework for discussing ethical issues in feminist research: a review of the literature', in V. Griffiths, et al (eds), 'Writing feminist biography? Using life histories', *Studies in Sexual Politics,* 19: University of Manchester.

6

Encouraging participation: ethics and responsibilities

MAXINE BIRCH AND TINA MILLER

Introduction

In many areas of social research the term 'participant' is used to describe the role undertaken by individuals invited to take part in a research project. The shift in terminology from research subject to research participant is firmly located in academic professional discipline codes of conduct, such as the British Psychological Society (2009) and British Sociological Association (2002). In feminist qualitative research the term 'research participant' reflects many positive developments in how the researcher approaches, understands and maintains the research relationship. In this chapter we explore how this notion of participation coincided with our understanding of 'being good researchers' and forming 'good research relationships'. When we examined our experiences of encouraging research participation we found that a dissonance had occurred between the ideal of 'participation' presented in ethical codes of behaviour, our hopes of encouraging the research respondent to feel part of the process and what actually occurred during the research process itself. These experiences lead us to argue that there is a need for researchers to return to the concept of participation from a personal/political perspective and to nurture the very seeds of a feminist perspective. We also advocate that the doing of ethically responsible research requires the researcher to negotiate participation at the outset of a research project and be sensitive to the dimensions of participation that have been agreed – which may indeed be partial participation and which may shift.

We argue that two aspects of qualitative methodology, participant observation and longitudinal interviews, construct a specific type of research relationship characterized by sharing personal and private experiences over a long period of time. We have demonstrated elsewhere that this type of research relationship may involve acts of self-disclosure, where personal, private experiences are revealed to the researcher in a relationship of closeness and trust (Birch and Miller, 2000). It is precisely the quality of such a relationship that can provide access to the rich, deep data that the qualitative researcher seeks. The focus on the research relationship as a social relationship is indebted to the many creative researchers in the development of a feminist perspective during the 1980s and after. Early feminist researchers identified complex processes involved in friendship, rapport, interpretation, and power in the interview setting (Cotterill, 1992; DeVault, 1990; Finch, 1984; Oakley, 1981; Reissman, 1987; Ribbens, 1989; Smith, 1987) and this has continued (Holland, 2007; Roulston, 2010). This accumulated knowledge illuminates the many components of the research relationship and highlights certain imperatives to assess and guide research relationships. In turn, it is argued this has led to the emergence of a 'moral high ground' that can guide the feminist researcher towards 'good' quality research relationships (Price, 1996). In planning and executing the first stages of our respective research we found that we wished to position ourselves within this feminist 'moral high ground' and ensure 'good' relationships. For us, the notion of participation embodies specific ideals of how the researcher and researched should cooperate with each other in order to form a 'good', honest and reciprocal relationship. Within our research negotiations we used the term research 'participant' in order to create reciprocal feminist research relationships. However, the ideal of fully involving research respondents, for example by inviting comments on our interpretations of the research data, was hard to maintain over the different stages of the research process. We found that the research ideals of participation that we embraced at the outset eventually came into conflict with our personal goals of completing our projects and fitting into the requirements of the academic world. This conflict led us to desert the 'moral high ground' and reinterpret our earlier understanding of what participation should involve.

When reflecting upon our experiences we found we both shared feelings of guilt and worrying reminders of 'I should have done this' and 'I promised that'. At the end of our projects we felt dissatisfied that we had never fully achieved the 'real' participation in the research process we had originally argued for. During our projects we had reframed our understandings of participation and how this could be achieved at different stages of the research process. In this chapter we describe how the ideal of participation can be difficult to achieve in research relationships and we identify particular ethical concerns that can arise as a result when undertaking qualitative work. From this we develop research strategies that in the context of research practice can help to identify ethical concerns. We argue that the need to provide spaces for all research participants to consider the ethical dimensions of the research and how to address them constitute an 'ethics of responsibility'. We use this framework of ethical responsibility to challenge and change our research practices.

Why participation?

In order to embrace the complexity of understanding individuals and the social lives we construct and maintain, researcher's today are called upon to create reflexive and innovative research designs. As PhD students in the 1990s we inherited the reflexivity of feminism, the deconstruction of post-structuralism and the uncertainty of postmodernism. Our key influences at this time were: feminist reflexivity developed into an auto/biographical perspective (Ribbens, 1993; Stanley, 1990, 1992), the reflexive project of the self and constructing a gendered sense of self-identity (Giddens, 1991, 1992; Griffiths, 1995), the deconstruction of a postmodern self (Benhabib, 1992; Lather, 1994) and the growing awareness of narrative and stories in understanding lived experiences (Frank, 1995, 2010; Josselson and Lieblich, 1997; Reissman 2008). These influences have enabled us to build a model of the individual as a reflexive, relational matrix of self-awareness and understanding. This model is illustrated in Benhabib's words, 'Identity does not refer to my potential for choice alone, but to the actuality of choices, namely to how I, as a finite, concrete, embodied individual, shape and fashion the circumstances of my birth and family, linguistic, cultural and gender identity into a coherent narrative that stands as my life's story ... The question becomes: how does this finite embodied creature constitute into a coherent narrative those episodes of choice and limitation, agency and suffering, initiative and dependence?' (1992: 161). In gathering coherent narratives or life stories from an individual, the researcher must acknowledge their own part as a co-producer in such stories (Corradi, 1991). And it is this recognition of the dynamic and constituent nature of the research encounter in which data is generated that necessitates the need for all participants to be visible in the research process.

The present challenges of postmodernist feminist research are to bring together the contradictions, previously held in many modernist perspectives, such as agency and structure, objectivity and subjectivity, distance and involvement in to the research relationship (Lather, 1994). Here participation is perceived to be a methodological resource to bring together dualities and recognize the plurality of realities. Patti Lather argues that research designs can be 'interactive, contextualized and humanly compelling, because they invite joint participation in the exploration of research issues' (1994: 52). An active research relationship then involves the exchange of ideas and understanding, and is a shared enterprise. It is interesting to note that 10 years after the publication of the first edition of this book significant technological advances may indeed have democratized the research process in ways we could not have previously envisaged (see, for example, Chapters 2 and 11, this volume).

Participating in an ethical model of responsibility

Using the methodological strategies of participant observation and longitudinal interviews, we tried to explore the life stories of others while at the same time acknowledging the construction of our own (coherent) narratives as researchers. It is the reflexive analysis of personal research experiences that is central to the development of an ethical feminist model, which we propose here. This is based on an 'expressive-collaborative model' adapted and developed from the work of Margaret Urban Walker (1997, 2007). Walker proposes ethical responsibility as 'a socially embodied medium of mutual understanding and negotiation between people over their responsibility for things open to human care and response' (2007: 9). We suggest that this provides an additional framework for appreciating ethical dimensions alongside the 'ethics of care' present in many other feminist debates. Importantly Walker (1997) argues that an ethics of care may unintentionally reinforce essentialist notions of being a woman whereas the assessment of responsibilities broadens our ethical awareness beyond gendered constructions. In her work Walker identifies three levels of 'ethical narratives': the narratives that, first, present the individual's sense of moral identity, that is the presentation of a 'good' self, second, the narrative which seeks to maintain this ethical 'good' self, when relating to others, and, third, a recognition of narratives concerned with representing moral values that are dominantly held in the public sphere. These three narrative layers, Walker argues, constitute the *ethical components* of our life stories. For us it is the second level of ethical narrative, the self in relation to others that is essential in helping us to understand ethical issues in the research process. Researchers can develop 'practices of responsibility' (Walker, 2007: 9) in order to pay attention to the ethical issues that arise in their research practices. For example, our feelings of guilt as our own research goals became more instrumental as we jettisoned earlier intentions in order to finish our PhDs within particular time frames could have been openly reflected upon and discussed at the time with those participating in our projects. But what expectations did those who participated in our projects have? What did participation mean to them? We draw upon Walker's 'expressive-collaborative model' to examine these notions and practices of responsibility in relation to our specific projects (1997, 2007).

Maxine's examples arise from 'the therapy study' (Birch, 1996, 1998; Birch and Miller, 2000) and illustrate her experiences of trying to achieve joint participation in an ethnography, which attempted to develop an auto/biographical position in participant observation. The therapy study involved Maxine's membership in four therapy groups advertised and promoted in the context of alternative health. All the groups shared the explicit promise to enable members to discover and uncover dimensions of their sense of an inner self, which may have been hidden or masked as a result of the complexities of social life. Interviewing both the facilitators and other group members complemented data gathered from the researcher's membership of the groups. To maintain our focus in this chapter on the experiences of trying to achieve a participatory research style in participant observation, we direct the reader to other publications for further information on the project (Birch, 1996, 1998; Birch and Miller, 2000). In our discussion Maxine also draws on her study of the relationship between three urban friendship groups of young people and their smoking and non-smoking lifestyle stories. She gathered these stories from interview settings that are explored in relation to the model of ethical responsibility discussed earlier.

We also draw on two of Tina's studies to analyse research respondent's participation in the interview process. The first study explored take-up of antenatal care among Bangladeshi women living in southern Britain (Miller, 1995). This small-scale study employed an ethnographic approach involving Tina accessing and joining a language group established to teach English to Bangladeshi women. The second – longitudinal – study documented women's experiences of transition to first-time motherhood (Miller, 1998, 2000a, 2000b, 2005). Both these projects illustrate the differing perceptions of participation that can co-exist in research. This focus prompts Tina to question whether 'participants' want to participate in every aspect of the research process and to consider the ethics of imposing a particular research relationship that is not sought. (For more details about these last two studies see Miller and Bell, Chapter 4, this volume.)

Developing an ethics of responsibility: tracing ethical narratives in field notes

During the 'therapy study' Maxine recorded her field notes in two sections: one page for the observed actions of others, 'the concrete record' and the other page for Maxine's personal reflections on the events that had occurred, 'the intuitive, feeling record'. Keeping reflective sections distinct from field observations has been reported in ethnographic studies from the discovery of Malinowski's (1967) diaries to the retrospective analysis of the research relationship (Okley and Callaway, 1992). In the therapy study the concrete record provided the data for the analysis of storytelling that went on in the group. The 'intuitive, feeling record' provided the ethical narratives, which are analysed here. These ethical narratives were produced in relation to Maxine's sense of what is right and wrong in relation to others – the second level of ethical narrative identified in Walker's (1997) model. It is these ethical narratives that present the ethical dimension in the research process. Throughout the intuitive, feeling record of the field notes questions were raised on what, how and why certain interactions had occurred and what, how and why certain interactions had not. When Maxine went into the field as a member of the alternative therapy groups she went equipped with the methodological term 'auto/biographical ethnography' adapted from the works of Jane Ribbens (1993) and Liz Stanley (1992, 1993). For Maxine this hyphenated connection of auto/biography appeared to represent the 'me and you' in the research process and so offered the potential to encourage joint participation as described previously in the work of Patti Lather (1994). Maxine hoped that the methodological tool of auto/biography would enable her to explore the research relationship while engaged in the research process.

In the early stages of negotiating access to the alternative therapy groups Maxine found that the descriptive term 'auto/biography' gave her a tool that appeared sympathetic and conducive to the group's objective of discovering one's self. The facilitators of the groups warmed easily to the description of auto/biography as a methodological style. An unforeseen research 'bargain' occurred as the facilitators immediately detected a potential tool and wanted to participate in order to learn about this research style and use it to explore their work. However, the explanation at this stage of negotiation did not explicitly state the more complex academic understanding of auto/biography where the hyphenated connection could be reinterpreted to mean the story of others. A particular example of how auto/biography was presented and interpreted differently is illustrated in the following extract from Maxine's corresponding pages of field notes (see Box 6.1).[1]

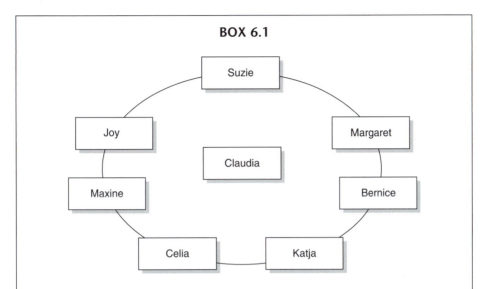

BOX 6.1

The group started with all the women introducing themselves. Summary of the round: Apart from Suzie we were all mothers, with Bernice and I being single parents. Five members worked in the alternative health fields with skills ranging from Astrology, Alexandra technique, Massage, Yoga, Acupuncture, Counselling. One woman was a psychologist and the other a secretary. We were all white. All of them had previous contact with the facilitator Claudia. During my turn to introduce myself I talked about my research, about autobiography and the other two groups involved. Claudia asked if the others were happy with this. All agreed but one.

I sat there in this candle lit room with all the other women looking at me. It was my time to explain my research role in the group. I felt quite uneasy. I tried to explain to the group how my research role would involve my own experiences in the group for the research. Had I deliberately underestimated how my research style would also be looking at the experiences of the group? I felt embarrassed to say. I could feel myself not saying everything. Too afraid that they would say no? After all the facilitator had agreed for my involvement to take place. Funny group they gave nothing away, they did not look pleased or interested. Slowly they went round most of them quietly agreeing this would be OK until ... She said she was a psychologist and that she was pregnant. Firstly from her background she did not want to be the subject of any research! God she had said it, the truth! Secondly she did not know if she could commit herself to the group due to the baby.

When Maxine discovered that one member of the group was also an 'academic' she felt that her presentation of an auto/biographical methodology had not disguised the actuality that participation in this project would not be exactly as Maxine had suggested. Maxine would be collecting the stories of *others* more than telling her own story. After this initial introduction the woman never returned to the group and

Maxine felt that her decision not to participate was based on knowing more about the potential research relationship than the others who had agreed to participate. Indeed, how ethical had it been for Maxine to 'disguise' the various interpretations of the term 'auto/biography'?

Maxine's field notes on her feelings subsequently record how her research role was never really discussed beyond this initial introduction in all the groups she attended. When Maxine was involved in the self-disclosure therapeutic activities as a group member she occasionally raised her role as a researcher in the group. However, this felt uncomfortable, as if the research role took away the authentic claim of being a group member. Maxine experienced tensions being a participant observer and found herself unable to perform the two competing roles within the therapeutic activities practiced in the groups. Outside of these therapeutic activities, when Maxine stopped being an active group member, she was able to concentrate on her research role once again and construct her field notes. In this way the field notes recorded the ethical narratives that arose from the two competing roles. The lack of reference to Maxine's research role was not the result of a planned strategy, but the way that being a member of the group evolved. The research role could re-emerge during breaks from the self-discovery activities undertaken. However, this felt like the research role being separated by a great sense of being 'real' in the different contexts of a therapy group member and a researcher. Maxine found that being a member of the group involved an ethical commitment to remain 'true' to her group membership. This may have been related to the precise character of the groups, where techniques of self-disclosure promoted this feeling of showing your 'real', 'true' self. Therefore the hyphenated connection in the textual representation of auto/biography began to symbolize the movement from being a 'Me' and sharing the present experiences of those being researched to being 'I', the researcher who recorded stories about the other 'Me's. The two roles continued to provide an ethical tension, as the more private and intimate aspect of the researcher's experiences could remain hidden from the public account of the research process, the field notes, whereas the private and intimate aspects of others could become the data. Ironically then Maxine's own participation was only partial in this context when compared to the other participants. The term auto/biography hid the researcher's task to record the stories of others and these others may not have fully appreciated whose experiences formed the research.

Some researchers argue that the possibility of practicing a feminist ethnography is continually evasive as 'equality with research subjects in the ethnographic approach masks a deeper, more dangerous form of exploitation' (Stacey, 1988: 22). The examples taken from Maxine's study could be seen to support this explanation of exploitation. Conversely, they illustrate the complexity of ethical issues. In order to develop an approach that embraces practices of responsibility as advocated by Walker (2007) the situational and trans-situational characteristics of ethical concerns in the field must be appreciated. The practice of ethnography is said to lead to a swamp, a 'murky quagmire' (Price, 1996) where you can never predict what issues become important. Qualitative research concerned primarily with narratives also requires the consistent negotiation of boundaries as the process unfolds (Birch and Miller, 2000; Josselson, 1996;

Reissman, 2008). Therefore if we are to fully embrace feminist ideals of participation, the participants in the research must be included and invited to take part in this negotiation.

In order for Maxine to meet an ethical responsibility, her research design should have identified *processes of participation*. For example, one strategy could be to increase the visibility of field notes and use them as an ethical research tool. Field notes from the other group members could complement the 'field notes' of the researcher. The field notes could have been shared and discussed, which would have raised the research role within the more immediate setting. Regular slots could be timetabled for 'ethical talk' so both the researcher and the participant disengage from the research topic and talk openly about the research process. In this way, ethical narratives could be produced jointly in the spirit of full participation. It would be this model of 'ethical talk sessions' or what Seyla Benhabib refers to as an 'open-ended moral conversation' (1992: 9) that could promote the practice of joint participation. In this way the relativity of situational and trans-situational ethical concerns could be addressed by applying a regulatory procedure at all times. As Benhabib has noted, 'In ethics, the universalizability procedure, if it is understood as a reversing of perspectives and the willingness to reason from the other's (others') point of view, does not guarantee consent: it demonstrates the will and the readiness to seek understanding with the other to reach some reasonable agreement in an open-ended moral conversation' (1992: 9). If this interpretation of a 'universalizability procedure' is taken into the research relationship, this means not only presenting the 'knowing' of the area being researched from joint participation, but also the understanding of the research relationship from each other's point of view.

Yet the call for an understanding of the research relationship from the perspectives of participants together with the researchers' own reflexive account of the research process, can pose further dilemmas. While it is good research practice to reflect on and acknowledge the differing perspectives of all those involved it is also necessary to question how far those we gather data from actually want to participate. In her qualitative research on take-up of antenatal care among Bangladeshi women, Tina experienced difficulties accessing this largely hidden group (Miller, 1995). Eventually a small group of women were 'volunteered' into the research by a powerful gate-keeper (see Miller and Bell, Chapter 4, this volume). Although they could be argued to have 'participated' in the research that took place over several months, their participation was limited in a variety of respects. Even though Tina entered the research embracing feminist notions of reciprocity (see discussion of this in Mauthner, 2000), sensitivity and power sharing for example, the initial problems of access led to women participating in the study who would almost certainly not identify themselves as 'participants'. 'Reluctant respondents' would more accurately convey their perception of their role in the research.

This raises the ethical concern of how far participation in any fully participatory sense is actually desired by those we research and how far we may be imposing a particular relationship on those we seek to collect data from. While it can be argued that we can and should develop practices of responsibility this does not automatically mean that those whose lives we wish to research will share, or embrace, our vision. Any notion of 'open-ended moral conversations' (Benhabib, 1992) or ethical talk sessions as suggested earlier would almost certainly have not been recognized and/or welcomed by the Bangladeshi women who Tina interviewed. Their perceptions of Tina were as an interviewer who was there to collect information. These perceptions persisted in spite of Tina's efforts to attend their language group, join in sewing activities and help with the crèche (helping organize the crèche had been part of the research bargain struck with the gate-keeper). Eventually a number of the women agreed to be interviewed, some individually and some in a group, but Tina felt they participated *reluctantly*. It was also apparent that their expectations, as with many of the people we research, were that the process of being interviewed involved responding to a set of structured questions and that once the interview was over so too was their involvement in the research. Indeed, on reflection, it may be that the women finally agreed to be interviewed in order to bring to an end the research relationship that Tina had sought to establish. Tina had no further involvement or communications with the group once the data had been collected.

Learning from these experiences Tina included an end-of-study questionnaire in her longitudinal research on women's experiences of transition to first-time motherhood (Miller, 2000a, 2000b, 2005). The rationale behind this questionnaire was to ask the mothers about their experiences of *being* participants in the study. This piece of longitudinal research had involved the women participating in three interviews over the course of approximately one year during which they first became mothers (see Miller and Bell, Chapter 4, this volume). The longitudinal dimension of the research together with the particular focus on mothering and motherhood – an experience that Tina shared with the women – led Tina to feel that fuller participation was possible in this study. Yet the longitudinal element only served to highlight the ways in which goals can shift as the research process unfolds. Tina found that while her feelings of gratitude to the women who agreed to participate remained throughout the study – and continue today – her notion of what participation should involve shifted as academic pressures took precedence. At the outset, Tina made two distinct commitments to the women who participated. The first was to return the tapes of the interviews to them once they had been fully transcribed, which she did. The second was to send them the findings of the study, and this commitment was eventually met. However, good intentions of sending accessible forms of the research and its findings were not realized. Shortage of time and work demands resulted in Tina sending them an unedited version of her 'Findings' chapter from her thesis. In practice, participation was limited to the data collection phase in both Tina's studies and the women who were interviewed/participated appeared to have had no other expectations. Again this prompts us to consider the ways in which we may be in danger of imposing research relationships, based on particular notions of participation, that are not sought by those whose lives we set out to study (but see Chapter 2, this volume, for new considerations for researchers and research relationships).

Similarly, in Maxine's therapy study, ethical concerns arose once she came to the analysis of her fieldwork data and the interview transcripts. In the later stages of analysis and writing up, Maxine's ethics of responsibility were transposed to the academic field where it was easier not to keep the research participants informed. The significance of the ethical research relationship was altered. It was in the later stages of the analysis and the final production of the report that Maxine chose not to maintain communication or participation with the research respondents. To work within an expressive-collaborative model (Walker, 2007) Maxine should have maintained communication and invited joint interaction at all stages. But, as both Maxine and Tina found, attempting to achieve a responsibility to participants in combination with meeting institutional and academic demands can involve many tensions. Tina's research experiences lead her to both acknowledge the *ideal* of participation represented in Walker's practices of responsibility within an expressive and collaborative model, and to question its applicability in all research settings. Tina would argue that while we should never enter into what could be seen as exploitative research relationships, we must be clear at the outset about the commitments we are making to those who take part. Our aim then should be to honour those commitments – which may not necessarily involve participants in anything more than the data collection phase. Further clarity is needed so that particular interpretations of 'participation' are transparent from the outset. This is not to say that researchers must slavishly adhere to prescriptive guidelines but rather they should be encouraged to reflect upon the dimensions of participation that they wish to invite and promote during their research. The aim then is not to prescribe one particular form of ethically responsible research but to acknowledge the need to embrace an ethics of responsibility in the context of diverse and shifting research settings and relationships.

Ethical terms and practical guidelines

We could then identify ethical narratives produced in the research process in order to develop an ethics of responsibility guide for researchers. This guide could be used to promote opportunities for ethical reflection by all involved and to acknowledge the co-production of certain elements – and the power of the researcher to produce the final research story. This guide could also provide the researcher with a choice of terms to indicate certain practical decisions and strategies followed. Qualitative research methods of collecting and analysing data are constantly evolving and demand different ethical negotiations. For example developing an ethical covenant is posed as a critical agreement when working with visual methods in performance and auto-ethnographic fields (Denzin and Lincoln, 2011). In areas of feminist biographical and narrative qualitative research, this agreement would have to be negotiated and renegotiated throughout the research process. Questions of 'what becomes data' as discussed in relation to both offline and online research (see Chapter 2, this volume) remain pertinent to all fields of research.

In her research with young people and their 'smokey stories' (Birch, 2001) Maxine also wanted to achieve ethical research strategies. She has used her role of 'being' a mother of teenage children and belonging to a local neighbourhood as a route to access three friendship groups of young people. Clearly, in this study, ethical concerns are immediately raised as she has access to a much broader framework of situated knowledge than usually available in an interview setting. Maxine is familiar with the areas where these young people live; she has heard other stories about their housing estates, and information about their families. This 'insider' knowledge places the information gathered in the interviews in a richer context. However, it also necessitates the need for a clearer guide for ethical responsibility. Being in the 'field', whether this is before or during the research implies a particular aspect of being, belonging and participating in social life, such as 'being a mother and belonging to a community' or 'being a member of a therapy group and belonging to a friendship network'. This suggests that when researching life experiences that are shared, the need to be more ethically reflexive becomes essential. The constant re-negotiation and re-mapping of personal and relational ethical judgements is then vital when researching familiar, intimate and sensitive areas of social life.

A further addition to the qualitative researcher's role is that of 'bricoleur' (Denzin and Lincoln, 2008: 5–8). The description of the qualitative researcher as a 'bricoleur', a professional do-it-yourself person, succinctly conveys the many tasks and overlapping perspectives and paradigms found within the qualitative researcher role. For example, the bricoleur could be encouraged to develop a set of close-knit practices specific to the 'situational and trans-situational' ethical problems we discuss here. We suggest that these close-knit set of practices could then be linked to a framework of ethical responsibilities that demands close attention be paid to the processes of participation. Yet practices of responsibility must also acknowledge the different interpretations of participation that are possible and within this the potential power of the researcher to impose ongoing participation that is not sought or wanted.

To seek full and active participation from our research participants – throughout a project – demands that not only we, but also those whose lives we research, share a common interest and understanding of the research enterprise. For many this would require a fundamental shift in the ways in which research is conceptualized. Yet to not embrace the possibility of full participation may mean that particular positions become reinforced. If we constantly permit interpretations to depend upon the researcher and the academic community and ignore the participation of the 'research participant' we may be in danger of reinforcing particular ways of knowing and particular forms of knowledge. Why are 'we', as White, academic women being so secretive, especially when we are researching areas of familiar experiences? Are we fearful of being marginalized if we challenge existing academic conventions? Researchers must be encouraged to look for flexible research practices and different ways to produce the final research story (see Chapter 11, this volume, for more reflections on this point). Against the demands for academic conformity, feminists must continue to seek to produce different writing strategies such as those argued for by Laurel Richardson (2005). Regrettably, it appears that the production of feminist research knowledge is still constrained by the structures of academic credibility as identified by Dorothy Smith in 1987. In the context of increasing pressures from a hierarchical higher education system, where research funding and quality assurance define particular measures of academic prestige these debates have become even more important.

Conclusion

Our argument is for closer attention to be paid to the various dimensions of participation in qualitative research if participation is to represent more than just a semantic shift. We have acknowledged the need as feminist researchers to work from a position that is continually, ethically sensitive, to those whose lives we investigate, honouring research commitments made. We have discussed our difficulties in maintaining participation in our research projects and we have noted the need for research designs to identify the processes of participation. If research participants are willing (and able) to take a fully participatory role then researchers must develop different styles of writing that may challenge academic conventions but will reflect the co-production of research accounts. Such an enterprise depends upon the negotiation of an active research relationship in which the exchange of ideas and understanding forms a rich seam that runs throughout the research. Our aim here then, is not to prescribe one particular form of ethically responsible research, but to insist on the need to embrace an ethics of responsibility in the context of diverse and shifting research settings and relationships.

Note

1 All names have been changed.

References

Benhabib, S. (1992) *Situating the Self: Gender, Community and Postmodernism in Contemporary Ethics.* Cambridge: Polity Press.

Birch, M. (1996) 'The Goddess/God within: the construction of self identity through alternative health practices', in K. Flanagan and P. Jupp (eds), *Postmodernity, Sociology and Religion.* London: Macmillan. pp. 83–100.

Birch, M. (1998) 'Re/constructing research narratives: self and sociological identity in alternative settings', in J. Ribbens and R. Edwards (eds), *Feminist Dilemmas in Qualitative Research.* London: Sage. pp. 171–85.

Birch, M. and Miller, T.A. (2000) 'Inviting intimacy: the interview as 'therapeutic opportunity', *International Journal of Social Research Methodology, Theory and Practice,* 3 (3): 189–202.

Birch, M. (2001) 'Smokey stories: an exploration of young people's narratives in the maintenance of smoking and non-smoking lifestyles', unpublished paper, School of Health and Social Welfare, Open University.

British Psychological Society (2009) 'Code of ethics and conduct. Guidance published by the Ethics Committee of the British Psychological Society'. Available at: http://www.bps.org.uk/sites/default/files/documents/code_of_ethics_and_conduct.pdf (accessed August 2011).

British Sociological Association (2002) 'Statement of ethical practice'. Available at: http://www.britsoc.co.uk/equality/Statement+Ethical+Practice.htm (accessed August 2011).

Corradi, C. (1991) 'Text, context and individual meaning: rethinking life stories in a hermeneutic framework', *Discourse and Society,* 2 (1): 105–18.

Cotterill, P. (1992) 'Interviewing women: issues of friendship, vulnerability and power', *Women's Studies International Forum,* 15 (5/6): 593–606.

Denzin, N.K. and Lincoln, Y.S. (2008) *The Landscape of Qualitative Research,* 3rd edn. Thousand Oaks, CA: Sage.

Denzin, N.K. and Lincoln, Y.S. (2011) *The Sage Handbook of Qualitative Research,* 4th edn. Thousand Oaks, CA : Sage.

DeVault, M. (1990) 'Talking and listening from women's standpoint: feminist strategies for interviewing and analysis', *Social Problems,* 37 (1): 96–116.

Finch, J. (1984) '"It's great to have someone to talk to": the ethics and politics of interviewing women', in C. Bell and H. Roberts (eds), *Social Researching: Politics, Problems, Practice.* London: Routledge and Kegan Paul. pp. 166–80.

Frank, A. (1995) *The Wounded Storyteller.* Chicago, IL: The University of Chicago Press.

Frank, A. (2010) *Letting Stories Breathe: A Socio-Narratology.* Chicago, IL: The University of Chicago Press.

Giddens, A. (1991) *Modernity and Self-Identity.* Cambridge: Polity Press.

Giddens, A. (1992) *The Consequences of Modernity.* Cambridge: Polity Press.

Griffiths, M. (1995) *Feminisms and the Self. The Web of Identity.* London: Routledge.

Holland, J. (2007) 'Emotions and research', *International Journal of Social Research Methodology,* 10 (3): 195–209.

Josselson, R. (ed.) (1996) *Ethics and Process in the Narrative Study of Lives,* vol. 4. Thousand Oaks, CA: Sage.

Josselson, R. and Lieblich, A. (eds) (1997) *The Narrative Study of Lives,* vol. 5. Thousand Oaks, CA: Sage.

Lather, P. (1994) *Getting Smart: Feminist Research and Pedagogy Within/in Postmodern (Critical Social Thought).* London: Routledge.

Malinowski, B. (1967) *A Diary in the Strict Sense of the Term.* London: Routledge and Kegan Paul.

Mauthner, M. (2000) 'Snippets and silences: ethics and reflexivity in narratives of sistering', *International Journal of Social Research Methodology, Theory and Practice,* 3 (4): 287–306.

Miller, T. (1995) 'Shifting boundaries: exploring the influence of cultural traditions and religious beliefs of Bangladeshi women on antenatal interactions', *Women's Studies International Forum,* 18 (3): 299–309.

Miller, T. (1998) 'Shifting layers of professional, lay and personal narratives: longitudinal childbirth research', in R. Edwards and J. Ribbens (eds), *Feminist Dilemmas in Qualitative Research.* London: Sage.

Miller, T. (2000a) 'An exploration of first time motherhood: narratives of transition'. PhD dissertation, Warwick University.

Miller, T. (2000b) '"Losing the plot". Narrative construction and longitudinal childbirth research', *Qualitative Health Research,* 10 (3): 309–23.

Miller, T. (2005) *Making Sense of Motherhood: A Narrative Approach.* Cambridge: Cambridge University Press.

Oakley, A. (1981) 'Interviewing women: a contradiction in terms', in H. Roberts (ed.), *Doing Feminist Research*. London: Routledge and Kegan Paul.

Okley, J. and Calloway, H. (eds) (1992) *Anthropology and Autobiography*. London: Routledge.

Price, J. (1996) 'Snakes in the swamp', in R. Josselson (ed.), *Ethics and Process in the Narrative Study of Lives*, vol. 4. Thousand Oaks, CA: Sage.

Reissman, C.K. (1987) 'When gender is not enough: women interviewing women', *Gender and Society*, 1 (2): 172–207.

Reissman, C.K. (2008) *Narrative Methods for the Human Sciences*. Thousand Oaks, CA: Sage.

Ribbens, J. (1989) 'Interviewing: an "unnatural situation"?', *Women's Studies International Forum*, 12 (6): 579–92.

Ribbens, J. (1993) '"Fact or fictions?" Aspects of the use of autobiography written in undergraduate sociology', *Sociology*, 27 (1): 81–92.

Richardson, L. (2005) 'Writing: a method of inquiry', in N.K. Denzin and Y.S. Lincoln (eds), *Handbook of Qualitative Research*, 3rd edn. Thousand Oaks, CA: Sage. pp. 959 –78.

Roulston, K. (2010) *Reflective Interviewing: A Guide to Theory and Practice*. London: Sage.

Smith, D. (1987) *The Everyday World as Problematic: A Feminist Sociology*. Milton Keynes: Open University Press.

Stacey, J. (1988) 'Can there be a feminist ethnography?', *Women's Studies International Journal*, 11 (21): 227.

Stanley, L. (ed.) (1990) *Feminist Praxis. Research, Theory and Epistemology in Feminist Sociology*. London: Routledge.

Stanley, L. (1992) *The Auto I Biographical T: The Theory and Practice of Feminist Autolbiography*. Manchester: Manchester University Press.

Stanley, L. (1993) 'On auto/biography in sociology', *Sociology*, 27 (1): 41–52.

Walker, M. U. (1997) 'Picking up pieces lives stories and integrity', in D. Tietjens Meyers (ed.), *Feminists Rethink the Self*. London: HarperCollins.

Walker, M.U. (2007) *Moral Understandings: A Feminist Study in Ethics*. Oxford: Oxford University Press.

7

'Doing rapport' and the ethics of 'faking friendship'

JEAN DUNCOMBE AND JULIE JESSOP

Introduction

This chapter centres on discussion of some of the ethical, feminist, emotional and methodological issues associated with how rapport is gained, maintained, and 'used' in qualitative interviews. Our interest in rapport was stimulated by our own research,[1] where we found that in order to persuade some of our women interviewees[2] to talk freely, we needed consciously to exercise our interviewing skills in *'doing* rapport' with – or rather *to* – them. Uncomfortably, we came to realize that even feminist interviewing could sometimes be viewed as a kind of *job* where, at the heart of our outwardly friendly interviews, lay the instrumental purpose of persuading interviewees to provide us with data for our research, and also (hopefully) for our future careers.

Our discomfort in our research interviews has broader analogies and deeper roots. For example, there are strong parallels between 'doing rapport' and the kinds of 'emotion work' that women, in particular, perform in their relationships by simulating empathy to make others feel good (Hochschild, 1983). Hochschild has argued that the spread of jobs where women are paid to simulate empathy represents the 'commercialization' of human feeling, and those who do such work run the risk of feeling, and indeed actually *becoming,* 'phoney' and 'inauthentic' (Hochschild, 1983). Seen in this light, feelings of 'insincerity' that we sometimes experience as interviewers can be linked to the pressures of commercialization in the 'job' of qualitative interviewing; even within feminist research (see also Bott, 2010).

An obvious starting point for a discussion of ethical issues associated with rapport is the early seminal article by Ann Oakley, which has played a large part in opening up feminist discussion of this 'commonly used but ill-defined term' (Oakley, 1981: 35). Oakley criticized the model of 'rapport' advocated in methods textbooks for being instrumental, hierarchical and non-reciprocal, qualities she characterized as would-be 'professional' and 'scientific', and basically masculine. By aiming to suppress the role of gender and individual personality in interview relationships, this model failed to engage with major feminist and ethical issues. As an alternative, Oakley advanced the now familiar argument that feminist researchers and their women subjects participate as 'insiders' in the same culture, where the 'minimal' social distance between them offers the basis for an emotionally empathetic, egalitarian and reciprocal rapport. However, she warned that the closer rapport that permits the feminist researcher to gain a deeper understanding of women's intimate lives and feelings also brings greater ethical problems:

> Frequently researchers . . . establish rapport not as scientists but as human beings; yet they proceed to use this humanistically-gained knowledge for scientific ends, usually without the informants' knowledge. (Sjoberg and Nett, 1968: 215–16)

> These ethical dilemmas are greatest where there is least social distance between the interviewer and interviewee. Where both share the same gender socialisation and critical life experiences, social distance can be minimal ... (From 'Interviewing Women: A Contradiction in Terms', Oakley, 1981: 55)

Somewhat ironically, Oakley has since criticized feminist proponents of qualitative methodology, on the grounds that their eagerness to claim 'preferentially to own the qualitative method' has become part of their own 'professionalizing agenda' within academia (Oakley, 1998: 716). However, we would suggest that this criticism distracts attention from two important but rather different trends, the first of which has taken place largely outside feminism. We believe that the expansion of 'consumer research' and various other interviewing jobs both in commerce and government, has high-lighted the value of research methods which persuade interviewees to disclose their more private and 'genuine' thoughts. As a result of which, the ability to 'do rapport' by 'faking friendship' in relatively less-structured[3] qualitative interviews has become a set of 'professional' and 'marketable skills', and generally with a training sanitized of any concern with broader ethical issues. In order to tap into wider debates, we would suggest that the skills of 'doing rapport' have become commodified, with little discussion of the function of rapport in 'agenda setting' and 'the management of consent' in the interview situation – terms used by Lukes to describe the hidden use of power in relationships (Komter, 1989; Lukes, 1974).

The second trend has been within feminism (although not exclusively), where the earlier, relatively uncritical acceptance of feminist claims for a special rapport between women has been challenged by a much more sceptical debate concerning the limits and ethical problems of 'feminist' qualitative research methods (see Edwards and Mauthner, Chapter 1, this volume).

These broad trends will now be outlined and examples from our own research will be drawn upon to illustrate and explore some of the ethical dilemmas associated with the concept and practice of rapport. We hope to convey how ethical problems emerge, overlap, and change unpredictably during interviews, and also to indicate how our awareness of these ethical dilemmas has changed as our 'careers' have developed from interviewing on behalf of other researchers, to interviewing for 'our own' research.

The commodification of rapport: 'agenda setting' and 'the management of consent'

We have suggested that there has been a trend towards the professionalization, or more accurately, the commercialization or 'commodification', of the skills of 'doing rapport' in less-structured qualitative interviews. We now explore in more detail what we mean, and how this trend differs from the 'would-be professionalism' criticized by Oakley. Nevertheless, both these trends are alike in their neglect of the broader ethical issues integral to the inequalities of power in the interviewing process (but see Reeves, 2010). Chief among these issues in relation to rapport is the 'management of consent'.

The most important difference in approach between the two models of rapport that we have discussed so far, is well summarized in the following description of what is involved:

> Rather than trying to expunge the personality of the interviewer and to standardise interviews, this [more personalised] approach demands that interviewers should *manage* their appearance, behaviour and self-presentation in such a way as to build rapport and trust with each individual respondent. (O'Connell Davidson and Layder, 1994: 122–3, emphasis added)

There are close parallels here with Hochschild's (1983) discussion of the 'management of emotion', as a passage from another methods text makes clear:

> *Rapport is tantamount to trust*, and trust is the foundation for acquiring the fullest, most accurate disclosure a respondent is able to make ... When you are warm and caring, you promote rapport, you make yourself appealing to talk to, and, not least, you communicate to your respondents, 'I see you as a human being with interests, experience, and needs beyond those I tap for my own purposes' ... In an effective interview, both researcher and respondent feel good, rewarded and satisfied by the process and the outcomes. The warm and caring researcher is on the way to achieving such effectiveness. (Glesne and Peshkin, 1992: 79, 87, quoted in O'Connell Davidson and Layder, 1994: 123, emphasis added)

We would argue that, in equating the process of 'doing rapport' with trust, and failing to question the insincerity of 'faking friendship', this passage exhibits a disturbing ethical naivety.

In order to achieve good rapport, however, interviewers are sometimes advised to adopt a special kind of naivety (Kvale, 1992), or what Glaser and Strauss (1967) characterise as a pretence awareness, where they convey overall ignorance about what interviewees say, while at the same time promoting rapport by giving the occasional knowing glance. Interviewers also learn that they should consciously dress and present themselves in a way that sends the correct messages to the interviewee. That is, they must seat themselves not too far away but not too near; maintain a pleasant, encouraging half-smile and a lively (but not too lively) interest. They should keep eye contact, speak in a friendly tone, never challenge, and avoid inappropriate expressions of surprise or disapproval; and practice the art of the encouraging but 'non-directive "um"'. If this is 'friendship', then it is a very detached form of it.

The development of techniques for 'doing rapport' has been reinforced by the adoption of counselling skills and language into the repertoire of the qualitative interviewer: 'Rogers's writings on therapeutic interviews have been a source of inspiration for the development of qualitative interviewing for research purposes' (Kvale, 1992: 24). Writings about counselling stress the need to minimize social distance and establish rapport and trust, by projecting an air of genuineness and empathy with the client. Counselling interviewers are trained to listen to 'what is said between the lines' as well as to the 'explicit description of meanings ... The interviewer may seek to formulate the "implicit message", "send it back" to the subject, and obtain an immediate confirmation or disconfirmation of the interviewer's interpretation of what the interviewee is saying ...' (Kvale, 1992: 32). Apart from this process of 'reflection', training in counselling discusses the use of pauses and how to be comfortable with (the 'sound' of) silences.

The skills of doing rapport also supposedly include the ability to draw boundaries around the range of subject matter and to limit the emotional depth of the interview; this is the 'purpose' in the apparently informal 'conversation with a purpose'. Kvale, for example, employs a mining metaphor to distinguish between 'qualitative research' interviews whose aim is to gather knowledge, and 'therapeutic interviews' that attempt to change subjects' lives: 'knowledge is understood as buried metal and the interviewer is the miner ... The interviewer researcher strips the surface of conscious experiences ... the therapeutic interviewer mines the deeper unconscious layers' (1992: 3).

This process of qualitative interviewing is generally seen as benign, leading the interviewee to valuable personal insights and enabling the researcher to contribute to a wider understanding of individual's lives and problems. Indeed this is the image of interviewing cherished by most qualitative researchers. However, the goals and potential outcomes of the interview are not the sole ethical issue to be considered. If interviewees are persuaded to participate in the interview by the researcher's show of empathy and the rapport achieved in conversation, how far can they be said to have given their 'informed consent' to make the disclosures that emerge during the interview?

It is clearly impossible for interviewees to give their *fully informed* consent at the outset of an essentially exploratory qualitative interview whose direction and potential revelations cannot be anticipated (Wise, 1987; Miller and Bell, Chapter 4, this volume). Some researchers have suggested that consent requires an ongoing process of discussion, reflection, and re-negotiation of trust throughout the interview. However, as Kvale (1992: 115) has pointed out, this approach depends on unrealistic assumptions of equality and 'rationalism' in research relationships, particularly where the interviewee may not share the interviewer's goals. We would also suggest that such *continual* intervention would inhibit the development of rapport and give the interviewer too intrusive a 'voice' in the construction of the interview dialogue. Under commercial (or professional) pressure to obtain results, there is a danger that, rather than engage in such complex negotiations which might entail the risk of refusal, interviewers will find it more convenient to rely on their skills in 'doing rapport' to persuade interviewees to disclose the information they seek.

Unfortunately, the process of 'doing rapport' may lead the interviewer into some of the serious ethical and emotional difficulties that can develop unanticipated during the interview. For example, as Kvale warns, there is a danger that 'close personal rapport ... may lead the research interview moving into a quasi-therapeutic interview', and indeed 'some individuals may [deliberately] turn the interview into therapy', although Kvale also confidently claims: 'The interviewer feels when a topic is too emotional to pursue in the interview' (1992: 149, 155). However, in practice even skilled interviewers may find it difficult to draw neat boundaries around 'rapport', 'friendship' and 'intimacy', in order to avoid the depths of 'counselling' and 'therapy' (Birch and Miller, 2000). With deeper rapport, interviewees become more likely to explore their more intimate experiences and emotions. Yet they also become more likely to discover and disclose experiences and feelings which, upon reflection, they would have preferred to keep private from others (Finch, 1984; Oakley, 1981; Stacey, 1988), or not to acknowledge even to themselves. Indeed, by doing rapport 'too effectively' interviewers run the risk of breaching the interviewees' right *not* to know or reflect upon their own innermost thoughts (Duncombe and Marsden, 1996; Larossa et al., 1981).

Ethical issues must inevitably arise where, increasingly, relatively unsuspecting interviewees are confronted by qualitative interviewers who are armed with a battery of skills in 'doing rapport' in interview relationships in order to achieve disclosure. In effect, by 'doing rapport' the interviewer 'sets the agenda' of the encounter and 'manages the consent' of the interviewee. This can work to close down or obscure any opportunities for the interviewee to challenge part or the whole of the interviewing process because this would appear a breach of the interviewer's ('faked') friendship. Under these circumstances, rapport is *not* 'tantamount to trust'. Instead, *'doing rapport'* becomes the ethically dubious substitute for more open negotiation of the interviewee's fully informed consent to participate in the interviewing process (see Birch and Miller, Chapter 6, and Miller and Bell, Chapter 4, this volume).

The limitations of woman to woman rapport

As Hey (2000) points out, the literature on 'doing rapport' often conveys the curious impression that interviewers (and counsellors) are being trained to do through artifice what most women supposedly do 'naturally' and 'spontaneously' as a consequence of their gendered subordination and socialization: for example, expressing empathy and tuning in to the moods of others (Miller, 1986); doing 'emotion work' to make others feel good (Hochschild, 1983); seeking communication through 'rapport talk' (Tannen, 1991); and listening to, and understanding, what remains unsaid 'between the lines' (Devault, 1990) (although see Duncombe and Marsden, 1998).

However, this somewhat over-generalized picture is becoming increasingly challenged by a number of feminist researchers in differing ways. Significantly, rather than explore how to 'do rapport' by 'faking friendship', some researchers are focusing on the conditions and ethical problems where rapport does *not* occur because the social and emotional distance between researcher and interviewee proves too great (see Hey, 2000).

This shift in emphasis can be seen as a result of wider feminist debates centred on the role of research (see Gillies and Alldred, Chapter 3, this volume). Initially, through disagreement about their goals and approaches, feminist researchers encountered dilemmas concerning the kinds of 'rapport' and 'openness' to be negotiated in the research relationship. Such dilemmas have worked to highlight the tensions between achieving an openness that enables women to speak 'in their real voices' (Ribbens, 1998: 17) and an 'Openness to complete transformation ... [that] lays the groundwork for friendship, shared struggle, and identity change' (Reinharz, 1992: 68). All qualitative interviewers inevitably play a part in the construction of the interview, yet it seems to us that the explicit goal of transformation implies a more active analytical and interventionist role for the feminist researcher, whose voice may come to 'overlay' that of her subject. In fact, McRobbie (1982) doubts whether feminist researchers have either the capacity or the right to attempt to transform their subjects' lives.

Even in research with the more limited goal of understanding women's lives, differences of power arise almost inevitably from the researcher's ability to shape the interview 'dialogue' and to put together her version of the subject's lived reality, which, however, the subject herself may reject (Stacey, 1990; Wise, 1987). In addition, Wise (1987) and Phoenix (1994) have doubted whether shared womanhood can bridge differences of social class, ethnicity, sexual orientation and so on. Indeed, other feminists have pointed out that failures of empathy and rapport in the course of researching power may be evidence of important differences of perspective that need to be explored and defined rather than negotiated away (Cain, 1990; Smart, 1984).

Similar issues concerning rapport arise where researchers attempt to negotiate with interviewees the subsequent production of reports, data analysis and publication. Ideally, it is sometimes suggested, consent should be renegotiated at each stage (Kelly, 1988; Luff, 1999; Stacey, 1990). Yet some feminists argue that such negotiations are merely attempts to enlist interviewees' help in their own 'objectification' (Cain, 1990), since even the feminist (sociological) researcher must inevitably control the analysis (Ramazanoglu, 1989; see also Doucet and Mauthner, Chapter 8, this volume).

A consequence of these various differences between researchers and interviewees is that rapport in actual interviews may be less encompassing than the 'feminist ideal' outlined above. For example, when Luff interviewed potentially anti-feminist women from a powerful 'moral lobby', she sometimes experienced the expected lack of empathy, yet she was also surprised to feel what she described as 'moments of rapport' with women she expected to dislike (Luff, 1999). She stresses that feminist interviewers should reflect on both what is going on *but also how they feel about such moments,* as evidence of how aspects of women researchers' 'fractured' subjectivities and identities may sometimes mirror those of interviewees but, equally importantly, sometimes clash (Harding, 1987: 8). However, in describing her own feelings, Luff confesses:

> Listening to views, nodding or saying simple 'ums' or 'I see', to views that you strongly disagree with or, ordinarily, would strive to challenge, may be true to a methodology that aims to listen seriously to the views and experiences of others, but can feel personally very difficult and lead to questioning of the whole research agenda. (1999: 698)

Luff worried that simulated friendliness might appear to support views irredeemably opposed to her own feminist beliefs. In practice, she found she could 'do rapport' (as we have called it) in relationships where she felt no empathy, but she guiltily suspected that her research was semi-covert. Her interviews with 'powerful' women offer a useful reminder that the balance of power is not always tilted mainly in the interviewer's favour. For example, after interviewing lone fathers, McKee and O'Brien (1983) have commented on men's tendency to take control, and how as women they had to assume a 'professional' asexual social distance in order to discourage unwanted male advances (McKee and O'Brien, 1983).

The above outlines the two trends we identified earlier: the 'commodification' of the skills of 'doing rapport', and feminist discussions of the limitations of what might be called the 'ideal feminist research relationship'. Luff's description in particular echoes our own ethical dilemmas as researchers, and we now explore our own research experiences in more detail.

Our own research experience of ethical problems with rapport

With hindsight, our own early attitudes to research were influenced by 'feminist' expectations that rapport would be easily achieved with women interviewees, but also (via graduate methodology training) by the 'professional' literature on 'doing rapport'. From both perspectives, rapport appeared ethically unproblematic and we pictured a 'good interview' as a reciprocal exchange, where our (genuine or simulated) expressions of empathy would ensure that interviewees would willingly make intimate disclosures. We were therefore unprepared for the disjunctures between these expectations and the ethical and emotional dilemmas that we experienced in practice – the feeling that we were intruding or even inflicting pain, or the way that pressures to collect data for our employers or our own research sometimes clashed with our sense of ethics.

Initially we were keen to establish ourselves as good interviewers, so although we often empathetically 'heard' our subjects' reluctance to be interviewed, we also felt (like salespersons) that to do our *jobs* properly we must deploy all the charm we could muster to get ourselves through the door so we could ask our questions. But once inside, to gain a 'good interview' we would have to work harder at doing rapport to get our interviewees to 'open up' more fully. However, we were unprepared to discover how widely many of these encounters could vary, or to experience the complexity of our personal reactions to doing rapport.

Hardly surprisingly, we found it more difficult to achieve rapport where we did not spontaneously feel empathy with our interviewees. For example, in an early study of youth training schemes (YTS), Jean felt she established a 'genuine', if shallow, rapport with the YTS trainees and with the more conscientious employers who took training seriously, because she was 'on their side'. But with the more exploitative employers and trainers (who provided neither jobs nor training), she knew she was faking rapport to 'betray' them into revealing their double standards; and sometimes while smiling at them she also smiled to herself, thinking: 'What a revealing quote.' However, in analogous situations, Julie felt uncomfortable and personally compromised when she found that, in order to gain a 'good' interview, it seemed necessary to smile, nod, and appear to collude with views she strongly opposed.

In later research on household finances, Jean disagreed profoundly with the would-be 'scientific' detachment adopted by her employer and colleagues. Yet she discovered that establishing close rapport could bring disclosures that were outside the scope of the research and occasionally beyond her capacity to handle. For example, one aggrieved wife showed Jean the knife she said she planned to use to kill her husband, whom she described as a confidence trickster who had deceived her. Another wife confided that, despite an injunction against her pathologically violent husband, she still allowed him back into the house to sleep with her, unknown to her children, or to the police and social services who were trying to protect her and her family. 'Doing rapport' had gained Jean the confidences of 'friendship', yet she felt bound by the ethics of confidentiality not to call on others to intervene. More minor dilemmas arose where interviewees asked Jean to switch off the tape, inviting her collusion in concealing what they had to say from 'her boss' and 'the outside world', but setting Jean the temptation still to use the material.

In Julie's first interview as a paid research officer, she too was confronted with ethical dilemmas resulting from the 'over effectiveness' of her attempts at doing rapport. Her interviewee was a man whose wife had recently left him after 22 years, and he immediately protested that he did not know why he had agreed to participate because he did not feel comfortable in talking about his feelings. Nevertheless, prompted by her training and the desire to establish herself as an interviewer, Julie tried all the harder to put him at his ease, smiling, empathizing, and stressing that participation was voluntary. Eventually, he was persuaded to reveal experiences from 20 years before that he had never even told his wife – the disclosure of which was emotionally upsetting and resulted in tears. Although Julie had alerted him to the fact that she was not a counsellor, she felt she had betrayed him into revealing more of his feelings than he would have wished, and more than she could handle (although after agreeing to further interviews, he felt he had been helped). Overall, Julie recognized that her reactions were a complex mixture of guilt and sympathy for her interviewee, and worries over the power her technique had given her, but nevertheless edged with a sense of satisfaction that she had gained a level of self-disclosure her employer would welcome.

As contract researchers, both Julie and Jean sometimes felt resentful and even possessive that the hard-won insights from their interviews might then be appropriated by their employers and misinterpreted, misused or even discarded. Julie, in particular, felt she knew which 'good quotes' her employer would take up, but regretted how much of the deeply emotional content the employer would then regard as outside the remit of 'her' research. Both Julie and Jean felt there was inevitably loss or distortion when someone else attempted to analyse data abstracted from the emotional context of the rapport through which it had been generated. (There are echoes here of debates concerning attempts to archive qualitative data for re-analysis; see Mauthner et al, 1998 and Natasha S. Mauthner, Chapter 10, this volume.)

The differences accruing to specific interviewer positions were emphasized for Julie when she realized how, as a paid research assistant, her sense of 'doing a job' had relieved her from taking full responsibility when interviewees were upset by what she regarded as 'her employer's' research. Once conducting her own research, however, she felt personally responsible, and consequently tended to steer interviewees away from potentially sensitive areas and to stop the interview at signs of distress, although she was then faced with the fact that her interviews might not achieve the degree of emotional disclosure that characterised the 'good interview' (Birch and Miller, 2000).

Ethical problems also arose in Jean's attempt to explore the 'interior' of marriage by probing the disagreements and 'secrets' that couples keep from the outside world, and sometimes from one another and even themselves. Fully informed consent could not be negotiated in advance, but Jean hoped that by maintaining good rapport, interviewees would feel comfortable enough to participate. However, she later recognized that by using rapport in this way, she was disguising rather than solving the ethical problems that remained integral to her research.

Such problems were less pressing where Jean found it more difficult to establish good rapport: some working-class husbands, in particular, were reluctant to discuss their emotions, and their wives in turn seemed to fear their husbands would condemn them for any disclosure of 'marital secrets'. After keeping a child in the room to inhibit the development of rapport, one working-class mother concluded, almost triumphantly: 'There, I don't suppose you found out much, did you!' However, there was an illuminating moment of rapport in an otherwise sticky interview with another working-class woman, when she discovered that Jean (like herself) had suffered postnatal depression and she trusted Jean enough to become more open and vulnerable, although social distance returned when the discussion moved to other areas.

The value of shared experience in promoting rapport was more evident to Jean in interviews with liberal middle-class women whose tastes and lives seemed closer to her own. These interviews became enjoyable conversations, where intimate emotional disclosures came so easily that the boundaries between research and friendship seemed to blur. Yet Jean came to realize that again such 'over easy' rapport entailed pitfalls. For example, when interviewees said: 'You know what I mean', she tended to reply: 'I know', partly deliberately to build rapport but also intuitively because she felt she genuinely *did* know. Only on listening to the tapes later did she realize how 'reading between the lines' brought the risk that she might project her own understanding onto the interviewees' relationships.

Such 'over rapport' sometimes created more obvious ethical (and methodological and feminist) problems in joint interviews where couples who were nursing grievances against one another were still comfortable, or aggrieved, enough to argue in Jean's presence. Some wives invited Jean to ally herself with them in condemning their husbands, who naturally then became hostile and reluctant to participate. With such interviews Jean experienced very mixed feelings: satisfaction in capturing such revealing data on tape, yet (particularly on re-hearing the tapes) guilt that her presence might have fuelled conflicts she should have tried to smooth over or silence.

More subtly, Jean also began to worry that probing about love and intimacy might disturb relationships where couples (usually wives) had 'worked hard' emotionally to achieve a balance. For example, whenever Jean asked one wife about her husband's views, the wife began by saying, 'We think . . .' but then hesitated and switched to, 'Well, *I* think', until she reluctantly began to realize during the interview how little her husband ever disclosed to her. Similarly, in response to a question on displays of affection, she began by saying, 'Oh yes, we like to cuddle ...', but then she corrected herself as she realized she was always the initiator, 'Well, *I* like to cuddle', adding thoughtfully, 'I'd never thought of that before'. Although the interviews ended with Jean engaging in 'repair work' to reaffirm that such couple relationships were 'all right, really', she could not dispel the thought that some couples or individuals might be betrayed by the rapport that she had established into learning too much about the imbalances of affection and power in their relationships.

The fact that interviews restricted to one visit might leave interviewees with unresolved pain, was brought home to Jean when some time after one interview she encountered a woman who had cried bitterly about intimate events in her personal life. Yet although they came face to face and she started visibly, obviously recognizing Jean, the interviewee walked past without a nod, perhaps now feeling that she had revealed too much of herself and recognizing that Jean was not, after all, a 'friend'.

Indeed, for both of us, later chance encounters with former interview subjects provided illuminating insights into how far there had been a blurring of boundaries between the temporary 'faked friendship' that we had induced by doing rapport, and 'real' friendship characterized by emotional empathy and continuity over time. For example, in repeated interviews with one subject, Julie felt a lot of effort was required in order to 'do her job' and establish rapport. However, she persevered over several months and eventually gained sufficient trust for the interviewee to disclose incidents and emotions that were extremely painful to her. Yet the disparity of this relationship (from Julie's perspective) was revealed soon after, when this participant rang Julie at home to suggest meeting up for coffee. Although Julie chatted politely and talked about how the woman was now feeling, she felt she did not 'have time' to meet; she had 'done her job' in relation to that particular piece of research, and she was now too busy cultivating new 'friends' on the next research project (see also Rogers and Ludhra, 2011).

Jean had a similar experience when someone whom she did not immediately rec-ognize rushed over and embraced her in the street and began chatting in a most friendly way about Jean's family and job. It took Jean several minutes to realize who this was, and she was left feeling slightly affronted by the 'assumption of familiarity' that was evident. Jean remembered that the interview (two years earlier) had been dif-ficult, with little real rapport or 'reward' so that, in an effort to put the interviewee at her ease, she had disclosed more about herself than usual. In effect, she had begun to engage in what was supposed to be the behaviour of a 'real' friend, although now, at a distance from, the interview, it no longer seemed appropriate to make the effort of expressing a friendship she did not feel.

This kind of blurring of boundaries between real and faked friendship seems more likely to occur in research where the interviewing process involves repeated visits. For example, Julie interviewed one woman five times over a 10-month period after her husband and friends had abandoned her, and listened empathetically to experi-ences that they sometimes had in common. In the last interview, when Julie asked her what she had gained from the research, she replied, 'Well, apart from anything else, I've made a friend'. However, this claim only brought home to Julie the falseness of the situation where the interviewee did not recognize how Julie's 'faking of friend-ship' had been part of her job. Julie's strong personal discomfort was later com-pounded when she could not immediately recall the interviewee's name when they met in the street. This, and similar experiences, in which it becomes apparent that a 'role' is being played, highlights the falsity of interview 'friendships' and leads to reflection on how interviewees themselves may be projecting a 'self that is specific to the situation'.

These later encounters with former interviewees offer intriguing insights about our different individual understandings of the unspoken interview 'contract', that is, how much of 'ourselves' we were prepared to give by way of 'doing rapport', and what we expected our interviewees to give us in return. In some interviews, Jean felt uncomfortable because her participants could feel that her research on inti-macy might be intrusive and potentially exploitative; yet at the same time she wondered how far her interviewees might be acting a part to conceal their 'real' selves, as she felt that she herself was doing. In contrast, Julie experienced almost the reverse reaction with some of her interviewees, feeling that they were 'intrud-ing' upon her when they 'called her bluff' by trying to take up and pursue the rap-port she had established in the interview as if it had been real rather than 'faked' friendship.

Another way of looking at these episodes is that they provide further illustrations of how interviewees may exercise power in their relationships with interviewers, not only through withholding the data that interviewers want, but by transgressing (or failing to recognize) the hidden 'rules' or 'cues' as to how interview relationships are 'supposed' to develop. In our interviews such 'transgressions' took the form of partici-pants rejecting our faked offers of 'friendship', or alternatively taking up the offer too enthusiastically as if it were genuine. Our contrasting personal responses to such 'transgressions', both as interviewers and *individuals,* highlight how the insights that we gain from research are influenced by both personal and social differences, and how ethical dilemmas permeate the whole experience of research interviewing.

Conclusion

Our discussion of the ethical issues associated with rapport started with what we called the 'ideal feminist research relationship' where spontaneous and genuine rapport supposedly leads more naturally to reciprocal mutual disclosure. We have contrasted this ideal with research relationships in which the interviewer is influenced by commercial pressures to 'do rapport' by 'faking friendship' in order to encourage the interviewee to open up. In practice, of course, all interviewing relationships, including women's interviews with women, are situated somewhere along a spectrum between the extremes of more genuine empathy and relationships with an element of 'faking'. However, interview relationships raise common ethical problems, to the extent that they encourage or persuade interviewees to explore and disclose experiences and emotions which – on reflection – they may have preferred to keep to themselves or even 'not to know'.

These ethical tensions are associated with the misuse of the interviewer's power of persuasion, exercised through the ideologies of shared 'womanhood' or alternatively shared 'friendship'. We have shown how claims for a special status for shared womanhood have been challenged even from within feminism. Feminist researchers must, therefore, inevitably face ethical dilemmas concerning the balance between the possibly adverse individual emotional consequences of their interviews for their interviewees, as against the more abstract gains to feminism and public education that may result from their research. We have also argued that in this 'ethical equation' we need to take into account the influence of professionalization, as a specific instance of a more general trend towards the 'commercialization' or 'commodification' of rapport.

It was our sense of alienation from the kinds of rapport that we felt we needed to establish in our interviews that led us to this exploration of the ethics of rapport. On further reflection, we became aware that some aspects of our graduate training, and the literature on the skills of qualitative interviewing, tapped into a more general trend towards seeing such skills in terms of their marketability, with a consequent neglect of their ethical implications. In short, the skills of 'doing rapport' are becoming 'commodified'.

We have suggested that the commodification of the skills of 'doing rapport' raises ethical questions concerning how far interviewers are able to 'set the agenda' for the interview and to 'manage the consent' of interviewees to participate in disclosing more or less private and intimate information. Our advice is that interviewers should continue to worry about these issues as they emerge in each piece of research and each individual interview. However, interviewers should remember that interviewees are not totally powerless, and that they can withhold their participation – as long as interviewers do not 'do rapport' too convincingly.

Notes

1 Julie has interviewed husbands and wives (not couples) between separation and divorce, and interviewed divorced mothers, divorced fathers and their new partners as part of her PhD on post-divorce parenting. Jean has researched youth training schemes, as well as wives, husbands (and other kin), for studies of household finances, and of love and power in couple relationships.

2 We use the term 'interviewee' because we feel that 'subject' claims too much and 'respondent' claims too little participation in the research.

3 Confusion arises because the term 'qualitative' is now used indiscriminately to refer to fairly structured interviews intended for quantitative computer analysis, which have virtually nothing in common with flexible ('unstructured' or 'semi-structured') 'conversations with a purpose' that rely at most on topic guides. Whereas Oakley deplored attempts to depersonalize and structure relationships in what she argued should be personal and flexible research relationships, our concern is with the spread of a commercial and phoney 'personalization' in the realm of more flexible methods.

References

Birch, M. and Miller, T. (2000) 'Inviting intimacy: the interview as "therapeutic opportunity"', *Social Research Methodology, Theory and Practice,* 3: 189–202.

Bott, E. (2010) 'Favourites and others: reflexivity and the shaping of subjectivities and data in qualitative research', *Qualitative Research,* 10: 154–173.

Cain, M. (1990) 'Realist philosophy and standpoint epistemologies or feminist criminology as a successor science', in L. Gelsthorpe and A. Morris (eds), *Feminist Perspectives on Criminology.* Buckingham: Open University Press. pp. 123–40.

Devault, M. (1990) 'Talking and listening from women's standpoint: feminist strategies for interviewing and analysis', *Social Problems,* 37: 96–116.

Duncombe, J. and Marsden, D. (1996) 'Can we research the private sphere?', in L. Morris and E. Stina Lyon (eds), *Gender Relations in Public and Private.* London: Macmillan.

Duncombe, J. and Marsden, D. (1998) '"Stepford wives" and "hollow men"? Doing emotion work, doing gender and "authenticity" in intimate heterosexual relationships', in G. Bendelow and S.J. Williams (eds), *Emotions in Social Life.* London: Routledge.

Finch, J. (1984) 'It's great to have someone to talk to: the ethics and politics of interviewing women', in C. Bell and H. Roberts (eds), *Social Researching.* London: Routledge and Kegan Paul.

Glaser, B.G. and Strauss, A. (1967) *The Discovery of Grounded Theory.* Chicago, IL: Aldine.

Glesne, C. and Peshkin, A. (1992) *Becoming Qualitative Researchers: An Introduction.* New York: Longman.

Harding, S. (ed.) (1987) *Feminism and Methodology.* Milton Keynes: Indiana University Press and Open University Press.

Hey, V. (2000) 'Troubling the auto/biography of the questions: re/thinking rapport and the politics of social class in feminist participant observation', *Genders and Sexualities in Educational Ethnography,* 3: 161–83.

Hochschild, A.R. (1983) *The Managed Heart: The Commercialization of Human Feeling.* Berkeley, CA: University of California Press.

Kelly, L. (1988) *Surviving Sexual Violence.* Cambridge: Polity.

Komter, A. (1989) 'Hidden power in marriage', *Gender and Society,* 3: 2.

Kvale, S. (1992) *Interviews.* London: Sage.

Larossa, R. et al. (1981) 'Ethical dilemmas in qualitative family research', *Journal of Marriage and the Family,* 43: 303–13.

Luff, D. (1999) 'Dialogue across the divides: "moments of rapport" and power in feminist research with anti-feminist women', *Sociology,* 33 (4): 687–703.

Lukes, S. (1974) *Power: A Radical View.* London: Macmillan.

Mauthner, N.S., Parry, O. and Backett-Miburn, K. (1998) 'The data are out there, or are they? Implications for archiving and revisiting qualitative data', *Sociology,* 32 (4): 733–45.

McKee, L. and O'Brien, M. (1983) 'Interviewing men: taking gender seriously', in E. Garmarnikov, et al. (eds), *The Public and the Private.* London: Heineman.

McRobbie, A. (1982) 'The politics of feminist research: between talk, text and action', *Feminist Review,* 12: 46–57.

Miller, J.B. (1986) *Towards a New Psychology of Women.* Harmondsworth: Penguin.

Oakley, A. (1981) 'Interviewing women: a contradiction in terms', in H. Roberts (ed.), *Doing Feminist Research.* London: Routledge and Kegan Paul.

Oakley, A. (1998) 'Gender, methodology and people's ways of knowing: some problems with feminism and the paradigm debate in social science', *Sociology,* 32 (4): 707–31.

O'Connell Davidson, J. and Layder, D. (1994) *Methods, Sex and Madness.* London: Routledge.

Phoenix, A. (1994) 'Practicing feminist research: the intersection of gender and "race" in the research process', in M. Maynard and J. Purvis (eds), *Researching Women's Lives from a Feminist Perspective.* London: Taylor & Francis.

Ramazanoglu, C. (1989) 'Improving on sociology: the problems of taking a feminist standpoint', *Sociology,* 23: 427–42.

Reeves, C.L. (2010) 'A difficult negotiation: fieldwork relations with gatekeepers', *Qualitative Research,* 10 (3): 315–31.

Reinharz, S. (1992) *Feminist Methods in Social Research.* Oxford: Oxford University Press.

Ribbens, J. (1998) 'Hearing my feeling voice', in J. Ribbens and R. Edwards (eds), *Dilemmas in Feminist Research: Public Knowledge and Private Lives.* London: Sage.

Rogers, C. and Ludhra, G. (2011) 'Research ethics: participation, social difference and informed consent', in S. Bradford and F. Cullen (eds), *Research and Research Methods for Youth Practitioners.* London: Routledge,

Sjoberg, G. and Nett, R. (1968) *A Methodology for Social Research.* New York: Harper and Row.

Smart, C. (1984) *The Ties That Bind: Law, Marriage and the Reproduction of Patriarchal Relations.* London: Routledge and Kegan Paul.

Stacey, J. (1988) 'Can there be a feminist ethnography?', in *Women's Studies International Forum,* 11 (1): 21–27.

Stacey, J. (1990) *Brave New Families: Stories of Domestic Upheaval in Late Twentieth Century America.* New York: Basic Books.

Tannen, D. (1991) *You Just Don't Understand: Women and Men in Conversation.* London: Virago.

Wise, S. (1987) ''A framework for discussing ethical issues in feminist research: a review of the literature', in V. Griffiths, et al. (eds), *Writing Feminist Biography 1: Using Life Histories. Studies in Sexual Politics.* Manchester: Manchester University Press.

8

Knowing responsibly: ethics, feminist epistemologies and methodologies

ANDREA DOUCET AND NATASHA S. MAUTHNER[1]

Introduction

Feminist discussions of ethics have tended to be separated into those that address research practice and those that concern knowledge construction processes as framed in philosophical or epistemological terms. On the one hand, feminist researchers who conduct qualitative research have documented the numerous ethical dilemmas that can arise during data collection and fieldwork, many of which revolve around issues of honesty and lying, power and privilege, and the overall quality of the relationships between researcher and researched (Hale, 1991; Patai, 1991; Reinharz, 1992 Wolf, 1996; Zavella, 1993; see also Duncombe and Jessop, Chapter 7, this volume). Parallel to this body of literature, there has been an enhanced focus by feminist philosophers and theorists on ethical issues surrounding the construction of knowledge (see Alcoff and Potter, 1993; Antony and Witt, 1993; Code, 1987, 1991; Duran, 1994; Lennon and Whitford, 1994; Gillies and Alldred, Chapter 3, this volume).

The scholars cited above, and many others, draw attention to the 'relations between knowledge and power' (Tanesini, 1999: 3; Flax, 1992: 451) as well as issues of advocacy (Code, 1995), subjectivity and objectivity (Code, 1993; Longino,1993), and the political and ethical dilemmas involved in reconciling or choosing between relativism and/or realism (Lazreg, 1994; Seller, 1988; Smith, 1999). While methodological and epistemological discussions about ethics have made important contributions to feminist practice, theory and epistemology, our concern here is that they have largely remained separate and parallel discourses (but see Maynard, 1994). This chapter aims to find paths towards greater integration between feminist research that reflects on issues of ethics and methodology *and* feminist scholarship on epistemology and ethics.

We began our work for this chapter by searching for feminist scholars who link ethics, methods, methodologies and epistemologies in explicit terms. We found a noteworthy example in the work of Canadian philosopher Lorraine Code (1984, 1987, 1988, 1991, 1993, 1995; see also Burt and Code, 1995; Code et al., 1983).[2] In connecting concrete discussions of innovative, alternative and experiential participatory research practice (for example, Burt and Code, 1995) with abstract philosophical discussions about knowing, knowers and knowledge production (for example, Code, 1987, 1995), Code's work has centred on, among other things, a consistent concern with 'recognizing the ethical dimensions of knowing' (Griffiths and Whitford, 1988: 19), as framed in intertwined methodological and epistemological terms. In her writing and theorizing, she constantly interchanges the terms 'knowing well', 'knowing responsibly' and 'epistemic responsibility', thus underlining the weight of social and political responsibility attached to those who are involved in 'power-based knowledge construction processes' (Code, 1995: 14). She argues that the explanatory capacities of theories, and of policies based upon them, 'depend upon their having a basis in responsible knowledge of human experience' (1988: 187–8) and that '(k)nowing well, being epistemically responsible has implications for people's individual, social and political lives' (1987: 10). For Code, thus, there are ethical issues involved in research *relationships*, as well as in being *accountable* within the varied sets of relations that comprise any given research project. Following on from Code, our chapter takes up her invitation to consider, in both methodological and epistemological terms, what it means to 'know well', to 'know responsibly' and to attain a high degree of 'epistemic responsibility'.

Our chapter develops two arguments that point to concrete ways of conducting ethical research practice, as well as to dilemmas that occur while attempting to do so. Our arguments about linking ethics, methods, methodologies and epistemologies focus specifically on data analysis processes because, for qualitative researchers, these are significant sites where everyday accounts are translated or transformed into academic, theoretical and policy-related knowledges. Moreover, data analysis processes constitute sites where methods, methodologies and epistemologies are fully entangled. The arguments developed in this chapter, thus, focus ethical dilemmas, which revolve around issues of relationships and accountability in data analysis processes.

Our first argument focuses on research *relationships*. We underline the importance of attempting to maintain 'relationships' with our research respondents/subjects during data analysis processes, particularly with subjects who may not 'fit' our theoretical, epistemological and political frameworks. While pointing to the importance of attempting to do this, we also highlight inherent tensions. In recognizing a responsibility to *research respondents*, we also know that there are other research relationships that incorporate issues of 'responsibility'. That is, processes of 'knowing well' and 'responsibly' are wrought with tension and complexity because research involves multiple sets of relationships and commitments to varied persons, communities and interests (see also Bell and Nutt, Chapter 5, this volume; Seale, 1999). As pointed out by Code, those who are involved in the processes of knowledge production have an ethical responsibility to those from whom/for whom knowledge is produced as well as to others who are involved in the production of theory, knowledge and policy. While ethical issues in research are most often, and with justification, centred on the researcher's relationship with and to research respondents, we argue in this chapter that in addition to this important focus, there are other research relationships that should be attended to in ethical discussions. These 'other', often unseen, relationships include the ones we have, or create, with many different communities: our readers; the users of our research; and the varied knowledge communities that influence our work, including 'interpretive'

(Fish, 1980), 'epistemological' (Longino, 1990; Nelson 1993) and academic communities (Haraway, 1991). From the beginning of a research project and far after its completion, a researcher and their work exist in many complex sets of relationships (see also Bell and Nutt, Chapter 5, this volume). In recognizing these multiple contexts which influence our research processes, and within which research endeavours occur, we are inevitably drawing attention to potential conflicts of interests and possible ethical dilemmas. Our chapter is thus informed by a concept of 'ethics' that relates to a wide sense of 'acting responsibly' as researchers who have an obligation and commitment not only to research participants but also to those who read, reinterpret and take seriously the claims that we make.

Our second argument is about ethical issues of *accountability*. Here we highlight that one way of building a relationship with our other sets of research relationships – those of reader, users and varied knowledge communities – is to be as transparent, as is reasonably possible about the epistemological, ontological, theoretical and personal assumptions that inform our research generally, and our analytic and interpretive processes specifically. In this vein, we are employing a very wide concept of reflexivity. We conceptualize reflexivity not only in terms of social location, but in terms of the personal, interpersonal, institutional, pragmatic, emotional, theoretical, epistemological and ontological influences on our research (see Mauthner and Doucet, 2003). Reflexivity is often configured as a methodological issue, where it is up to the researcher's discretion to decide how much and what to reveal about themselves. In speaking about the ethical significance of reflexivity, we are referring to its broader relevance to issues of honesty, transparency and overall accountability in research.

In order to illustrate methodological and epistemological ethics in the context of data analysis processes, we draw on three case studies. The second and third include brief illustrations from our own doctoral research projects, about which we have written several collaborative and individual pieces on knowledge construction processes with a particular emphasis on data analysis (Doucet, 1998; Mauthner and Doucet, 1998, 2003; Mauthner et al., 1998). Our studies, while separately conceived and carried out shared a common focus in that they were both qualitative studies on women and men's parenting and employment lives: Andrea's was a study of heterosexual couples attempting to share housework and child care (Doucet, 2000, 2001) while Natasha's focused on women's experiences of motherhood and postnatal depression (Mauthner, 1999, 2002). Both studies involved multiple interviews, innovative and participatory methods of data collection, and 'the data' were analysed in the context of a research group while using a particular adaptation of the 'voice centred relational method' of data analysis.

In addition to our own work, we also draw largely on a case study that occurs in a completely different academic discipline and in another time in history. This is a case study on the work of American geneticist Barbara McClintock (1902–1987) as discussed by Evelyn Fox Keller (1983, 1985). We selected McClintock as an exemplary case of 'knowing well' for two reasons. First, we were initially drawn to her story by an intriguing paradox that remained at the centre of her work and her life. Second, we are interested in broadening out the dominant feminist way of reading this case study and to suggest that she is an interesting and important case study of 'knowing responsibly' and thus of ethical research practice. Although McClintock's subjects of study were plant subjects and not human subjects, we nevertheless argue that the wider implications of her work have relevance for feminist ethical discussions in both methodological and epistemological terms.[3]

The central paradox that attracted us to the work and life of Barbara McClintock is well described by Keller who writes about her as a scientist who was able 'to make contributions to classical genetics and cytology that earned her a level of recognition that few women of her generation could imagine' (Keller, 1985: 158) and yet, paradoxically, McClintock's life was marked by both 'success and marginality' (Keller, 1985: 159). That is, even though McClintock was named a Nobel Laureate and was showered with numerous other awards and international praise for her research and her landmark discovery of genetic transposition,[4] her work remained for decades largely 'uncomprehended and almost entirely unintegrated into the growing corpus of biological thought' (Keller, 1985: 159). Keller maintains that one key explanation for McClintock's marginality was 'not because she is a woman but because she is a *philosophical and methodological deviant*' (1985: 159; emphasis added). That is, part of the reason for her persistent location on the periphery of mainstream science, both philosophically and methodologically, is found in the often cited description that McClintock gives of her scientific matter under study: '... these were my friends ... you look at these things, they become part of you. And you forget yourself' (McClintock, cited in Keller, 1985: 165). In a world characterized by positivist empiricist models of knowing and knowers as detached, distanced and objective, McClintock's unconventional view of maize and corn plants as her 'friends' was clearly out of sync with the precepts and approaches of her scientific colleagues.

Ironically, it is precisely this appreciation of the radical and unconventional way in which McClintock developed and maintained her *research relationships*, albeit with corn plants, that has attracted the most attention from feminist scholars, both in the realms of epistemology (Alcoff and Potter, 1993; Bar On, 1993; Belenky et al., 1986; Fox Keller, 1985; Longino, 1990; Tanesini, 1999) and methodology (Reinharz, 1992: 234). A recurrent feminist reading of the significance of McClintock's work is that she developed 'feminist ways of knowing' (Belenky et al., 1986) through developing a close relationship with the plants that she was studying. This intimacy with her research subjects that allowed her to 'hear what the material has to say to you' and to develop a profound 'feeling for the organism' (Keller, 1983: 198) is often used as a metaphor for social scientists conducting responsive interviewing practice (for example, Gilligan et al., 1990) and, for feminist philosophers interested in the role of emotions, feeling and connection in knowledge construction (for example, Griffiths and Whitford, 1988). Returning to the words of McClintock:

> I start with the seedling and I don't want to leave it, I don't feel I really know the story if I don't watch the plant all the way along. So I know every plant in the field. I know them intimately and I find it a great pleasure to know them. (McClintock cited in Keller, 1983: 198)

We want to propose a different reading of the significance of this case study of McClintock from ones most often proffered from feminist scholars. That is, we examine this as a case study of 'knowing well' and 'responsibly' in that her story illustrates the ethics of research relationships in two ways. First, she attempted to maintain relationships with subject that did not 'fit' her theoretical frameworks and analytical concepts. Second, her work demonstrates a wide concept of reflexivity, which incorporates theoretical, ontological and epistemological reflexivity. Each of these points will be examined, first through McClintock's work and then with brief reference to how these issues have played out in our own research.

Ethics and maintaining relationships with research subjects

In her book *Reflections on Gender and Science*, Keller writes on McClintock:

> Her work on transposition in fact began with the observation of an *aberrant pattern* of pigmentation on *a few kernels of a single corn plant*. And her commitment to the significance of this *singular pattern* sustained her through six years of solitary and arduous investigation – *all aimed at making the difference she saw understandable.* (1985: 163; emphasis added)

Not only did McClintock develop and maintain a close and 'loving' relationship with her research subjects, but she also focused in on the uniqueness of each research subject, even those subjects whose characteristics fundamentally challenged the theoretical, ontological and epistemological perspectives that she started out with. This is how McClintock describes the process of coming to challenge mainstream explanations:

> If the material tells you 'it may be this', allow that. Don't turn it aside and call it an exception, an aberration, a contaminant … The important thing is to develop the capacity to see one kernel (of maize) that is different and make that understandable … If something doesn't fit there's a reason, and you find out what it is. (Cited in Keller, 1985: 162–3)

McClintock saw, heard and felt something that was not immediately comprehensible, at least within the dominant theoretical, ontological and epistemological frameworks of her field. Yet she maintained a relationship with her research subjects during ongoing data analysis. The commitment to maintain, rather than cut off, relationship during this prolonged analysis set her apart from her colleagues working in the same field of research. Speaking again through Keller, McClintock writes:

> 'I feel that much of the work is done because one wants to impose an answer on it … They have the answer ready and they know (what they want) the material to tell them'. Anything else it tells them they don't really recognize as there, or they think it's a mistake and throw it out … (Cited in Keller, 1983: 179)

McClintock's apparent refusal to 'twist her data', particularly the aberrant patterns, to fit more acceptable mainstream scientific explanations constitutes an ethical issue because she faced the dilemma of deciding what to incorporate or reject, what to emphasize, and ultimately what to disclose about her analysis processes. In the end, she took the risk of alienating herself from her scientific community, and chose instead to maintain a close relationship with the perspective being offered by the research subjects who were largely scientific 'misfits'. The ethical dilemma illustrated by McClintock's story is that of honouring some relationships and cutting off others and the difficult choices over doing this within, or against, certain 'epistemological communities' (Longino, 1993; Nelson, 1993). That is, will we alienate ourselves from a particular epistemological or scientific community, as McClintock did, if we pursue certain explanations and make particular knowledge claims? And if we know this is possible, what path will we choose and to whose harm? This dilemma is especially profound in cases where established scientific communities, at times with weighty mentors, have the power to censure some stories and promote others (Haraway, 1991: 106).

From McClintock we learn about the courage and determination it takes to 'stay with the data'; and the price she paid ultimately for remaining faithful to her data. The dilemmas qualitative researchers face in analysing their data are not dissimilar. It can be remarkably difficult to 'listen to the data' amidst the political, theoretical, epistemological, ontological and institutional pressures that can bear down on us at this stage of research (Mauthner and Doucet, 2003). Moreover, the often isolated and invisible nature of the data analysis process compounds the vulnerability of both researcher and research participants. The analysis of data usually takes place 'back in the office', in isolation from our respondents, research users and colleagues. We often find ourselves alone with our data and generally speaking few other people will see this 'raw' data. In the words of Miriam Glucksmann, these subdued moments of the research relationship are rife with 'ethical considerations' and endowed with issues of 'trust':

> ... ethical considerations enter equally, if not more, into the stage of processing the data as into the interview situation. Usually the researcher has sole access to and total control over the tapes or transcripts. No one else oversees which parts she selects as of significance ... Each researcher is left on trust to draw the difficult line between interpreting the data in terms of its relevance to her research questions as opposed to twisting it in a way that amounted to a misrepresentation of what was said. (1994: 163).

Data analysis is where the power and privilege of the researcher are particularly pronounced and where the ethics of our research practice are particularly acute because of the largely invisible nature of the interpretive process (Mauthner and Doucet, 1998). Looking back at our research processes, we now realize that it was during our data analysis processes that similar ethical dilemmas surfaced in our work. It was there that we encountered moments of struggling to reconcile dominant political or theoretical conceptions with contrasting accounts and emergent concepts that we were 'hearing' in our data. We will illustrate this dilemma by drawing on an example from Andrea's work.

In Andrea's research, there was evidence of this ethical issue of maintaining relationships with subjects or respondents who did not fit into her initial theoretical framework. Influenced by many excellent works on gendered divisions of domestic labour that were emerging in Britain in the early 1990s, Andrea began her data analysis work by looking for 'success stories' as represented in the accounts of women who successfully maintained autonomous identities as workers with their parenting practices and identities. As her analysis work progressed, however, she began to 'read' and 'hear' her data in different, at times contradictory, terms. Specifically, her increased reading of literature on the 'ethic of care', combined with the birth and care of her own children, saw her gradually coming to the view that many studies on gender divisions of domestic labour were underpinned by liberal feminist conceptions of autonomous, self-sufficient, and individualistic beings (see Doucet, 1995). Subject accounts which did not fit into these liberal feminist theoretical frameworks were those that espoused more connected and relational ways of being and acting; these included accounts that prioritized domestic lives, particularly the care of children, over and above employment identities and practices. Indeed, in other research studies similar accounts offered by research respondents were sometimes inadvertently treated as being either deficient or as trapped within gendered ideologies (see Doucet, 1995, 1998).

Rather than seeing a 'problem' in and with women's accounts that articulated the value of care giving and the importance of challenging 'male stream' models of full time work, Andrea attempted to hear her respondents accounts from within alternative theoretical frameworks informed by 'the ethic of care' and 'relational' ontologies; these included notions of 'selves in relation' (Ruddick, 1995: 211), of 'relational beings' (Jordan, 1993: 141), of human relations as 'interdependent rather than independent' (Tronto, 1995: 142), and of daily practices as embedded in a complex web of intimate and larger social relations (Gilligan, 1982).[5] That is, in contrast to employing an ontology of self-sufficient human beings that emphasized where women were successful in their attempts to achieve greater autonomy from their children and their household lives, the adoption of a relational ontology enabled Andrea to also hear how women and men defined domestic work and responsibility in intrinsically relational terms, between persons as well as between social institutions (see Doucet, 1998, 2000, 2001).

In analysing interview transcripts from 46 individuals and 69 interviews, it quickly became clear early on that relationships could not be maintained with *each and every* respondent. Grouping respondents into heuristic categories where they shared some elements of daily practice or underlying ideological assumptions was a first way of dealing with the complexity of understanding respondents' diverse lives and accounts. Maintaining relationships with certain respondents allowed Andrea to find ways of articulating novel concepts that were not as clearly heard within academic discourses. Nevertheless, it is also important to point out that while this can be conceived as ethical practice in that certain relationships were valued and maintained, others were inevitably cut off and not given equal weight. In particular, when women and men espoused views on distinct and irreconcilable gendered differences between women and men, Andrea tended to down play these, as they were slightly outside of the analytical frameworks she was using.

While pointing to the importance of maintaining relationships with subject or respondents who do not initially fit ours, or our academic discipline's, dominant theoretical frameworks, it is also important to reiterate that we are not maintaining a thoroughly ethical position with *all* research subjects. Indeed it could be argued that in hearing some perspectives, we are cutting off others and thus perhaps acting unethically with some respondents. What we are highlighting here is the importance of recognizing that being uniformly ethical, in the sense of maintaining a close and connected relationship, is not possible with all respondents. This is partly because respondents are not a homogenous group, and partly due to the fact that in taking theoretical positions in our research, some accounts are heard with greater commitment and connection than others. The complexity of our multiple research relationships and commitments in research confounds our desire, however well intentioned we may be, to remain in relationship with all research respondents. This issue will become even more complicated in the next section.

Ethics and reflexivity in methodology and epistemology

In her analysis of McClintock's life and work, Keller asks an intriguing question: 'What enabled McClintock to see further and deeper into the mysteries of genetics than her colleagues'? (1983: 197). Keller argues that McClintock's insights grew, not only out of the close relationships she maintained with her research subjects, but also from her realization and admission that the theoretical, ontological and epistemological dimensions of her work had radically altered as a result of her research. Keller points to a dialectical process between methodology and epistemology/ontology/theory whereby McClintock's observations shifted her 'gestalt', which in turn modified how and what she observed. As an example, Keller refers to how McClintock gives an 'account of a breakthrough ... in analysis' pointing to how the geneticist 'describes the state of mind accompanying the shift in orientation that enabled her to identify chromosomes she had earlier not been able to distinguish' (1985: 165). In the process of utilizing innovative methods that allowed a certain 'listening' and 'responding' to the data, McClintock came to take on a changed conception of 'nature' and a different epistemological understanding of 'what counts as knowledge' (Keller, 1985: 166). These different epistemological, ontological and theoretical assumptions led, in turn, to radically different analytical questions to be asked of her subjects, and consequently to distinct readings of data, changed findings and a thoroughly altered story.

Keller's interpretation of McClintock's knowledge construction processes is an excellent case in point of the wide and strong reflexivity we are calling for. In reflecting on how it was that McClintock came to the claims and discoveries that she did, Keller reasons that it is not the fact that she was a White, middle-class, female scientist working within a world of men. Nor was it only her relational and connected way of doing research – her 'feeling for the organism' – that mattered to her work. Rather, it was the ontological, theoretical and epistemological assumptions that informed her work, her realization that they changed part way through her research, and her ability to make these transparent. Keller writes:

> I am claiming that the difference between McClintock's conception of nature and that prevailing in the community around her is an *essential key* to our understanding of her life and work. (1985: 167, emphasis added)

What is striking about McClintock's experience and account is her honest rendering of these reflexive processes. As qualitative researchers confronted with differing ways of interpreting a story, it is not just staying close to the research participants or subjects that merits recognition as an ethical issue, but the naming of the assumptions that lead us to read and tell the stories that we do (Doucet, 1998; Mauthner et al., 1998). These are not just methodological and epistemological issues, but also ethical issues in that they involve being as honest, transparent and accountable as possible with our varied audiences about the role our informing assumptions play in interpreting individual stories. This 'strong' and 'robust' reflexivity (Harding, 1992, 1998) within our research practice goes beyond situating ourselves in terms of gender, class, ethnicity, sexuality and geographical location. Indeed, as Daphne Patai points out, these locations, and their automatically associated power differentials, are often 'deployed as badges'; they are meant to represent 'one's respect to "difference" but do not affect any aspect of the research or the interpretive text' (1991:149). A robust conception of reflexivity means giving greater attention to the interplay between our multiple social locations and how these intersect with the particularities of our personal biographies *at the time* of analysing data (Doucet, 1998; Mauthner et al., 1998). This strong reflexivity also means being cognisant and open about the epistemological, ontological and theoretical assumptions that inform our work, and particularly as they shape our data analysis processes. Just as ethical reflections in fieldwork concentrate on issues of honesty/lying, power and relationships (for example, Wolf, 1996), these ethical issues of transparency and honesty in naming the influences on our knowing processes are also fundamental in providing responsible accounts of 'coming to know people' (Code, 1988).

In our own work, we have both become aware of how our theoretical and personal biographies affected our knowledge construction processes as well as the knowledges that we produced about women and men's lives. We would argue that a wide and robust concept of reflexivity should include reflecting on, and being accountable about, personal, interpersonal, institutional, pragmatic, emotional, theoretical, epistemological and ontological influences on our research, and specifically about our data analysis processes. We are now cognizant of how our respective backgrounds – personal, theoretical, ontological and epistemological – came to play a role in the analysis of our data and the findings we drew and made from our data. Moreover, as we highlight in the following section by drawing on an example from Natasha's work, it is with hindsight, as well as time and distance from our doctoral projects, that we have both been able to understand and articulate how our research was the product of these multiple influences (see also Mauthner and Doucet, 2003).

It is with the benefit of hindsight that Natasha became aware of the multiple influences – personal, institutional, theoretical and epistemological – that shaped her research and affected her knowing processes about women's experiences of postnatal depression. While she initially approached her doctoral research from a positivistic background in experimental psychology, her disenchantment with the discipline and its positivist paradigm led her to move to a social and political sciences department in the first year of her doctorate. Despite the physical move, she still felt intellectually caught between two paradigms. While her explicit theoretical and methodological position was one in which she rejected notions of the detached, neutral, 'objective' researcher, she nevertheless felt a positivist pressure to render herself, her voice, and her influence invisible in her research. This was compounded by the fact that, having not experienced motherhood herself, she viewed the women she was interviewing as 'experts' about motherhood and postnatal depression. Her tendency to prioritize the women's accounts also resulted from her desire to react against the dominant research traditions and theories in her field, in which mothers' views are devalued and disregarded (Mauthner, 1998, 2002). And here, she was influenced by feminist standpoint epistemology and the notion of 'giving voice' to marginalized groups such as women and particularly women with mental health problems. Her approach also reflected the epistemological and ontological assumptions underpinning the methodological and theoretical tradition she was using in analysing her data in which there is a tendency to romanticize women's 'voices' and 'subjectivities'.

As Natasha's research progressed, she also incorporated relational theory into her doctoral theoretical framework and into her 'hearing' aid through which she listened to the women's accounts. This was partly facilitated through her discontent with existing theoretical explanations and partly through institutional influences in that she began to work with a visiting feminist academic who introduced relational theory and associated methodological approaches to her university department. Increasingly, she began to listen to the women's stories of depression and mothering through a 'relational filter' – listening for a relational 'self', prioritizing her analysis on relational issues in women's accounts, and constructing a relational interpretation of postnatal depression. This shift in ontological, theoretical approaches meant that her understandings of postnatal depression altered radically and she began to posit alternate understandings to those that were dominant in academic and public discourses.

In speaking about these processes together, and in looking back on our knowing processes, we are now aware of the multiple influences that came to matter greatly in our work. Moreover, as in the McClintock case study, our theoretical and ontological concepts changed over the duration of our projects' evolution, partly due to personal and institutional influences in our research, and these changes profoundly affected the knowledges that we each produced. These changes were not fully known to us while we were in the thick of data analysis, and while under institutional pressure to complete our projects. It was only much later that the breadth and width of our reflexive processes was revealed to us. In this sense, we would argue that the theoretical and epistemological life of a project, and the knowledges it creates, lives on long after the project work has been formally completed. When we speak about accountability in research, it is perhaps best configured in this very long-term way as a process through which researchers engage in a conversation with those who read, re-read, critique and utilize their work and also in relation to one's evolving thinking about theoretical, methodological and epistemological issues. In being reflexive about these processes with our readers, we want to argue that this increases ethical research practice in that it allows for greater accountability on the part of the researcher while simultaneously instilling trust in the reader who know something about how knowledge was constructed.

One dilemma that is raised here is that since some of these critical assumptions affecting our knowledge production may not be readily available or known to us at the time of conducting our research, it may be that reflexivity and accountability are ultimately limited. That is, in spite of our attempts to be highly reflexive, we concur with Grosz who maintains that 'the author's intentions, emotions, psyche, and interiority are not only inaccessible to readers, they are likely to be inaccessible to the author herself' (1995: 13). We have argued elsewhere that it may be more useful to think in terms of 'degrees of reflexivity', with some influences being easier to identify and articulate at the time of our work while others may take time, distance and detachment from the research (Mauthner and Doucet, 2003). In a similar way, it may be that there are *degrees of ethical accountability* in that it may be that we can be as open and transparent as is reasonably possible at each stage of our knowing processes but that it may take time and engagement with varied academic communities – interpretive or epistemological – before we can actually clearly articulate the multiple influences on our research. One way of increasing the likelihood of this strong reflexivity and thus enhancing our ethical research practice along the lines of being accountable is to create dedicated times, spaces and contexts within which to be reflexive. In our own case, a research group set up around data analysis assisted us in beginning to think critically about the assumptions informing our work and thus in acquiring some degree of reflexivity in our research (see also Siltanen et al., 2008).

There is also a further dilemma pointed to here in the processes of being reflexive and being accountable in our research. Given that, as argued above, a wide and robust conception of reflexivity may only become meaningful and enacted during our data analysis processes, and indeed after the completion of the projects, it may not always be possible to be completely honest and transparent with our *research respondents* about the wide array of assumptions influencing our research. As mentioned above, research respondents are not a homogenous group and saying too much about what influences our research at any given moment may hinder our projects' attempts at data collection. That is, in cases where we have differing world views and political assumptions than those held by some of our research respondents, we may risk their inclusion if we speak too much about the research's informing assumptions. Of course we can and should let research respondents know some of the assumptions that inform our work. Indeed many researchers have experimented with varied ways of involving their participants throughout the project's stages, especially during data analysis and writing up (Borland, 1991; Denzin, 1998; Edwards, 1993; Ribbens, 1994). While this is laudable, we would also maintain that with large samples of diverse research respondents, this is not always possible and the ethics of doing this very much depend on the project's overall purposes and focus. Moreover, we are arguing that, as this is only one of many relationships that occurs in research, we must also be careful to recognize that we also have commitments to our other sets of research relationships, including with those persons and communities who will read, use and build on our knowledge. What we are pointing to here is that the stronger weight of being transparent and accountable in our reflexivity can sometimes be found in the relationship between researcher and reader and user of the research. The larger implication here is that rather than frame ethical issues exclusively or mainly in terms of our relationships with respondents, other important research relationships also require recognition and attention.

In this section, we have pointed to a complex and wide conception of reflexivity as being an ethical issue that relates to being as transparent as possible about theoretical, ontological and epistemological conceptions, while also recognizing that this wide conception of reflexivity also incorporates interpersonal and institutional contexts of research, all of which can have a profound effect on our research (see Mauthner and Doucet, 2003). We have also drawn attention to what we now regard as the limited extent of our reflexive processes at the time of our research. We point out how, with the benefit of hindsight, we have reached a greater understanding of the range of influences that shaped our research. We also want to suggest that the particular conceptions employed by researchers are less important than the *epistemological accountability* involved in making these conceptions as transparent as possible for the many communities who have a relationship to, and interest in, our work (Mauthner and Doucet, 2003).

Conclusion

In this chapter, we attempted to follow Lorraine Code's initiative to reflect on intertwined ethical, methodological and epistemological processes and to consider what it means to 'know well', to 'know responsibly' and to attain a high degree of 'epistemic responsibility'. Using the life and story of American geneticist Barbara McClintock as an illustrative case study, this chapter argued for the inseparability of ethics, research practice and the construction of knowledge. First, we argued that attempting to build 'responsible knowledge' involves maintaining relationships, or staying in relation, with research subjects, particularly those who may not fit our theoretical, epistemological and ontological models. We emphasized particularly the importance of these continuing relationships during data analysis processes. Second, we argued for a 'robust' concept of reflexivity that goes beyond the usual calls for researcher location.

This is a reflexivity that includes reflecting on social as well as political and institutional locations but also involves transparency and accountability about the theoretical, epistemological and ontological assumptions that inform and influence our knowledge construction.

Several implications emerge from the arguments made in our chapter. The first is that data analysis is rife with ethical issues because it exposes power and privilege in relationships, decision making around maintaining or curbing relationships with research subjects, and the potential for profound and varied relational violations. In arguing that data analysis processes are ethically infused, we also suggest that data analysis methods are not neutral techniques that are solely methodological. In this vein, we challenge the distinction which was drawn by Sandra Harding between methods, methodologies and epistemologies[6] and which has been utilized, in turn, by several feminist researchers (for example, Collins, 1991/2000; DeVault, 1996). Contrary to this view, we argue data analysis processes are key sites for drawing together ethics, methodology and epistemology and thus are key sites of responsible knowledge construction.

The second key implication arising from this chapter is that reflexivity, as an integral part of knowing processes, is also an intensely ethical issue. While feminist researchers often draw attention to the importance of reflexivity as an ethical aspect of our commitment to the women from whose experiences we construct knowledges, we also have an 'epistemic responsibility' to the women (and men) who read our work and indeed to any person who takes our knowledge claims seriously. While we cannot always know or name the multiple of influences on our research at the time of conducting it (see Grosz, 1995; Mauthner et al., 1998), we can be as reflexive as possible in the very wide sense that we have outlined in this chapter. In recognizing that knowledge construction requires a range of commitments and relationships to large groups of knowers, both participants and readers alike, we then recognize the critical importance and ethical weight that 'robust' reflexivity plays in our knowing processes. '(I)f we are to ensure that we know responsibly and well' (Code, 1995:43), greater sustained attention must be accorded to the ethical aspects of our data analysis procedures and to putting in place strong enactments of reflexivity throughout our knowing processes.

A third implication of what we are arguing is that, as argued in the Introduction to this edition, research may be best served by 'situational' or contextualized ethics. That is, each research project will have to decide on a number of ethical issues: how to enact a process of including the perspectives of research subjects who would seem to challenge our initial theoretical frameworks; which relationships to emphasize and which relationships to play down; how much and how far to be accountable and to whom. Being ethical in research practice may involve *varied degrees* of ethical responsibility and accountability. Furthermore, these processes can be greatly assisted through the creation of supportive 'knowing' communities that can aid us in our attempts to maintain our varied research relationships as well as to be accountable within these relationships.

Finally, the arguments we are positing in this chapter lead to a wide concept of ethical practice, one that focuses on relationships and accountability and recognizes the importance of attending to these issues throughout and beyond the research process. Just as the methodological literature, including feminist contributions to methodological debates, has concentrated overwhelmingly on data collection processes (see Mauthner and Doucet, 1998), it may also be the case that ethical discussions in methodology have concentrated heavily on research relationships with respondents during data collection. This partly mirrors the separate discourses on feminist ethics in methodology and feminist ethics in epistemology. It also mirrors a continuing division in research that feminist empiricists have, to their credit, astutely tried to draw together: the 'context of discovery' and 'the context of justification' (see Longino, 1990, 1993). That is, while feminists have ably described the influences on data collection processes at the 'discovery' phase of the research, little attention has been accorded to the context of *justification*. Much greater attention should be given to the epistemological questions of justifying and validating one's knowledge claims and of building and maintaining relationships with the readers and users of our research, as well as the academic, interpretive and epistemological communities within which this research is conceived, carried out and reviewed. Our view is that ethical research practice must attend to the close connection between both the context of discovery and the context of justification by attending to the continuous, fluid and complex relationships that constitute qualitative research projects throughout the varied contexts and processes of knowledge construction. In order to actualize ethical research practice, there needs to be a wider understanding of the multiple commitments that research entails and the long-term quality of 'knowing well' and 'knowing responsibly'.

Acknowledgements

We remain indebted to the mothers and fathers who participated in our respective research studies. We are grateful to Melanie Mauthner, Maxine Birch and Tina Miller for their critical commentary on this chapter as well as to the members of the Women's Workshop on Qualitative/ Household Research. We also thank Carol Gilligan, Martin Richards and R.M. Blackburn for the support and insights they have provided to us in our work. Financial support for the research that informs this chapter was provided by the Commonwealth Association, the Social Sciences and Humanities Research Council of Canada, and the Medical Research Council of the United Kingdom, respectively.

Notes

1 Like many of the other chapters in this volume, our contribution was written 10 years ago when we were still in the early stages of our thinking on reflexivity and responsible knowing. We have since widened and deepened our approach to these matters in at least three ways. First, we have continued to reflect together on intertwined issues of subjectivity,

relationality, reflexivity, and narrative in our research practice (Doucet and Mauthner, 2006, 2008; Mauthner and Doucet, 2003, forthcoming) as well as what it means to enact 'responsible knowing' in the context of team-based or collaborative research (Mauthner and Doucet, 2008). Second, Andrea has expanded her attention to the epistemological significance of relationality between researchers, readers and epistemological communities (Doucet 2008). Finally, Natasha has explored how the entanglement of ontology, epistemology and ethics highlights the ethical and moral responsibility we have for the knowledge we produce, for the realities we bring into being, and for the methods we use in doing so (see Mauthner's Chapter 10, this volume).

2 While we maintain the shape of this chapter as it was etched a decade ago, our future attention to this topic will incorporate some of Lorraine Code's recent thinking on her concepts of 'knowing responsibly' and 'epistemic responsibility', both of which are central to this chapter. We note, for example, that she has further developed her epistemological approach within a framework that she terms 'ecological thinking' (Code, 2006, 2008); this approach 'is not simply thinking *about* ecology or *about* 'the environment' but rather a 'revisioned mode of engagement with knowledge, subjectivity, politics, ethics, science, citizenship, and agency that pervades and reconfigures theory and practice' (Code, 2006: 5).

3 If we return to these issues in the future, we will seek to interweave this chapter's central case study of Keller's compelling narrative of Barbara McClintock with Code's equally compelling narrative of marine biologist and conservationist Rachel Carson. There are intriguing overlaps in how these two feminist philosophers, Keller and Code, draw on the radical thinking of two female scientists to demonstrate the interconnections between relationality, epistemology and ethical research practice. Parallel to Keller's story of McClintock, which we address briefly below, Code refers to how Carson practiced 'ecological thinking' and 'responsible knowing' though the 'explanatory power of an attentive concentration on local particulars (and) specificities' (Code, 2006: 50), a 'careful understanding to and about the precise circumstances of a particular species, community group, or society' and 'the power and value of the small' (Code, 2008: 199).

4 Put simply, genetic transposition is the view that 'genetic elements can move in an apparently co-ordinated way from one chromosomal site to another' (Keller, 1983: 199). Keller also writes about the significance of this discovery to McClintock: 'For her, the discovery of transposition was above all a key to the complexity of genetic organisation – an indicator of the subtlety with which cytoplasm, membranes and DNA are integrated into a single structure. It is the overall organisation, of orchestration, that enables the organism to meet its needs, whatever they might be, in ways that never cease to surprise us' (Keller, 1983: 199).

5 In addition, this view can be viewed as akin to sociological accounts that highlight the self in symbolic interactionist terms (Blumer, 1969; Mead, 1934; Smith, 1999).

6 In *Feminism and Methodology*, Harding distinguishes between a method as 'a technique for (or way of proceeding in) gathering evidence' and a methodology 'as theory and analysis of how research should proceed' (1987: 2–3). She also states that epistemological questions should not be confused with issues of method or methodology.

References

Alcoff, L. and Potter, E. (eds) (1993) *Feminist Epistemologies*. London: Routledge.

Antony, L.M. and Witt, C. (eds) (1993) *A Mind of One's Own: Feminist Essays on Reason and Objectivity*. Boulder, CO: Westview Press.

Bar On, B.A. (1993) 'Marginality and epistemic privilege', in L. Alcoff and E. Potter, E. (eds), *Feminist Epistemologies*. London: Routledge. pp. 83–100.

Belenky, M.F., Clinchy, B.M., Goldberger, N.R., et al. (1986) *Women's Ways of Knowing: The Development of Self, Voice, and Mind*. New York: Basic Books.

Blumer, H. (1969) *Symbolic Interactionism: Perspectives and method*. Englewood Cliffs, NJ: Prentice Hall.

Borland, K. (1991) '"That's not what I said": interpretive conflict in oral narrative research', in S. Gluck and D. Patai (eds), *Women's Words: The Feminist Practice of Oral History*. London: Routledge. pp. 63–75.

Burt S. and Code, L. (1995) *Changing Methods: Feminists Transforming Practice*. Peterborough, Ontario: Broadview Press.

Code, L. (1984) '"Toward a "Responsibilist" epistemology', *Philosophy and Phenomenological Research*, 45 (1): 29–50.

Code, L. (1987) *Epistemic Responsibility*. Hanover: Brown University Press.

Code, L. (1988) 'Experience, knowledge and responsibility', in M. Griffiths and M. Whitford (eds), *Feminist Perspectives in Philosophy*. Bloomington, IN: Indiana University Press. pp. 187–204.

Code, L. (1991) *What Can She Know? Feminist Theory and the Construction of Knowledge*. Ithaca, NY: Cornell University Press.

Code, L. (1993) 'Taking subjectivity into account', in L. Alcoff and E. Potter (eds), *Feminist Epistemologies*. New York: Routledge. pp. 15–48.

Code, L. (1995) 'How do we know? Questions of method in feminist practice', in S. Burt and L. Code (eds), *Changing Methods: Feminist Transforming Practice*. Peterborough, Ontario: Broadview Press. pp. 13–44.

Code, L. (2006) *Ecological Thinking: The Politics of Epistemic Location*. New York: Oxford University Press

Code, L. (2008) 'Thinking about ecological thinking', *Hypatia*, 23 (1): 187–203.

Code, L., Ford, M., Martindale, K., et al. (1983) *Is Feminist Ethics Possible?* Ottawa: CRIAW/ICREF.

Collins, P.H. (1991/2000) 'Black feminist epistemology', in P.H. Collins (ed.), *Black Feminist Thought: Knowledge, Consciousness and the Politics of Empowerment*. London: Routledge. pp. 251–71.

Denzin, N.K. (1998) 'The art and politics of interpretation', in N.K. Denzin and Y.S. Lincoln (eds), *Collecting and Interpreting Qualitative Materials*. London: Sage. pp. 313–44.

DeVault, M. (1996) 'Talking back to sociology: distinctive contributions of feminist methodology', *Annual Review of Sociology*, 22 (1996): 29–50.

Doucet, A. (1995) 'Gender equality and gender differences in household work and parenting', *Women's Studies International Forum*, 18: 271–84.

Doucet, A. (1998) 'Interpreting mother-work: linking methodology, ontology, theory and personal biography', *Canadian Woman Studies*, 18 (2–3): 52–58.

Doucet, A. (2000) ''There's a huge gulf between me as a male carer and women': gender, domestic responsibility, and the community as an institutional arena', *Community, Work and Family*, 3: 163–84.

Doucet, A. (2001) '"You see the need perhaps more clearly than I have": exploring gendered processes of domestic responsibility', *Journal of Family Issues*, 22 (3): 328–57.

Doucet, A. (2008) '"On the other side of (her) gossamer wall": reflexive and relational knowing', *Qualitative Sociology,* 31: 73–87.

Doucet, A. and Mauthner, N.S. (2006) 'Feminist methodologies and epistemologies', in C.D. Bryant and D.L. Peck (eds), *Handbook of 21st Century Sociology,* vol. 26–32. Thousand Oaks, CA: SAGE Publications. pp. 36-42.

Doucet, A. and Mauthner, N.S. (2008) 'What can be known and how? Narrated subjects and the listening guide', *Qualitative Research,* 8 (3): 399–409.

Duran, J. (1994) *Knowledge in Context: Naturalized Epistemology and Sociolingusitics.* London: Rowman and Littlefield.

Edwards, R. (1993) *Mature Women Students: Separating or Connecting Family and Education.* London: Taylor & Francis.

Fish, S. (1980) *Is There a Text in This Class? The Authority of Interpretive Communities.* Cambridge, MA: Harvard University Press.

Flax, J. (1992) 'The end of innocence', in J. Butler and J.W. Scott (eds), *Feminists Theorise the Political.* London: Routledge. pp. 445–63.

Gilligan, C. (1982) *In a Different Voice: Psychological Theory and Women's Development.* Cambridge, MA: Harvard University Press.

Gilligan, C., Brown, L.M. and Rogers, A. (1990) 'Psyche embedded: a place for body, relationships and culture in personality theory', in A.I. Rabin, R. Zucker, R. Emmon, et al. (eds), *Studying Persons and Lives.* New York: Springer. pp. 86–147.

Glucksmann, M. (1994) 'The work of knowledge and the knowledge of women's work', in M. Maynard and J. Purvis (eds), *Researching Women's Lives from a Feminist Perspective.* London: Taylor & Francis. pp. 149–65.

Griffiths, M. and Whitford, M. (1988) 'Introduction', in M. Griffiths and M. Whitford (eds), *Feminist Perspectives in Philosophy.* Bloomington, IN: Indiana University Press. pp. 1–28.

Grosz, E. (1995) 'Sexual signatures: feminism after the death of the author', in E. Grosz (ed.), *Space, Time and Perversion.* London: Routledge. pp. 9–24.

Hale, S. (1991) 'Feminist method, process and self criticism: interviewing sudanese women', in S.B. Gluck and D. Patai (eds), *Women's Words; the Feminist Practice of Oral History.* London: Routledge. pp. 121–36.

Haraway, D. (1991) *Simians, Cyborgs and Women.* New York: Routledge and Kegan Paul.

Harding, S. (1992) *Whose Science? Whose Knowledge?* Milton Keynes: Open University Press.

Harding, S. (1998) *Is Science Multicultural? Postcolonialism, Feminisms and Epistemologies.* Bloomington, IN: Indiana University Press.

Jordan, J. (1993) 'The Relational Self: A Model of Women's Development', in J. V. Mens-Verhulst, K. Schreurs & L. Woertman (eds.), *Daughtering and Mothering: Female Subjectivity Reanalysed.* London: Routledge and Kegan Paul. pp. 131–9.

Keller, E.F (1983) *A Feeling for the Organism: The Life and Work of Barbara McClintock.* New York: W.H. Freeman.

Keller, E.F. (1985) *Reflections of Gender and Science.* New Haven, CT: Yale University Press.

Lazreg, M. (1994) 'Women's experience and feminist epistemology: a critical neo-rational approach', in K. Lennon and M. Whitford (eds), *Knowing the Difference: Feminist Perspectives in Epistemology.* London: Routledge. pp. 45-62.

Lennon, K. and Whitford, M. (1994) *Knowing the Difference: Feminist Perspectives in Epistemology.* London: Routledge.

Longino, H. (1993) 'Subjects, power and knowledge: description and prescription in feminist philosophies of science', in L. Alcoff and E. Potter (eds), *Feminist Epistemologies.* New York: Routledge. pp. 101–20.

Longino, H. (1990) *Science as Social Knowledge: Values and Objectivity in Scientific Inquiry.* Princeton, NJ: Princeton University Press.

ETHICS IN QUALITATIVE RESEARCH

Mauthner, N.S. (1998) '"It's a Woman's Cry for Help": A Relational Perspective on Postnatal Depression', *Feminism & Psychology*, 8: 325–55.

Mauthner, N.S. (1999) '"Feeling low and feeling really bad about feeling low": women's experiences of motherhood and postpartum depression', *Canadian Psychology*, 40: 143–61.

Mauthner, N.S. (2002) *The Darkest Days of My Life: Stories of Postpartum Depression*. Cambridge, MA: Harvard University Press.

Mauthner, N.S. and Doucet, A. (1998) 'Reflections on a voice centred relational method of data analysis: analysing maternal and domestic voices', in J. Ribbens and R. Edwards (eds), *Feminist Dilemmas in Qualitative Research: Private Lives and Public Texts*. London: SAGE Publications. pp. 119–44.

Mauthner, N.S. and Doucet, A. (2003) 'Reflexive accounts and accounts of reflexivity in qualitative data analysis', *Sociology*, 37 (3): 413–31.

Mauthner, N.S. and Doucet, A. (2008) 'Knowledge once divided can be hard to put together again', *Sociology*, 42 (5): 971–85.

Mauthner, N.S. and Doucet, A. (forthcoming) *Narrative Analysis: The Listening Guide Approach*. London: SAGE Publications.

Mauthner, N.S., Parry, O. and Backett-Milburn, K. (1998) '"The data are out there, or are they?" Implications for archiving and revisiting qualitative data', *Sociology*, 32: 733–45.

Maynard, M. (1994) 'Methods, practice and epistemology', in M. Maynard and J. Purvis (eds), *Researching Women's Lives from a Feminist Perspective*. London: Taylor & Francis. pp. 10–26.

Mead, G.H. (1934) *Mind, Self, and Society: From the Standpoint of a Social Behaviorist*. Chicago, IL: University of Chicago Press.

Nelson, L.H. (1993) 'Epistemological communities', in L. Alcoff and E. Potter (eds), *Feminist Epistemologies*. London: Routledge. pp. 121–59.

Patai, D. (1991) 'U.S. academics and third world women: is ethical research possible?', in S.B. Gluck and D. Patai (eds), *Women's Words; the Feminist Practice of Oral History*. London: Routledge. pp. 137–54.

Reinharz, S. (1992) *Feminist Methods in Social Research*. Oxford: Oxford University Press.

Ribbens, J. (1994) *Mothers and their Children: A Feminist Sociology of Childrearing*. London: Sage.

Ruddick, S. (1995) *Maternal Thinking: Towards a Politics of Peace*, 2nd edn. Boston, MA: Beacon Press.

Seale, C. (1999) *The Quality of Qualitative Research*. London: Sage.

Seller, A. (1988) 'Realism versus relativism: towards a politically adequate epistemology', in M. Griffiths and M. Whitford (eds), *Feminist Perspectives in Philosophy*. Bloomington, IN: Indiana University Press. pp. 169–86.

Smith, D. (1999) *Writing the Social: Critique, Theory and Investigations*. Toronto: University of Toronto Press.

Siltanen, J, Willis, A. and Scobie, W. (2008) 'Separately together: working reflexively as a team', *International Journal of Social Research Methodology*, 11 (1): 45–61.

Tanesini, A. (1999) *An Introduction to Feminist Epistemologies*. Oxford: Blackwell Publishers.

Tronto, J. (1995) 'Care as a basis for radical political judgements' (Symposium on care and justice), *Hypatia*, 10: 141–49.

Wolf, D.L. (1996) 'Situating feminist dilemmas in fieldwork', in D.L. Wolf (ed.), *Feminist Dilemmas in Fieldwork*. Boulder, CO: Westview. pp. 1–55.

Zavella, P. (1993) 'Feminist insider dilemmas: constructing ethnic identity with "Chicana Informants"', in L. Lamphere, H. Ragone and P. Zavella (eds), *Situated Lives: Gender and Culture in Everyday Life*. London: Routledge. pp. 42–62.

9

Eliciting research accounts: re/producing modern subjects?

PAM ALLDRED AND VAL GILLIES

Introduction

The research interview is not a clear window onto the interviewee's experience, rather it is the joint production of an account by interviewer and interviewee through the dynamic interaction between them. This is now widely accepted among qualitative researchers, particularly those informed by feminist research debates, but what are the implications in terms of the responsibility the researcher bears for the perform-ance elicited or for the account produced and how it functions politically?

The interaction in the research interview tends to elicit presentations of self that largely conform to dominant cultural forms because of the implicit expectations that shape the interview process. At a general level, this is because strangers who seek to connect with each other will adopt an established mode of communication, but in more particular ways, it is also about the 'space' constructed for an interviewee to occupy, given the presumptions about research that both interviewee and researcher bring to the interview. It is some of the more particular layers of expectation about research interviews that we will explore here. Research interview practices must be seen as 'helping' or 'suggesting' that participants employ conventional modes of self-expression and so perform as (or within a narrow range of difference from) the 'stand-ard' subject. This standard subject is of course an historically particular model of individual who, within Western cultures, is understood through modernist principles as bounded, rational and autonomous. What if, therefore, research interviews do not merely look in upon, but actively serve to produce modern subjects? That is, provide a particular social experience through which we experience and in some ways are active in producing ourselves as modernist individuals. What are the ethical implica-tions of research practices that exert a pressure to conform to cultural expectations? And what are the political implications of research accounts that then serve to rein-force the centrality and superiority of this Western model of the self?

The research interview has been a key tool for feminist and other critical research-ers in the social sciences. As we argued in Chapter 3, such researchers have sought either to enable muted or marginal perspectives to be validated and more widely acknowledged in the public sphere, or have aimed to empower research participants through consciousness raising or action research. Research embodies modernist principles, at least embracing notions of progress and enlightenment that have attracted feminist theorists' and philosophers' criticisms of its epistemology. Another consequence of the modernist foundation of social research is that it, unsurprisingly, rests on a modernist model of the subject. This model is critiqued by feminist and psychoanalytic scholars for its mythical rationality, boundaried and radical independence, and by cultural and political theorists for the way it has functioned to bolster a sense of the superiority of the Western subject against the inferiority of its Others. Its hegemonic status is corroborated by the understanding of the subject in social research. Our research practice is usually located in a framework that assumes and enforces particular conditions of subjectivity, irrespective of the sensitivity with which we strive to recognize difference at later analytic stages. Therefore, as researchers, we elicit performances of self in which radical difference is suppressed by virtue of contemporary understandings of research, of ethical practice, of rapport and of the consenting, self-speaking subject.

We will explore the ethical implications of our argument that interviews elicit performances of the modernist subject on two levels. The first level concerns those who take part in the research. For some, being interviewed might be constraining or prescriptive, extending everyday pressures to be 'normal', while for others, or at other times, it might be a comforting affirmation of one's 'normality' or sociability. We will discuss some of the subtle, unintentional ways in which interviews can be normalizing for participants. The second level relates to ethical concerns associated with broader political relations. If, as feminists (or social and cultural theorists), we are critical of the cultural norms of Western subjectivity, are we justified in reinforcing this model of the self in our accounts, even when we believe the research has a progressive impact locally? But how else do we make powerful claims to know that can have any influence today? And, how can we conceive of ethical research practice without founding it on the modernist subject? This tension arises from the attempt to build feminist/critical research on the foundations of modernist understandings of knowledge and the subject, and the impossibility of escaping understandings through which we are ourselves formed.

This chapter explores some of the *implicit* ways in which ethical research practice relies on this modernist subject. Feminists, such as Erica Burman (1992) and Elspeth Probyn (1993), have urged that researcher reflexivity should concern relations not only 'in the field', but also 'in the academy and beyond' and so we discuss the presence of assumptions about the subject at different stages of the research process. We argue that ethical scrutiny of research should consider its impact at a cultural, not only an individual level, that is, in relation to the notion of the subject, not only its participants. We hope to contribute to feminist debates about research by highlighting the way in which even when presuming the modernist subject is not unethical at the immediate or individual (participant) level, by eliciting and representing this mode of subjectivity, we bolster its arrogant normativity and perpetuate its exclusions. Identifying the modernist subject as a culturally particular ideal at least interrupts its naturalization.

The modern subject(s) of research

The production of knowledge in the social sciences is a modernist project that rests on empirical realist understandings of truth and reality, which are core features of the Western epoch identified as modernity. If research is a modernist knowledge practice, it is not surprisingly based on a modernist notion of the subject. This is the Cartesian subject, whose cognitive processes operate independently of emotion and according to the rules of abstract rationality (Henriques et al., 1998/2004). Also referred to as the psychological subject, the individual celebrated in liberal humanism is the model of personhood presumed in post-Enlightenment thought. Historically there have always been those who failed to live up to this ideal for reasons attributed to their own inadequacy or pathology: it was women's 'emotionality', 'mad' people's 'irrationality', children's 'instability' and 'immaturity' and the colonial subject's supposed cognitive inferiority. Attributing failure to match the 'ideal' to the psychology or make-up of the individuals in these particular groups, meant that the normality of the model itself went unquestioned.

However, critiques from many perspectives have shown this unitary, rational subject to be untenable. Feminist scholars have long identified its presumption of masculinist ideals, and post-colonial theorists, postmodernists and post-structuralists have developed critiques of its 'independence' and cognitivism, and questioned assumptions about 'development' and rationalism (Burman 1994/2008, 2008). This Cartesian subject 'whose self-consciousness acts as guarantor of meaning', is challenged 'both by versions of psychoanalysis (Althusser, 1971; Frosh, 1987) and discourse analysis (Parker, 1992), which see the subject as being fragmented and constituted within language' (Marks, 1996: 115). Michel Foucault emphasized the modernity of the notion of the subject as the self-centred, constitutive agent of history and of its own biography (Henriques et al., 1998/2004). His work has been central in showing how discourses and practices function to constitute subjectivities in historically specific ways and how power operates through processes that produce subjectivity. This is why for many feminists and others, post-structuralist approaches offer not an abandonment of a political subject, but a better way of understanding the operation of power than seeming acquiescence to hierarchical power relations and adoption of 'false consciousness'. This affords us a more complex understanding of the relationship between culture and the psyche, but also explains why the subjectivity constituted through Western modernity is not vanished by deconstruction in academic seminar rooms. Since we are ourselves subjects of its formation, we are materially and psychologically invested in it. As feminist post-structuralists have shown, the idea that our desires would fall in line with our politics is itself rationalist (Walkerdine, 1990; Weedon, 1987).

The very idea of interviewing someone is rooted in particular understandings about what being a person is, about communication between two people and about how knowledge can be generated by the posing of questions by one and recording of responses by another. The account an individual provides in an interview is seen as a snapshot of their perspective. The expectation is that they are responsively reflexive and can 'represent' themselves to us. 'Giving primacy to interviewees' talk about their experience . . . suggests that their speech may refer to themselves as a unified, authentic subject' whereas social constructionist theory has warned that 'giving our "subject" a "voice" involves the fantasy that it is possible to have unmediated direct knowledge of experience (James and Prout, 1990)' (Marks, 1996: 115). Social research interviewing is viewed here as a practice that rests on and reiterates the dominant construction of the individual, so that even research which tries to introduce broader ethical considerations and a degree of reflexivity into its practice, tends to construct the interviewee as the rational, self-reflexive modernist subject (for example, David et al., 2001; Marks, 1996).

Those who were historically excluded from full (modern) subject status were not viewed as potential research subjects (Blackman, 1996; Hogan, 1998; Hood et al., 1999; Rose, 1985) because they are seen as unable to participate in the (polite, rational, reflexive, 'middle-class') interaction required to negotiate an interview, or were not trusted to respect the 'contract', or because communication might fall outside the bounds of expected interaction, where transgressions of that mode of being might be experienced as so disruptive as to breach the implicit contract between interviewer and interviewee. However, in the second half of the 20th century, the in-depth interview has been an important tool for progressive social researchers from the Chicago School and left-wing sociologists of the 1960s onwards, as a way of allowing marginalized perspectives greater recognition. Feminist theorists and activists and 'race' theorists and multiculturalists have shown that dominant (White, European, androcentric) ways of seeing the world are not the only ways and have used it to gain some recognition of other perspectives by the mainstream and for validating them among marginalized groups. More recently it has provided a tool for researchers to hear the views of children and young people across the disciplines as well as in Childhood and Youth Studies.

However, some feminist and post-structuralist writers have pointed out that even progressive, reflexive and ethically well thought through research can prompt interviewees to narrate themselves through the dominant discourses of subjectivity, ultimately reinforcing the implicit rules of subjectivity by which contemporary individuals are expected to govern and regulate ourselves. Deborah Marks (1996) argues this and illustrates it through her own interviews with young people who had been excluded from school. She hoped to provide a supportive ear as someone not associated with the school regime. However many of the young people narrated themselves through discourses of repentance and 'responsibility' for their 'bad behaviour'. Reluctantly, she recognized that the interviews functioned as yet another site for these pupils to produce themselves as reformed characters, as reflexive, self-regulating (and therefore now trustworthy) individuals. She employed the Foucauldian notion of governmentality to understand how her interviews functioned in a regulatory way, not only in a restrictive sense, but also in a productive sense (Foucault, 1988; Rose, 1989, 1993). They were productive or performative in that pupils performed, and thereby actively 'produced' themselves as subjects within the dominant meanings of 'bad behaviour' and legitimate sanction. The interviews were therefore normalizing in that they invited pupils to regulate themselves in line with the school's discourse of responsibility and justice.

The notion of performativity, from Butlerian queer theory, maps the same collusive and resistive possibilities for subjects, but helpfully, the term (unlike 'normalizing' and 'regulation') does not foreclose the question of whether this is against the interests of the subject (Butler, 1990). The complexity of such an evaluation is suggested by Marks' (1996) example, where accepting the school's discourse of justice might help a particular pupil avoid further sanctions at this particular time. Interviews can therefore function to 'invite' or enable people to occupy particular subject positions which can function in normalizing and regulatory ways, through their own will and through the production of certain desires, rather than in a coercive or sanction-threatening way (Foucault, 1988; Henriques et al., 1998/2004; Rose, 1993).

Not only may interviewing function to reinforce a particular model of subjectivity for those who participate in research, but because it elicits performances of the modern subject and then represents these in authoritative accounts, it reinforces this model as the cultural norm. Research participants who might be seen as marginal subjects face particular risks because any indications of straying from the ideal subject are more likely to be attributed to their own failings or developmental limitations, rather than pointing to the limitations, assumptions or fabrications of the model of research. As Burman (1994/2008) has argued 'descriptive' norms when presented authoritatively come to function prescriptively, and eventually as norms in the sense that deviation from them becomes problematized or pathologized. The fact that interviews elicit a narrow range of expressions of subjectivity becomes a problem when, as public representations, they exert a normative effect due to the value explicitly and implicitly accorded to the status of research accounts. Just as eliciting a modernist performance is not necessarily damaging to the individual, the wider political implications associated with bolstering such cultural norms while undesirable generally, might be positive for particular groups. We discuss the dilemma this raises about our use of research in the next section.

Thoroughly modern Millies?

Feminist theorists (Haraway, 1990; Hollway, 1989; Lather, 1991) have described how our knowledge practices are so predicated on modernist understandings that one can scarcely avoid using metaphors of light and vision or the 'further up the mountain' narrative of progress towards the Truth (Kitzinger, 1987; Rorty, 1980). The modernist understanding of how we come to know something constructs perceiving as a neutral, objective process and so obscures and negates the role of the researcher in constructing knowledge. We inevitably perceive through the lens of our own cultural perspective, and feminists and anthropologists in particular (see, for instance, Nencel and Pens, 1991) have agonized about how we can hear and represent the views of those from perspectives different to our own, considering the compromises others make to be understood on (and literally in) the researcher's terms (Grossberg, 1989). At the same time as the particularity of perspective is under-recognized, the researcher is, implicitly, centre-stage. Our skill and insight are seen as allowing us access to 'knowledge', but our perspective and points of reference are naturalized, bolstering the centrality of the (modernist) self who 'knows' and the marginality of those (who are often Other in some way) who are known, in their (sometimes quirky) objectified states (Probyn, 1993). Feminists and others have problematized this subject/object split, and post-colonial and psychoanalytic theorists critique the (political and intra-subjective) violence of the hierarchical relation between self and Other (for example, Venn, 1985). Several chapters in Ribbens and Edwards (1998) examined the relation research can create between researcher and researched, for instance, Standing's exploration of interviewing stigmatized mothers and Alldred's discussion of research with children or on childhoods.

The knowledge relations produced between researcher and researched is so inevitably hierarchical that some (for example, Patai, 1991: 139) believe that it is not possible 'in the actual conditions of the real world today – to write about the oppressed without becoming one of the oppressors'. While we may not wish to fully accept her conclusion that when the research relation overlays existing structural inequalities research can never be ethical, her argument highlights how even critically considered work might still bolster particular dominant understandings or power relations. James Scheurich (1997) describes how the 'Western modernist imperium is constituting our common, everyday assumptions about researchers, research, reality, epistemology, methodology, etc.' and identifies what we might call the institutionalized racisms and imperialisms of the unintended political consequences of how research functions on a cultural level:

> Even though we researchers think or assume we are doing good works or creating useful knowledge or helping people or critiquing the status quo or opposing injustice, we are unknowingly enacting or being enacted by 'deep' civilizational or cultural biases, biases that are damaging to other cultures and to other people who are unable to make us hear them because they do not 'speak' in our cultural languages. (Scheurich, 1997: 1)

The implication is that despite the political intentions of researchers, research can reinforce not only the particular and narrow range of ways of being a 'modern subject', but the broader political relations that stem from the modernist foundation of the research enterprise. However, research attempting to move beyond conventional, positivist assumptions to allow for a model of subjectivity as unfixed and performative, would itself generate another set of ethical issues. What does a radical openness to different 'ways of being' look like in practice, given that researchers too are formed as modern subjects? And if we could imagine it, enacting it would probably be compromised by understandings of good practice in research, as is embodied in professional bodies' codes of conduct and standards asserted by university research ethics committees, as well as, in all probability, by our common-sense understanding of (and commitment to) treating interviewees 'decently'.

In current good practice around 'informed consent' it is now expected that research-ers take responsibility for informing would-be participants of the aims, methods and funders of a study and the use to which the findings will be put, before they are asked to decide if they will participate. Standard good practice also involves asking if an interview can be taped and explaining the practice of anonymous write-ups, the use of pseudonyms where case studies or quotations are used, etc. This is the explicit research 'contract'. But there is also an implicit 'contract' regarding the ways in which both parties are expected to act, and next we discuss aspects of this that relate to the inter-view interaction. As Burman (1992) highlighted, the parts of this that are concerned with the relationship once back 'in the academy', including, significantly, the researcher's right to interpret participants' words, is seldom made explicit, even in participatory or collaborative research. With the increasing significance of legal dis-course, the research 'contract' is moving towards a more literal one. The legal frame-work is founded on the modern subject – to whom individual rights are accorded and from whom rational, cognitive agency is expected. The paradox is that it would be unethical in current conditions not to adopt practices that assume the modernist sub-ject, and yet we can see how the ideas underpinning these practices are not ultimately ethical themselves.

Thus, while research may be considered ethical if it results in recognition or respect for an individual's subject status, reinforcing this status in itself can raise serious ethical concerns. Ethical considerations are more tangible when research can be rec-ognized as impacting directly on people's lives, rather than indirectly through the cultural politics of representation. As researchers we are accustomed to considering the former, but far less the latter. Nevertheless, this ethical tension is often evident. For instance, research which seeks to 'hear the views of Black women' might uninten-tionally reinforce the centrality and 'normality' of White women in contrast to whom Black women's difference marks them as Other. The dilemma we face as researchers is that in making powerful claims to 'know' in order to effect desirable social change, we may inadvertently bolster such hierarchical and normative political relations.

As researchers we occupy a position that rests upon and reinforces modernist knowl-edge practices and the commodification of knowledge. We elicit particular kinds of responses from research participants because the social 'space' of the interview is not as open to diverse ways of being as we might hope, but we might judge that the political gains for a particular group of being represented outweigh performative and/ or representative compromises, either despite normalization or perhaps because of what inclusion in full modern subject status means for them. Thus, the modernist foundations of research limit radical political intentions, requiring us to hold in ten-sion realizable but often reformist aims with more radical aspirations.

Recognizing these compromises can help us to identify when there are strategic gains in modernity's own terms for those still marginalized within them, and when we want to challenge the frameworks that result in such exclusions, competition and individualism. Discussions of feminist research strategies in the social sciences (for example, Alldred, 1996; Burman, 1998; Ribbens and Edwards, 1998) echo debates about the merits of the human rights framework, for instance, where the specific potential impact may be progressive, but the framework as a whole is Western and naturalizes the Western subject. Similar points have also been made about the way the liberal humanist individual is exported along with aid packages to 'developing' countries, with globalization functioning as cultural imperialism (Burman, 1995, 2008). The risk of unintentionally reifying particular meanings or agendas might create tensions even on the pragmatic level, among those involved. For instance, doing research about sex education can promote the shared aim of raising its status within schools, but it can be diverted by a national policy emphasis which justifies it narrowly in terms of reducing teenage pregnancy into a restricted focus on heterosexual sex, contraception and tacitly supporting the unqualified problematization of teenage pregnancy (David, 2001). Similarly, as one of us found, research which aimed to question the dominant discourse of parental involvement in education, functioned to reinforce it when teachers used the research itself to 'teach' this message (David et al., 2001) and because asking parents' permission to interview young children possibly fuelled guilt or anxiety about how involved they were in their children's education. Both cases risked reinforcing a dominant policy agenda, when the intention was for research to open it up for questioning.

Prompting this chapter is the tension we each experience between a belief in the potential political gains of feminist interview-based research, and yet recognition of the limitations and unintended corollaries of our own practice. This tension derives from a rethinking of key modernist beliefs in which researchers are schooled: first, that research knowledge is Truth, and second, that 'the truth' is necessarily progressive or emancipatory. In Chapter 3, we argued that in response to critiques of truth claims, feminist research can reformulate its aims from progress-through-knowledge to overtly political interventions. But still our sense that research can promote social justice, and our belief in the possibility of such 'progress' reveals our own modernist formation. This highlights our ambivalence because while we recognize that notions of 'progress' can operate in oppressive ways and require a (self-centring) assertion of value, we would not want to abandon them – yet.

The next sections concern particular aspects of research that serve to construct and affirm the modernist subject (to which 'non-standard' adults and children are expected to aspire). Although the practice as a whole is implicated, we will illustrate how interviewee subjectivity is constructed at three discrete moments: during the interview itself; in the understanding of consent to participate in research; and through the production of an interview transcript.

Eliciting performances of the modernist subject

It requires some distance from the interview to recognize as normative those features that were 'normal' at the time and made for 'successful' research interviews. The implicit expectations are difficult to recognize and only with hindsight can we see qualities that characterize most of the interviews we have conducted. This raises issues of selection and self-selection of/by participants, but we will focus here on normative expectations. The taken-for-granted modes of cooperative communication that function to construct the research subject in a particular way can often only be glimpsed when they are disrupted. When behaviour deviates from general norms of communication, even with subtle variations from the manner, tone and etiquette expected it can disrupt research relations. It might be seen as rude or inappropriate, perhaps even to the extent of breaching the 'research contract' between interviewer and interviewee. This contract of understanding between researcher and interviewee can be seen as having explicit elements, concerning anonymity and confidentiality and publishing intentions, but also implicit terms and conditions.

We can use our experience of discomfort in interviews to reveal our expectations and assumptions and to generate an understanding of how they might differ from those of the participants'. For instance, if an interviewee refuses the narrative task by speaking in a style that is unexpected or does not maintain particular interpersonal boundaries our expectations are disrupted. Being flirted with by an interviewee has felt uncomfortable and disorientating because of its breach of etiquette and its undermining of our professional role. Similarly, our feelings of disappointment at an interview can reveal our assumptions about good rapport, which is where we see our own personal investments in being a 'good' researcher and a 'nice' person. Where interviewees go beyond the interview brief or refuse/neglect our agenda we can feel used for participants' own ends. For example, in the course of research conducted by one of us on lesbian parenting, an interview was 'hijacked' and 'used' solely for the narration of a 'coming out' story (Plummer, 1995). At the time this was experienced as frustrating because the relevance to the research agenda could not be drawn out. Only retrospectively did this highlight how obliging all the other interviewees had been, how subtle the negotiation of and compromises over the 'agenda', and what demands were being asked of all participants, in terms of personal confidence and articulation of a stabilized sexual identity, trust and the establishing of political and supportive alliances. If interviewees do not perform as a reflexive subject or narrate themselves earnestly through a confessional, self-conscious account we might feel disrespected or that they are not taking the interview 'seriously'. Such surprises or moments of awkwardness can generate important insights when it comes to recognizing difference, and not only in communication styles. It is at these points that the contours of the room for manoeuvre in the position of 'interviewee' are more easily visible.

In our own research, we have both encountered situations where in order to conform to notions broadly accepted as good practice we have unintentionally imposed particular assumptions on interviewees. For example, out of a commitment to include non-White perspectives, when interviewing a couple from Bangladesh, it became clear to one of us that the structure and the content of the interview was predicated on White, Western assumptions about the nature of personhood and agency. The notion of personal decision making and individualism that underpinned the interview questions made little sense to this couple, who were in effect being asked to narrate themselves as Westernized modernist subjects.

Similarly, one of us interviewed a working-class father, and was disorientated by the random nature of his anecdotes, as his biographical 'narrative' moved backwards and forwards in time with few connecting themes. As a researcher, the compulsion was to try and 'untangle' his account and actively impose a chronological structure on his recollections in order to produce an ordered, cohesive story because the interview agenda assumed individual biographies would be articulated through a modernist discourse of linear development or reflexivity. Life stories are generally expected to have some degree of linearity, not necessarily in the telling, but in the narrative plot, and we expect insight, progress and development. Ironic anti-developmental narratives are possible (e.g. 'I'm getting worse! I don't learn, do I! It's just the way I am'), but the absence of *any* of the narrative conventions would probably be disturbing to hear. It sounds chaotic and confusing if there is no sense of their own reflection on their lives. We might interpret the interview as unsuccessful where an interviewee was not and did not account for his or her actions. Performing what we consider to be reflexive subjectivity is an unwritten rule of the interview. We may only ask for an account of a life (or aspect of it) but what we are really expecting is a self-conscious, reflexive account which describes and comments on (does some analysis of) that account. Not only do we expect the modern subject to illustrate narratives of personal enlightenment and improvement or reflection, but these rely on a sense of history or biography which, in turn, rely on a sense of identity. The telling of a narrative also requires a belief that this account is worthy of a researcher's interest (see Birch, 1998).

Reflecting on encounters that felt disturbing, upsetting or dissatisfying helps us recognize our active efforts to produce and control the interview process to prompt the construction of selves as modern subjects. In those interviews that 'passed' as successful ones, we must have organized and contained the conversation in order to obtain accounts that have a sense of structure and order (such as a linear chronology) and have probed and coaxed and steered away from certain topics in order to navigate a path through personal accounts that was recognizable to our research agenda.

Here we can see how the role of researcher is constructed too. We are seeking to perform similar goals and to perceive with a degree of abstraction, reflection and impartiality. In the negotiation of intimacy (over disclosures of distressing personal experiences in particular) are also our own personal boundaries and positionings and our understandings of this peculiar form of passing intimacy (and see Duncombe and Jessop, Chapter 7, this volume). We can use our awareness of the ways in which interview interactions can function to constrain as they invite particular modes of being, and how values accord to different behaviour even as we try not to be judgmental of participants ourselves. Although concern with researcher reflexivity arose from a critique of scientific objectivity, it too can be seen as modernist in its remedial promise. In addition to the concern to avoid providing an experience that interviewees find normalizing or constraining, eliciting particular performances through interviews means that these modes of being are more likely to predominate and direct our research reflections and are therefore further circulated in the authoritative cultural representations that are research reports.

The consenting subject

The idea of informed consent is central to ethical research practice, but unsurprisingly it too rests on an understanding of the individual as the modernist subject (Miller, 2005: ch. 7; Miller and Boulton, 2007). So even if we strive to conduct interviews that do not elicit and affirm only a narrow range of subjectivities, the explicit and implicit negotiations that precede this, 'speak to' this subject. 'Informed consent' involves the idea that good practice in research means providing 'adequate' information about the study for the researchers' side of the 'consent' procedure to be fulfilled and it constructs research participants as rational beings whose judgment must reflect and guarantee their own interests. This relies on the idea that the information researchers provide is unproblematic (correct, appropriate, accessible, adequate), that the subject has cognitive information processing skills and can make a rational decision in their own interests. As a consequence, responsibility then lies with the individual – a rational, autonomous subject who is in control of their own destiny. There is, therefore, little room to consider how the social context and emotional factors affect such 'processing' and 'decision making'.

Personal reflections on the research we have conducted with children and young people highlighted two limitations within an entirely rationalist approach to informed consent for participation in research. The first is concerned with what the would-be participant understood social research to be, since their general expectations of research would inform their decision, in addition to their more specific understandings of the interests, intentions and boundaries of the particular research/ers (Edwards and Alldred, 1999). The fact that future outcomes may not be fully knowable has been raised in relation to medical consent, but this also limits the ideal in social research where we cannot be sure of the personal or cultural impact our research conversations might have. The second limitation relates to the abstract ideal of the neutral setting that does not affect decision making. How 'freely' can we assume children's consent is in an institutional setting such as a school, in which meanings, both moral and educational evaluations ('helping' with research, being mature and articulate) are constantly made across a doubly determined (adult–child, teacher–pupil) power relation? Accessing children through their home environment is dependent on a similar power relation between parent/guardian and child, as one of us discovered when she attempted to arrange an interview with four children via their mother. Although the mother stated in advance that her children were happy to take part, it emerged during the course of the interview that they had been informed that they would be taking part just five minutes earlier.

The argument that children's consent to medical treatment or social research participation should be affirmed or renegotiated throughout the research process rather than consent having been given as a once and one for all at the start (Alderson, 1995; Alderson and Morrow, 2004; Morrow, 1999; Morrow and Richards, 1996) goes some way to reducing the pressure to make the right decision at the outset, and allows for changes of mind. Trying to open up space in this way (for processing, deciding, thinking and feeling differently) is the most we can do here, since 'informed consent' is still the best practice guideline, but unless we recognize these presumptions we can neither be more ethical to the particular subjects in question or recognize that our culturally particular ways of viewing the individual are presented as if they are inevitable.

In addition to reflecting upon the ways in which our research practices elicit particular performances from participants, and from ourselves, we must consider the way in which our representational practices may serve to depict subjectivity in particular ways. The interpretation of interviews may involve legitimate, unavoidable and unacknowledged processes of projection onto participants, and when we present research accounts we may question our claims about representation in both the literal and political senses of the word. However, next we will highlight one of the taken-for-granted representational processes in research where standard practice may serve to paint participants with greater uniformity, and in this way, reduce the range of subjective forms that research represents.

Producing transcripts

Collecting and processing data are active processes well before what we call 'analysis'. Researchers are 'processing the data' consciously and unconsciously as we make decisions about the form and conventions to use to represent the 'data'. The phrase 'data analysis' implies wrongly that there is a prior stage of data collection that occurs without the interpretive involvement of the researcher. It therefore constructs the object of study as fixed, observable, existing prior to, and independently of the researcher's gaze. Many theorists question positivist assumptions, such as that data analysis is merely the literal re-presentation of data, but few researchers draw on philosophical debates about ethics and representation. James Scheurich describes it as 'a creative interaction between the conscious/ unconscious researcher and the decontextualised data which is assumed to represent reality, or at least, reality as interpreted by the interviewee' (1997: 63). Unfortunately though, this creativity is 'severely bounded by the restrictions of modernist assumptions about selves, language and communication' (Scheurich, 1997: 63).

Analysis is often assumed to start once the tape of an interview has been typed up and a transcript printed out. The process of transcription – making a written account of the verbal interaction – is one of the least problematized parts of the research process, not generally recognized as an act of representation or embodying interpretation.[1] But transcription tends to affirm a particular theoretical position about the relation between language and meaning and when researchers focus on the mechanics of coding, they can fail to attend the complex ambiguities of language, communication and interpretation (Mishler, 1991).

As transcription has become both more routine and precise … emphasis on it as a technical procedure has tended to detach the process from its deeper moorings in this critical reflection on the intractable uncertainties of meaning-language relationships. (Mishler, 1991: 260)

Technical procedures, adopted to ape the systematic rigor of scientific method, mask these uncertainties and 'the unstable ambiguities of linguistically communicated meaning' (Scheurich, 1997: 63). They therefore obscure the active role of the researcher in making meaning of interviewees' utterances.

Transcription is not the straight-forward, passive process it is assumed to be because representing inter-subjective interaction on a two-dimensional page entails some compromises. Even rendering the speech alone on the page entails some distinct simplifications and there are strong conventions for it. Grammar and punctuation are required to make verbalizations conform to the rules of written English. But as we punctuate, we produce sentences from what are often streams of phrases and clauses and we therefore attribute and fix meaning. Transcribing interviews have demonstrated to us just how ambiguous unpunctuated words can be. For instance, it is surprisingly common for a speaker to begin a negative statement with a 'yes' ('Yeh, no, it's not like that'). The 'yes' is a social emollient, perhaps agreeing with or affirming the previous speaker. Putting a full-stop, rather than a comma, between the 'yes' and 'no' gives the 'yes' more emphasis which makes it seem more of an expression of opinion. Writing it as 'yeh' suggests a more casual tone, closer to an 'aha' than a decisive 'yes'. The simplification or loss of tone, pace and volume can mean that emotions are 'sanitized' from the account (Burman, 1992: 47, and see Hollway, 1989). Losing the subtleties of humour can misrepresent emotional tone and meaning. The significance of tone and the difficulty of representing it was highlighted for one of us when interviewing children who spoke sarcastically about wanting their parents to come into school (Edwards and Alldred, 1999). Their words alone contradicted what we understood to be their views and their sarcasm indicated a strength of feeling that '[laugh]' or an exclamation mark seemed to understate. In both these examples, erring on the side of 'meaning', so that we prioritize representing what we believe to be their views over pedantic literality about utterances, shows clearly how we inevitably draw on our own understanding of what the speaker intended, revealing the potential for projection in processes of 'perception'.

It is easy not to type every repetition, or to omit oddly used phrases that sit uneasily in a written sentence and it is hard to resist making sentences neater and arguments clearer when it merely involves transposing the word order slightly. Omitting the question tags that could be reassurance or agreement-seeking, makes an interviewee look more self-assured, the account more confident or rehearsed and the conversation more uni-directional – the delivery of their views – as opposed to being more of a dialogue. Resisting smoothing out hesitancy can leave them looking insecure, and punctuation that implies timing can distinguish clear qualifiers from hesitancy. In addition, it is more comfortable reading an account of an interview which spares us from seeing how messy our own speech is, our requests for affirmation or repetition of 'you know' and 'right'. We are put under pressure if we feel our affirming sounds or agreements will be read as reducing the 'impartiality' of our interview or the impact of the account. Furthermore, it is easy to 'amend' word order and 'correct' grammar without being conscious of doing them. The drive to 'sort out' the above is one illustration of how we iron out contradictions, automatically as well as deliberately, either to make the account 'readable', or to capture what we believe they meant, unintentionally, perhaps by convention or deliberately, in order to avoid making speakers look inarticulate. It can be a conscious dilemma when literal quotations might seem unfair because the messiness of the spoken word may be attributed to the particular participant.

Decisions about what and how to transcribe are often made arbitrarily or unconsciously, so when the task of transcription is passed to someone else, detailed communication about what constitutes a 'non-significant' utterance is required. Different projects and styles of analyses will attribute different significance to word repetitions, half-word utterances and 'innit's, and draw the line differently around the ethics of transcribing interruptions from third parties, 'post-interview' talk or discussion of the research contract itself.

Transcripts are artefacts and we should acknowledge that we researchers produce, rather than retrieve them shell-like from the seabed. We are active in producing the particular account and that transcript therefore bears traces not only of ourselves as interviewer, as the culturally situated and particular individuals we are, but also as interpreters. Transcripts do not contain pearls of wisdom allowing insight into the essential truths of other beings. Transcribed interviews function as if their wholeness was more than an arbitrary framing, suggesting a certainty which represents the interview authoritatively. Even if we try to qualify, the production of a transcript embodies a claim of literal representation, and of unmediated access to an authentic, unified subject. These illustrations show how decisions about meaning are being made in the supposed neutral process of transcription, where the demands of communication mean that we err on the side of normalizing in order to render an account more fitting of a modernist subject. Our instinct to produce representations of participants that veer towards the norm as subjects whose communication is at least manageably linear and logical is also our own investment in ourselves as modern subjects. It is easy to imagine how an interview that did not feel successful or a transcript that felt very difficult to work with might not be included in a study and this is the kind of unintentional way in which research ends up representing a narrower range of people, experiences and ways of being.

The politics of research

It is because the representations of subjectivities we produce are given the status of research knowledge that their circulation in the public sphere confirms and bolsters the notion of the unitary rational subject. The authority of research means that such accounts function in normative ways, where what is written as descriptive ends up functioning prescriptively (Burman, 1994/2008). We can, however, use our recognition of the extent of our interpretive involvement in 'representative' processes to interrupt its implied objective status. We can also admit our own investments in this model of the subject – again at both levels – directly as we are boosted by the interaction, and indirectly as the cultural privileging of the hegemonic Western form to which we subscribe and for the most part probably succeed in performing. However, bolstering this cultural notion has implications both for Western individuals who struggle to live up to the ideal, as well as for the global relations it reaffirms. This is why we argue that researcher ethics should be concerned not only with the individuals who are directly touched by the research, but also with the cultural political and power relations research promotes or sustains.

In producing ourselves as modernist subjects and eliciting similar performances from interview participants through research practices, we reify this model at a cultural level, thereby sustaining its normative pull. The roots of research lie in the modernist project making the reproduction of the modernist subject in research accounts almost inevitable. Therefore we are not suggesting that this dilemma can be resolved, only that we can and should be more reflexive about the way our practice colludes with the elevated status of the modern subject. Awareness of the way in which we, as researchers, actively reproduce dominant cultural accounts of individual subjectivity works to de-naturalize taken-for-granted assumptions about personhood, opening up greater space to challenge normative, restrictive constructions. While we cannot transcend or deny our (or others') investments in the modernist subject, we would want to promote research that, through its own ethical practices or representational function, eschews uncritical acceptance of the culturally dominant mode of subjectivity in favour of a recognition of more diverse ways of being.

Note

1 Although since this chapter was first published, transcription has received slightly more attention in some research methods textbooks, many still omit this as a stage to be theorized or reflected upon.

References

Alderson, P. (1995) *Listening to Children.* London: Barnardos.

Alderson, P. and Morrow, V. (2004) 'Ethics, social research and consulting with children and young people children', *Youth and Environments,* 17 (1): 148–74.

Alldred, P. (1996) '"Fit to parent?" developmental psychology and "non traditional" families', in E. Burman, P. Alldred, C. Bewley, et al. (eds), *Challenging Women: Psychology's Exclusions, Feminist Possibilities.* Buckingham: Open University Press. pp. 141–59.

Alldred, P. (1998) 'Discourse analysis, ethnography and representation: dilemmas in research work with children', in J. Ribbens and R. Edwards (eds), *Feminist Dilemmas in Qualitative Research: Public Knowledge and Private Lives.* London: Sage: Sage.

Althusser, L. (1971) 'Freud and Lacan', in, *Lenin and Philosophy and Other Essays.* London: New Left Books.

Birch, M. (1998) 'Reconstructing research narratives: self and sociological identity in alternative settings', in J. Ribbens and R. Edwards (eds), *Feminist Dilemmas in Qualitative Research: Public Knowledge and Private Lives.* London: Sage.

Blackman, L. (1996) 'The dangerous classes: retelling the psychiatric story', *Feminism and Psychology,* 6 (3): 361–79.

Burman, E. (1992)'Feminism and discourse in developmental psychology: power, subjectivity and interpretation', *Feminism and Psychology,* 2 (1): 45–60.

Burman, E. (1994/2008) *Deconstructing Developmental Psychology.* London: Routledge.

Burman, E. (1995) 'Developing differences: gender, childhood and economic development', *Children and Society,* 9 (3): 121–42.

Burman, E. (ed.) (1998) *Deconstructing Feminist Psychology.* London: Sage.

Burman, E. (2008) *Development: Child, Image, Nation.* London: Taylor & Francis.

Burman, E. and Parker, I. (1993) *Discourse Analytic Research, Repertoires and Readings of Texts in Action.* London: Routledge.

Butler, J. (1990) *Gender Trouble: Feminism and the Subversion of Identity.* London: Routledge.

JDavid, M. (2001) '"Teenage parenthood is bad for parents and children": a feminist critique of the restructuring of the governance of family, education and social welfare policies and practices', in M. Bloch and T. Popkewitz (eds), *Restructuring the Governing Patterns of the Welfare State.* New York: Routledge.

David, M., Edwards, R. and Alldred, R (2001) 'Children and school-based research: "informed consent" or "educated consent"?', *British Educational Research Journal,* 27 (3): 347–65.

Edwards, R. and Alldred, P. (1999) 'Children and young people's views of social research: the case of research on home-school relations', *Childhood: A Global Journal of Child Research,* 6 (2): 261–81.

Foucault, M. (1988) 'Technologies of the self', in L.H. Martin, H. Gutman and P.H. Hutton (eds), *Technologies of the Self: A Seminar with Michel Foucault.* London: Tavistock.

Frosh, S. (1987) *The Politics of Psychoanalysis.* London: Macmillan.

Grossberg, L. (1989) 'On the road with three ethnographers', *Journal of Communication Inquiry,* 13 (2): 23–36.

Haraway, D. (1990) 'A manifesto for cyborgs: science, technology and socialist feminism in the 1980s', in L. Nicholson (ed.), *Feminism /Postmodernism.* London: Routledge.

Henriques, J., Hollway, W., Urwin, C., et al. (1998/2004) *Changing the Subject: Psychology, Social Regulation and Subjectivity.* London: Routledge.

Hogan, D. (1998) 'Valuing the child in research: historical and current influences on research methodology with children', in D. Hogan and R. Gilligan (eds), *Researching Children's Experiences: Qualitative Approaches.* Dublin: The Children's Research Centre, Trinity College. pp. 1–9

Hollway, W. (1989) *Subjectivity and Method in Psychology.* London: Sage.

Hood, S., Mayall, B. and Oliver, S. (1999) *Critical Issues in Social Research: Power and Prejudice.* Buckingham: Open University Press.

James, A. and Prout, A. (eds) (1990) *Constructing and Reconstructing Childhood, Contemporary Issues in the Sociological Study of Childhood.* London: Falmer Press.

Kitzinger, C. (1987) *The Social Construction of Lesbianism.* London: Sage.

Lather, P. (1991) *Getting Smart: Feminist Research and Pedagogy With/in the Postmodern.* London: Routledge.

Marks, D. (1996) 'Constructing a narrative: moral discourse and young people's experience of exclusion', in E. Burman, G. Aitken, P. Alldred, et al. (eds), *Psychology, Discourse, Practice: From Regulation to Resistance.* London: Taylor & Francis. pp. 114–30

Miller T, and Boulton, M. (2007) 'Changing constructions of informed consent: qualitative research and complex social worlds', *Social Science and Medicine,* 65 (11): 2199–211.

Miller, T. (2005) *Making Sense of Motherhood: A Narrative Approach.* Cambridge: Cambridge University Press.

Mishler, E.G. (1991) 'Representing discourse: the rhetoric of transcription', *Journal of Narrative and Life History,* 1 (4): 255–80.

Morrow, V. (1999) 'If you were a teacher it would be harder to talk to you: reflections on qualitative research with children in school', *International Journal of Social Research Methodology,* 1: 297–314.

Morrow, V. and Richards, M. (1996) 'The ethics of social research with children: an overview', *Children and Society,* 10: 90–105.

Nencel, L. and Pens, P. (eds) (1991) *Constructing Knowledge: Authority and Critique in the Social Sciences.* London: Sage.

Parker, I. (1992) *Discourse Dynamics.* London: Routledge.

Patai, D. (1991) 'US academics and third world women: is ethical research possible?', in S. Berger Gluck and D. Patai (eds), *Women's Words: The Feminist Practice of Oral History.* London: Routledge. pp. 137–153.

Plummer, K. (1995) *Telling Sexual Stories: Power, Change and Social Worlds.* London: Routledge.

Probyn, E. (1993) *Sexing the Self: Gendered Positions in Cultural Studies.* London: Routledge.

Ribbens, J. and Edwards, R. (eds) (1998) *Feminist Dilemmas in Qualitative Research: Public Knowledge and Private Lives.* London: Sage.

Rorty, R. (1980) *Philosophy and the Mirror of Nature.* Oxford: Blackwell.

Rose, N. (1985) *The Psychological Complex.* London: Routledge and Kegan Paul.

Rose, N. (1989) *Governing The Soul: The Shaping of the Private Self.* London: Routledge.

Rose, N. (1993) *Inventing Ourselves.* London: Routledge.

Scheurich, J. (1997) *Research Method in the Postmodern.* London: Falmer Press.

Venn, C. (1985) 'A subject for concern: sexuality and subjectivity in Foucault's history of sexuality', *Psych Critique,* 1 (2): 139–54.

Walkerdine, V. (1990) *Schoolgirl Fictions.* London: Verso.

Weedon, C. (1987) *Feminist Practice and Poststructuralist Theory.* Oxford: Blackwell.

10

'Accounting for our part of the entangled webs we weave'[1]: ethical and moral issues in digital data sharing

NATASHA S. MAUTHNER

Introduction

One of the most significant developments since we published the first edition of this book has been the steady growth of the digital data sharing movement, and the promotion of digital data sharing methods: the preservation, sharing and (re)use of research data through digital repositories. In the case of publicly funded research, most funding agencies now have data sharing policies expecting or requiring researchers to deposit their research data within digital depositories. Data management plans are also being increasingly required in university ethics and research governance frameworks. Moreover, the introduction of freedom of information legislation means that researchers may be legally forced to release their data. These developments have entailed important shifts in the research environment and in research practices: increasing prescription and regulation of research methods and practices; new moral discourses defining digital data sharing as 'good research' and 'good research practice'; the institutionalization of digital data sharing as a normative research practice; and the requirement that researchers seek research participants' informed consent to share their data.

The case for data sharing rests on three central pillars: a scientific, a moral, and an economic one. Data sharing is seen as 'good science'. It increases transparency by opening up our data and research processes for public scrutiny. It allows researchers to verify each others' interpretations by returning to the 'raw' data. It enables researchers to investigate data in new ways: by using new techniques or theoretical perspectives; by exploring data that were never analysed by the primary researchers; or by combining different datasets. Data sharing is also defined as 'good research practice'. As public sector workers undertaking publicly funded research we are seen to be accountable to the public. Making our research data more widely available is understood to be in the public's interest, and part our moral responsibility and duty. The UK Data Archive (UKDA) (2011), for example, suggests that researchers have a moral 'duty to wider society to make available resources produced by researchers with public funds (data sharing required by research funders)'. Finally, reusing data is seen as cost-effective and cost-efficient because it provides a better return on public investment in research. There is a further, often implicitly rather than explicitly articulated, political rationale for digital data sharing. This is the notion that digital technologies have the potential to democratize knowledge and empower researchers and research communities; and openness, including data sharing, are seen as necessary to unleash this transformative potential (see discussion in Mauthner and Parry, 2009, in press).

How are we to respond to these new expectations, requirements and discourses? I first began to ask myself this question 15 years ago. It arose directly out of my research experiences: having agreed, in an ESRC application, to comply with data sharing requirements I found that putting these into practice was changing the way in which I was doing research, raising new and unanticipated philosophical, ethical and moral tensions. I discovered that digital data sharing methods, practices and requirements were doing things beyond what they intended. Seeking informed consent to data sharing, for example, was doing more than just this. It was also changing the moral basis of my relationship with respondents. Furthermore, informed consent took on new meanings when used in a data sharing and digital context. Indeed, I found that 'old' methods (including informed consent, data anonymization, and reuse of data) were reconfigured through their use in new contexts, and in the process were raising new risks for respondents, researchers and qualitative research more generally. This led me to question the ethics of complying with data sharing requirements, and recommended ethical and legal guidelines, without better understanding these new methods. What else were digital data sharing methods doing, other than providing the means with which to preserve and reuse data? What new ontological, moral and political realities did their use bring into being? And what did this imply for my moral responsibilities as a researcher using these methods? These are the questions I have been grappling with since the late 1990s (Mauthner et al., 1998; Mauthner and Parry 2009, in press; Parry and Mauthner, 2004, 2005).

My purpose in this chapter is to make the argument that our ethical and moral responsibilities as researchers lie beyond the implementation of prescribed methods, and associated ethical and legal guidelines. Rather, as researchers we have responsibility for the very methods we use: for what they do when *put into practice* and for the risks they materialize in the *doing* of research. To support my claim, I demonstrate how digital data sharing methods are reshaping the research environment and research practices. I show how seeking informed consent, anonymizing data, and reusing digital data reconfigure the relationships we develop with our respondents, our moral responsibilities and commitments to respondents, our moral ownership rights over the data we produce, and the very nature of qualitative research. In developing these points, I draw on an interview I conducted in 1998 with George, a survivor of the Piper Alpha oil disaster, because it provided one of the first occasions in which I noticed these issues. I want to begin, however, with a discussion of the emergence of the digital data sharing imperative.

The emergence of the digital data sharing imperative

In the space of ten years, digital data sharing has gone from being a voluntary research practice to an almost universally expected (and in some cases required) one that has come to be defined as simply and unquestionably 'good research practice'. It is being incorporated into ethics and research governance frameworks and guidelines issued by universities (for example, Universities of Edinburgh and Oxford), funding agencies (see DDC, 2010; SHERPA, 2009), professional associations (for example, Statement of Ethical Practice for the British Sociological Association), data repositories (for example, UKDA), non departmental public bodies (for example, Joint Infrastructures Systems Committee), national and international science policy organizations (for example, OECD), and many other agencies within and beyond the UK. A decade ago, it was mostly up to researchers to decide whether and how to preserve and share their research data. Today, most funding agencies have data sharing policies requiring them to provide a data management plan if not lodge their data within a digital archive (Ruusalepp, 2008: 3). The ESRC's *Research Data Policy*, for example, requires grant holders to make their data available for reuse and can 'withhold the final payment of an award if data have not been offered for archiving to the required standard within three months of the end of the award' (2010b: 4). Universities are also beginning to develop data management plans and strategies requiring their researchers to address, at the outset of their projects, the question of data sharing.

Furthermore, the new Freedom of Information Act 2000 and Environmental Information Regulations Act 2004, both of which came into force in 2005, mean that researchers can be legally forced to release their data. Both acts provide the public with a right to access information held by a UK public authority, which includes most universities, colleges or publicly funded research institutions. The information requested can include research data and must be provided unless an exemption or exception allows an institution not to disclose it. Both acts are designed to ensure accountability and good governance in public authorities (Rusbridge and Charlesworth, 2010). To date there have been few legal requests for researchers to share their data. However, two cases are worth highlighting here. In April 2010, Mike Baillie, a dendrochronologist from Queen's University Belfast, was forced to release tree-ring data under the Freedom of Information Act. The Information Commissioner's Office ruled that Queen's University Belfast must release the data to the public because Baillie did all the work while employed at a public university. Baillie unsuccessfully contested this directive by claiming that the tree-ring data he had collected over a 40-year period were his own personal intellectual property (Baillie, 2010). In September 2011, the tobacco company Philip Morris International submitted a series of freedom of information requests to the University of Stirling to gain access to research data collected by a team of researchers over 10 years exploring attitudes towards smoking among 6000 teenagers and young adults. Scotland's Information Commissioner has dismissed the University's case for failing to release the information and has asked the university to respond to the demands made by Philip Morris (Christie, 2011).

Underlying these policy, regulatory and legal shifts is the principle of 'open access', and the notion that information, scientific results and research data are 'public goods' that society and individuals have an obligation to make available and that others should be able to access as a basic right (Willinsky, 2006). This principle lies at the heart of the OECD's (2007) *Principles and Guidelines for Access to Research Data from Public Funding*, a key policy document drawn on by funding and other agencies when developing data sharing policies (for example, ESRC, 2010b; MRC, 2011). The open access principle specifies that 'publicly funded research data should be openly available to the maximum extent possible' (Arzberger et al., 2004: 136). Over the past decade, open access to research data has been acknowledged as relevant to all forms of data, all disciplines and all researchers across the natural sciences, social sciences, and arts and humanities. As Arzberger et al. argue, the principle of openness to research data should apply 'to *all* science communities' (2004: 144; original emphasis) and they urge that this imperative is backed with 'formal policy frameworks and regulations' (2004: 146).

Emerging data sharing discourses, policies, legislation, and ethics and research governance frameworks are reshaping and transforming the research landscape. The question of whether and how to share data is increasingly being seen as a matter for public and regulatory bodies to decide, rather than as an issue for researchers to deliberate, using their professional judgment, expertise and knowledge of the particular case at hand. A new moral norm has been set whereby researchers are expected, are under moral pressure, and can be mandated to release information that is now regarded as public property where once it was viewed as more private in nature. For example, until recently, it was seen as good research practice within the social sciences to destroy data (particularly personal data) collected for research purposes once the data had been analysed and written up. This was reflected in data protection policies adopted by funding agencies and universities. Indeed, there are still tensions and contradictions between data sharing imperatives and data protection guidelines (and legislation) instituted by universities (Carusi and Jarotka, 2009). Furthermore, while universities – as employers of researchers – have long had legal ownership of research data, in practice researchers were recognized to have moral ownership and universities rarely exercised their ownership rights. With the introduction of freedom of information legislation, however, universities are coming under pressure to exercise these rights by demanding that researchers release their data where a freedom of information request has been made and upheld.

These changes mean that public and other bodies are increasingly regulating, taking responsibility for, and eroding researcher's control over research methods and practices. Qualitative researchers have long worked on the implicit assumption that their ethical priority is the protection of their respondents, and that ethical decision making is primarily their responsibility. Increasing regulation of research activities, however, means these working assumptions can no longer be taken for granted. Researchers are being asked (and possibly forced) to privilege their moral responsibilities to the public over their responsibilities and commitments to research respondents (who are, after all, specific members of the public). As I now go on to illustrate, this has far-reaching implications for how we do research, the nature of the research that we do, what we tell our respondents, the kinds of relationships we build with them, and the moral commitments and assurances we are able to make.

Becoming entangled with digital data sharing: surviving piper alpha and other oil stories

In 1998, I interviewed a man who had survived the explosion that took place on 6 July 1988 on the North Sea oil production platform, Piper Alpha, killing 167 men. George was one of the 62 survivors, and I came to talk to him as part of a three-year ethnographic study of work and family life in the oil and gas industry. It was a morning in late May when I interviewed him in his Aberdeen home. We sat in his basement kitchen, drinking tea, as he recollected the series of events that came together on that fateful night. The official story, George explained, was that human error had caused the disaster: there had been a problem with securing a safety valve on the platform. George's account, however, focuses on wider economic, political, cultural and social aspects of the industry. He talks about capitalism, commercial pressure, greed, demand for oil and an ingrained culture of fear within the industry with regards to shutting down a platform because of potential loss of revenue. He speaks about the high levels of unemployment at the time, job insecurity, the prevalence of contract work and what he describes as 'industrial apartheid' within the industry: a sense in which the lives of contract workers such as himself were expendable. He describes how codified health and safety measures based on helicopter evacuation plans were disconnected from the reality of being offshore. He gives a graphic account of how men he knew who had put their faith within these measures perished as they waited for the helicopter to arrive, despite the platform being engulfed in flames. He put his own survival, and that of others, to their abandonment of the health and safety guidelines and jumping into the sea.

It was in the context of writing the grant application for this ethnographic study, 15 years ago, that I first became aware of the issue of digital data sharing. In our application (co-written with Lorna McKee) to the ESRC, we had to complete a section of the form on 'Data collection and provision for the preparation and archiving of datasets'. This was a relatively new addition to the forms, and followed on from the recently introduced ESRC Datasets Policy in 1995. We were asked to outline any difficulties we envisaged in making the data available for secondary research, and this is what we wrote: 'We have some concerns over the confidential nature of data we anticipate collecting from both the families and the oil companies, particularly given that the proposed project would be a very focused study on a very discrete geographical area. However, provided the material was anonymised and all identifying features removed, and the research participants give their informed consent, we would be happy to offer our dataset to the Data Archive or any other data centre and make it available for secondary research.'

This paragraph reflects what were, and remain, the standard ethical and legal guidelines for data sharing, such as those recommended by the UKDA (2011): 'A combination of gaining consent for data sharing, anonymising data to protect people's identities and controlling access to data will enable sharing people-related research data – even sensitive ones – ethically and legally.' In cases where anonymization would result in too much loss of data content, they advise regulating access to the data. This can be done in a number of ways: secondary users may need specific authorization from the data owner to access data; confidential data can be embargoed for a given period of time; access can be restricted to approved researchers only; and restrictions can be placed on data downloading. There is a reminder to researchers, however, that 'Restricting access to data should never be seen as the only way to protect confidentiality. Obtaining appropriate informed consent and anonymising data enable most data to be shared' (UKDA, 2011). The UKDA houses the UK's largest collection of digital research data in the social sciences and humanities. It provides best practice guidelines (see Van den Eynden et al., 2011), and funding agencies such as the ESRC (2010a) refer researchers to the UKDA for advice and protocols on dealing with ethical issues in digital data sharing.

The UKDA suggests that following the recommended procedures will ensure that researchers share their data ethically and legally. Attempts to put these procedures into practice in my own research, however, raised ethical, moral, ontological and epistemological questions. I discovered that engaging in digital data sharing was not simply a matter of adding further procedures to my existing methodological and ethical tool box. This was because, although in one sense, these methods were not new – qualitative researchers are used to the idea of seeking informed consent, anonymizing their data, and analysing data generated by other researchers – when used in data sharing and digital contexts these methods were *doing new things*. They threatened to reconfigure the very nature of George's story, weaken the relationship of trust I wanted to build with him, and compromise my ability to honour my moral responsibilities and commitment towards him. Using 'old' methods in new contexts was raising new questions that I had not anticipated, and changing what I understood to be qualitative research. I was reluctant to lodge George's narrative, and others like it, in a digital archive not because I was opposed to the principle of data sharing but because I needed more time to understand and think about these methods before using them. What *else* were digital data sharing methods doing? What *else* was *I* doing by agreeing to share my data?

Seeking informed consent to data sharing

As already indicated, seeking informed consent to data sharing was and continues to be seen as fundamental to ethical practice. Moreover, within a context where data sharing is coming to be seen as normative, seeking informed consent is being defined as mandatory good research practice. The UKDA (2011) advises researchers that: 'Informed consent, both for people to participate in research and for use of the information collected, is an ethical requirement for most research.' The ESRC's *Research Ethics Framework* specifies that researchers who collect primary data 'should be aware that the ESRC expects that others will also use it, so consent should be obtained on this basis and the original researcher must take into account the long-term use and preservation of data' (2010a: 24). This means that, as a matter of course, researchers should be seeking their participants' informed consent to data archiving and sharing. Having secured this, they can then discuss with their respondents on what basis the data are to be made available to others: in an unedited form; with personal details anonymized; or through restricted access.

Although we had in principle agreed to do this in our ESRC application, putting this into practice proved more challenging. My existing practice had been to undertake interviews on the explicit understanding that the respondent's account would be treated in confidence, shared only with members of the research team, stored in a safe and secure place, and used in such a way that it would not be possible for others to identify them in any written reports or publications. This amounted to making an ethical and moral commitment on my part that I would, to the best of my ability, treat respondents, their identity, their privacy and their story with care. I made these moral assurances on the basis of confidence in my ability to follow through on them. I had control over how and where interviews and field notes were stored, who had access to them, and how they would be used by members of the research team (I recognize this may not always be the case, for example where research teams may not be well functioning). When George gives me his informed consent to use his narrative in the context of my own study, he is giving me permission to do so on the basis of what I have told him about my study, my research purposes and how I plan to take care of his story. His consent is given within these specific relational terms and conditions.

Why and how might seeking George's consent to archive and share his story reconfigure these moral ties, commitments and responsibilities? For his consent to be informed, I would have to explain to George what he was consenting to, and outline the risks and benefits of digital data sharing. We would need to discuss and agree on what basis to make his interview accessible. In a context where digital data loss, and illegal data access and use, are routinely featured in the media I would feel morally compelled to indicate that while every effort is made to ensure the security and ethical reuse of digitally stored data, placing his interview in a digital archive would lessen my and his control over what happened to the data and how it might be used. This is because I am no longer 'simply' asking George to trust *me* with his story. There are now as-yet-unknown third parties (however 'bona fide'), with as-yet-unknown intentions and purposes (however laudable and legitimate), to factor into the equation. I would have to explain to George that researchers reusing his interview would be required by the UKDA (2011) to sign an end use licence, which 'has contractual force in law, in which they agree to certain conditions, such as not to disseminate any identifying or confidential information on individuals, households or organisations; and not to use the data to attempt to obtain information relating specifically to an identifiable individual'. Nevertheless, I would also feel an obligation to explain that this in itself does not protect George against the potentially morally harmful effects of seeing his story interpreted through different lenses or used for different purposes.

Some researchers have argued that these moral concerns about the potential risks associated with consenting to data sharing are over paternalistic. The UKDA (2011), for example, argues that researchers have 'a duty to treat participants as intelligent beings, able to make their own decisions on how the information they provide can be used, shared and made public (through informed consent)'. Others suggest that these risks are unfounded because respondents are unlikely to read what researchers write about them in obscure journals (Thompson, 2003). These responses simplify the moral complexities involved. For one thing, working in a digital context makes our academic writings much more widely accessible and significantly increases the likelihood of our respondents reading, and responding to, what we write about them (see Tina Miller, Chapter 2, this volume). This means that the very nature and meaning of 'informed consent' change when used in digital and data sharing contexts. Given this, we must ask ourselves: How meaningful and ethical is it to ask respondents to give their *informed* consent to share their stories for future uses they have not been informed about? Furthermore, the ethical and moral issue is not only *whether* George will read, or feel morally harmed by, what is written about him. Rather, I have a moral responsibility to explain to him these potential risks because failure to do so risks breaching the relationships of trust that are fundamental to our research. Placing the onus on respondents to make decisions about data sharing overlooks the power differentials between researchers and respondents, and the fact that generally speaking, respondents will believe what we tell them and will entrust us with their stories *because they trust us to do the right thing*. Research works because respondents trust us, and because, for the most part, researchers do behave in responsible and professional ways. This places respondents like George in a vulnerable position. It heightens my own responsibility to think carefully about what I am asking of, and doing to, George by seeking his informed consent to data sharing: what the repercussions might be not only for George, but for others like him whose trust and participation we rely on for the very conduct of our research.

Furthermore, spelling out the potential risks of digital data sharing reconfigures the moral and ontological conditions in which I am doing research, conducting fieldwork, and building a relationship with George. In our interview, I was able to make an unspoken moral commitment to take care of his story if he trusted me with it. Within a digital data sharing context, it would be unethical for me to make this moral assurance because I have no knowledge of (and most likely little control over) how his story might be used at some future date. This is important because it means that seeking informed consent to digital data sharing constitutes *a different moral context* for George's story telling than seeking his informed consent to take part in my study and share his data just with the research team. Seeking informed consent is not simply an additional neutral ethical procedure that researchers must ensure they carry out and that leaves everything else unchanged. Seeking informed consent has moral and ontological effects: it constitutes *different moral and ontological conditions of possibility* for George's storytelling. It gives rise to different stories to those that might otherwise have been told. For example, knowledge that George's account might be lodged within an archive (consciously or unconsciously) may foster a 'public' rather than a 'private' narrative. Similarly, (and as I have subsequently discovered in a current project[2]) this might impact on my own interviewing style: on my willingness to share and expose personal experiences as part of building relationships of trust with my respondents, knowing these may no longer be shared only with George and members of my research team. The changes matter because they might make it more difficult to create the kinds of relationships that I see as critical to, indeed constitutive of, the narratives I am interested in: the quiet and vulnerable stories that are difficult to tell, and hear, in particular social, cultural and historical settings.

Importantly, the issue is not whether the practice of seeking informed consent prevents us from accessing *an already-constituted or given story*. Similarly, I am not suggesting that seeking informed consent affects the so-called rapport that we build with participants in such a way that they will be less likely to divulge a pre-existing 'personal story'. These assertions assume that realities and stories are pre-formed, waiting to be harvested, ontologically separate from the researchers who collect them, and the methods and practices they use to do so. My argument is that methods – in this case, the practice of seeking informed consent – are not merely neutral mediators between researchers and respondents' stories. Rather, they are performative: they provide the specific conditions of ontological possibility both for the stories that our respondents tell us, and for the untold stories they might otherwise have told had we used different methods. Seeking informed consent to data sharing is a boundary-drawing practice that (re)configures that which it helps to produce.

Anonymizing data for digital archiving

Given the personal nature of much of the data collected by social scientists, the UKDA (2011) advises researchers to anonymize the data they will lodge in a digital archive in line with agreements made with respondents during the informed consent process. They recommend using 'pseudonyms, replacement terms, vaguer descriptors or systems of coding … to retain maximum content' rather than simply removing or blanking out the information. They also recommend creating an 'anonymization log of all replacements, aggregations or removals made' and storing the log separately from the anonymized data files. Anonymizing George's interview, and those of others in our ethnographic study of the oil and gas industry, was a challenging prospect because it was focused on three specific communities within an identifiable geographical area. Interviews were carried out with several members of 52 families, community figures and human resource managers all living within what is a tight-knit 'oil' community. Even if the accounts were anonymized, many would remain identifiable by fellow family or community members. Anonymization, then, would not guarantee privacy, protection or confidentiality.

Furthermore, the protective power of anonymization is weakened within a digital context where the range of information available might enable identification of participants if combined with details taken from a dataset (see ESRC, 2010a: 25; Zimmer, 2010). The point is not only whether third parties might seek to identify anonymized respondents. Rather, the fact that digital technologies provide the possibility for doing so reconfigures the very nature and meaning of anonymization in a digital context.[3] This has implications for our ethical and moral responsibilities towards our participants and whether following the recommended guidelines of anonymizing narratives, and telling respondents that this will protect them, constitutes ethical practice when working within a digital context. As I indicated above, the nature, meaning and effects of long-standing methods and ethical practices are transformed, and need to be rethought, when used in a digital environment.

In order to avoid the lengthy and resource-intensive process of anonymizing data once they have been collected, the UKDA (2011) recommends that researchers keep some personal names and issues out of the interview conversation from the outset:

> Pre-planning and agreeing with participants during the consent process, on what may and may not be recorded or transcribed, can be a much more effective way of creating data that accurately represent the research process and the contribution of participants. For example, if an employer's name cannot be disclosed, it should be agreed in advance that it will not be mentioned during an interview. This is easier than spending time later removing it from a recording or transcript.

Researchers, the UKDA suggests, might extend this to other personal identifiers: names of friends, relatives, places, institutions, etc. Again, this practice is presented as benign in its effects. In practice, however, it helps constitute a new dataset for secondary researchers, one that is different to that being generated and used by the primary researchers. While the primary researchers who have set up the study and/or are conducting interviews can have access to and understanding of this personal information (for example, by virtue of having established the study and/or through unrecorded conversations with respondents), this information will never form part of the dataset being used by secondary researchers. Furthermore, asking informants to refrain from using personal identifiers in their narratives is an interview practice that gives rise to a specific relational context that in turn generates specific stories while excluding others. When I interviewed George, the degree of interest I expressed in the personal details and specificities of his life and experiences, and the fact that I remembered this information and used it throughout the interview to generate further questions and stories, played an important part in building a particular kind of empathic, understanding and responsive relationship with George. By conveying to George that I was listening to him carefully, taking an interest in the details of his story, trying to understand the significance of what he was telling me – in a word, that I cared – I was creating a specific set of relational conditions of possibility that had ontological effects: that allowed George to tell me this particular story, and not others.

Reusing digital data

When the ESRC brought in its Datasets Policy in 1995, as well as requiring its grant-holders to offer their data for deposit, it also asked grant applicants to demonstrate that data similar to those they were proposing to generate did not already exist. Indeed, the ESRC's most recent *Research Funding Guide* indicates that 'Any applicant, whose research proposal involves funds for primary data collection, must establish in the application that the required data are not already publicly available. This is to ensure that the ESRC does not duplicate its funding effort, for example, by funding the acquisition of data that are already available from the ESDS or some other data repository' (2011: 67). This policy is based on the ontological and epistemological assumption that doing primary and secondary research is the same thing; that primary and secondary researchers are analysing the same data (for example, George's interview transcript); and that this in turn represents the same singular external reality (George, his life, his experiences). This implies that the ontological unit of analysis that we work with is data alone: George's transcript is sufficient to make sense of his story. This is explicitly articulated in the afore-mentioned OECD report on *Principles and Guidelines for Access to Research Data from Public Funding*. Here data are defined as 'factual records (numerical scores, textual records, images and sounds) used as primary sources for scientific research, that are commonly accepted in the scientific community as necessary to validate research findings. A research data set constitutes a systematic, partial representation of the subject being investigated' (OECD, 2007: 14). This empirical realist understanding of research underpins the data sharing movement and has been taken up in qualitative research where researchers working from a mostly implicit realist perspective also assume that the data held within digital repositories provide more or less complete reflections of a singular reality (see Mauthner and Parry, 2009, in press; Mauthner et al., 1998). Primary researchers are understood to have collected self-contained and inherently meaningful nuggets of information, and deposited them within a data archive that secondary researchers can subsequently access in order to uncover new findings or generate new interpretations (for example, Bishop, 2007; Bornat, 2005; Corti and Thompson, 2004).[4] Digital data sharing discourses, policies and methods are therefore underpinned by, materialize, and render normative a particular philosophical understanding of qualitative research. George's digitally stored, anonymized, interview transcript is viewed as ontologically equivalent to my experience of 'being there' with George, in his kitchen, listening to his voice, taking in his story, noticing his body language, reading his facial expressions, watching his gaze, catching his hand gestures, noting the tilt of his head, feeling his emotions, taking in the children's clothes scattered around the kitchen, and much more. Normative understandings of digital data sharing recognize the importance of this interview and research context, but view it as additional and secondary to the primary ontological entity: data, in this case, the interview transcript (Mauthner and Parry, 2009).

Part of my ambivalence about sharing George's and other interviews was because I did not subscribe to this empirical realist understanding of qualitative research. I did not share the view that primary and secondary researchers are doing the same thing. This was because I knew from my experiences of reading colleagues' and students' data (in the context of research teams and doctoral supervision) that the material differences between first- and second-hand data mattered to my understanding of it: that the material specificities of our research encounters and practices are significant; that who does what in research makes a difference to what we know and how we know it (Mauthner and Doucet, 2008). When I interpret narratives from interviews I have conducted myself, I am drawing on this material specificity of the data to make sense of it. I am using much more than just the spoken words: I am using an embodied and tacit form of knowledge and understanding that come from 'being there' with my respondent. I am recollecting, in my mind and body, what it felt like to come to know this person. When analysing second-hand data I do not have access to this and securing the integrity of my interpretive process is dependent on including the interviewer's experientially derived knowledge of 'being there' with their respondent into my analytic process. It becomes necessary to discuss my analyses with the interviewer: not as an add-on but as an integral ontological part of the analytic process; and not in order to reach interpretive agreement or consensus, but to ensure the epistemological integrity and plausibility of my interpretations. These experiences told me that the material practices of our research matter. That the practices through which George's story was brought into being (the specificities of how I interviewed him), the practices through which I made sense of his narrative (the specific analytic methods I used, and how I used them), the practices through which his story is digitally archived (through anonymization and contextualization of data), and the practices through which secondary researchers access, download and analyse his interview all have ontological effects: they make a difference to what we will come to know, and not know, about George. These practices are productive and ontologically constitutive of knowledge: they are part of, and help constitute, what we are coming to know (Barad, 2007).

The notion of data sharing that is being promoted, prescribed and rendered normative is not neutral. It is rooted within a particular philosophical worldview: one that takes 'data' as its ontological unit of analysis while marginalizing the significance of these constitutive practices that I am highlighting. This understanding of digital data reuse has ontological, moral and political effects. It privileges one particular philosophical understanding of qualitative research over alternative frameworks. This raises questions over the ethics of prescriptive data sharing policies, governance frameworks, and information sharing legislation that render one worldview normative with the expectation that all researchers must conform to it. Indeed, it is reminiscent of what post-colonial feminist scholar Spivak (1988) calls 'epistemic violence', a term she uses to refer to the destruction of non-western ways of knowing and the domination of western ways of understanding.

Furthermore, the notion that data are free-floating individual things, with their own independent sets of determinate properties and meanings, depends on uprooting data from the contexts, conditions, relations and labour through which they are constituted. It is dependent on excluding practices, and the ontological and epistemological work performed by researchers and their methods. Casting away the socio-material moorings of data is morally consequential because it allows the emergence of a particular moral understanding of data: an instrumental view in which data are regarded as public property, a public good or a global commodity. It legitimizes a view in which data are no longer seen as morally belonging to those who produce them but rather can be regarded as belonging to the public. Rendering one particular ontological worldview as normative – in which data are understood as separate from their contexts of production – in turn helps to bring new moral realities and configurations into being whereby researchers' (physical, intellectual, emotional, epistemic) labour is no longer seen to constitute legitimate grounds for intellectual property or moral ownership rights over the data they produce. This in turn materializes new political realities because if data are understood as public property it legitimizes the regulation of research activities, the prescription of data sharing by public bodies, the legal enforcement of data sharing, and the notion that researchers have a moral obligation to the public that can (and sometimes should) over ride their obligations to their respondents.

We see some of these issues at play in the case I mentioned above of Mike Baillie. The case goes back to April 2007, when Doug Keenan, a London City banker and part-time climate analyst, asked Queen's University for all data from tree-ring studies by Baillie and others. The data covers more than 7000 years and contain measurements from 11,000 tree samples. The university turned down Keenan's request, citing a range of exemptions allowed under both the Freedom of Information Act and the European Union's Environmental Information Regulations. Keenan appealed to the information commissioner, who ruled that the data be released. Baillie described the ruling as a 'staggering injustice' (Baillie, 2010) and saw it as a direct offshoot of the information revolution, and the idea that research data can be demanded by anyone (Pearce, 2010). His tree-ring data, he argues, are his own personal intellectual property. He says: 'We are the ones who trudged miles over bogs and fields carrying chain saws. We prepared the samples and – using quite a lot of expertise and judgment – we measured the ring patterns. Each ring pattern therefore has strong claims to be our copyright' (Baillie, 2010). He further elaborates:

> when a dendrochronologist measures the widths of the growth rings in a sample, he or she has to make multiple decisions with respect to the starts and ends of the rings, problem rings, and so on. Repeated measurement of the same sample, will not give exactly the same measurements. The number of rings must be the same, but the actual measured widths will not be. This means that the ring pattern of a tree-ring sample carries the 'intellectual fingerprint' of the dendrochronologist who measured it, every bit as much as this text carries my intellectual fingerprint. In my opinion, tree-ring patterns are therefore intellectual property and should not be handed out as if they are instrumental climate data.

Baillie's argument is that he has moral ownership rights over his data because of the physical and intellectual effort and investment that went into producing the tree-ring data. Indeed, this is recognized in intellectual property and copyright law as 'sweat of the brow', whereby the creator of a work or a database has rights through diligence and effort. It is precisely this labour, however, that is rendered immaterial within emerging data sharing norms, discourses and practices. What we see in this case are the effects of taking up different philosophical and moral definitions and understandings of data and their reuse. When we agree to share our data, we are doing more than just this: we are signing up to a hegemonic understanding of data and data sharing, that is in turn entangled with, and helps to materialize, specific assumptions about the ethics and politics of knowledge production.

In the preceding sections, I have suggested that digital data sharing methods are doing more than just allowing us to preserve and reuse research data: they are reconfig-uring the landscape of research by redrawing boundaries, relationships and responsi-bilities. Seeking informed consent, anonymizing data and reusing data are performative practices. They bring into being particular ontological, epistemological, moral and political configurations of the world. They materialize specific ways of understanding research data and their moral status; who they do or should belong to; and who has legitimate authority, power and rights to make decisions over research data. Digital data sharing methods are entangled with much larger sets of discursive and material relations, arrangements and conditions. They are intertwined with wider technological, scientific, methodological, philosophical, ethical, moral, legal, historical, political, social, cultural and economic processes. When we use methods, we play a part in, and are responsible for, giving shape to these specific realities that we help to enact.

Taking responsibility for the methods we use and 'for the role that we play in the world's differential becoming'[5]

The ethical and moral issues raised by digital data sharing methods in qualitative research have been debated since the late 1990s. In the wake of the ESRC's introduction of its Datasets Policy in 1995, several researchers voiced ambivalence about the new policy (for example, Alderson, 1998; Griffin, 1997; Hammersley, 1997; Mauthner et al., 1998). They saw its potential benefits in terms of fostering the preservation of significant research studies; demystifying the qualitative research process; opening up for debate the question of data ownership; and using archived studies for historical and methodological research, as well as for teaching purposes. However, they also drew attention to what they regarded as pressing ethical and moral issues raised by the policy, and the methods it entailed. Hammersley (1997), for example, argued that revealing personal information through the preservation of their studies may be potentially damaging to researchers whose efficiency and competence could be assessed on the basis of archived materials. Alderson (1998) asked how researchers could provide ethical assurances to respondents given uncertainties over how data would be stored, used and interpreted. Griffin (1997) pointed to power differentials between potential data 'users', such as major private sector corporations and public sector institutions, and the data 'suppliers' or respondents who tend to be individuals from less privileged sections of society. And my colleagues and I raised questions about the notion of reusing 'data' taken out of their contexts of production, and what philosophical and moral understanding of data, qualitative research, and research relationships this implied (Mauthner et al., 1998; see also Parry and Mauthner, 2004, 2005). The intention of these early contributions was to initiate a debate about this new policy, foster critical reflection on its underlying assumptions and consider its potential implications for qualitative research methods and practices. These researchers were not seeking to oppose the use of these methods. Rather, they were asking how their use might change our practices as qualitative researchers, and with what philosophical, moral and political implications.

The debate that has ensued has been, at least in part, about the legitimacy of these questions and whether they lie within the bounds of our ethical and moral responsibilities. For the most part, qualitative researchers have taken the view that what is important is *using* the methods, and ensuring that we do so ethically and legally, rather than getting caught up in moral and philosophical deliberations. Mason (2007), for example, notes that data sharing debates have led to 'a culture of uneasy suspicion that there might be something ethically, morally or epistemologically dubious about 're-using' qualitative data'. She asks whether this 'is the most important question to be debating in the first place', and commends those researchers who have sought to 'push past the more moralistic overtones of the "re-use" debate to focus instead on what happens, what is involved, what can and cannot be achieved, when sociologists get on and do' secondary data analysis. Moore (2007) suggests that scepticism about digital data sharing methods is unwarranted because it relies on misguided assumptions about the 'the supposed "newness" of reusing qualitative data'. Digital data sharing, she suggests, is similar to existing methodological traditions in which researchers 're-use' data stored in historical and other archives, data they have collected earlier in their career, or data that has been generated by other members of a research team. In response to Richardson and Godfrey's (2003) concerns about how data sharing weakens moral ties and responsibilities between respondents and those reusing their narratives, Thompson reminds qualitative researchers that 'Ultimately it is important to remember that our prime purpose is to do research, not to enter into morally overwhelming relationships with interviewees and their families' (2003: 359). The implicit understanding has been that researchers' moral responsibilities extend no further than compliance with data sharing imperatives, and recommended ethical and legal guidelines. Much discussion has therefore focused on the development of sophisticated procedures and protocols for data deposit and reuse that address issues of informed consent, data anonymization, data contextualization, end user license agreements and access restrictions (see Bishop, 2009).

But this debate raises profound questions about the precise nature of our ethical and moral responsibilities as researchers, and where we draw the line around these. Is our moral responsibility to comply with emerging data sharing expectations, requirements and demands: to use prescribed methods in ethically, morally and legally recommended ways? Or, do we have a responsibility to contest and rework data sharing imperatives and their normative understandings of what we do? Should we resist the ways in which the data sharing movement is eroding researchers' autonomy and freedom to practice research that has philosophical and moral integrity as understood within their particular philosophical perspective? Should we insist that new methods, and the new ethical, moral and political challenges they give rise to, be better understood before their widespread implementation? How do we decide what constitute legitimate moral concerns? And what are the consequences of our inclusionary and exclusionary practices: of making the specific choices that we do?

In this chapter I have suggested that researchers have a moral responsibility for the very methods they use. The legitimacy of this claim is dependent on thinking about methods in ways that we are not accustomed to: in terms of what they do; in terms of what else they are entangled with; in terms of their performativity. Methods tend to be taken for granted. They are seen as neutral tools that mediate between researchers and researched, and that have no effects in and of themselves. As Law and Ury (2004) suggest, despite shifts towards more complex and performative understandings of social inquiry, method itself continues to be regarded as a reasonably secure framework: a set of neutral and innocent techniques or 'short-circuits that link us in the best possible way with reality, and allow us to return more or less quickly from that reality to our place of study with findings that are reasonably secure, at least for the time being' (Law, 2004: 10). In contrast, Law and Ury (2004) propose a performative understanding of method in which different methods do not generate different perspectives on a single reality but rather different realities. To say that methods are performative is to suggest that 'they have effects; they make differences; they enact realities; and they can help to bring into being what they also discover' (Law and Ury, 2004: 393; see also Law, 2004; Barad, 2007).

A performative understanding of research methods opens up questions of responsibility; or what Law and Ury (2004), drawing on Mol (1999), term 'ontological politics'. It raises questions about what realities we might or should bring into being. This means that methods, including those who use them, are neither neutral nor innocent; they have effects and consequences. They help enact certain realities while excluding others. 'Method', explains Law, 'unavoidably produces not only truths and non-truths, realities and non-realities, presences and absences, but also arrangements with political implications' (2004: 143). Methods are political. This insight is of critical importance for qualitative researchers because it enfolds a consideration of methods themselves – as entangled phenomena that are practised and imbued with 'normativities' and 'moralisms' (Law, 2004) – into our ethical responsibilities (an issue Andrea Doucet and I discuss in Chapter 8, this volume; and also addressed by Pam Aldred and Val Gillies in Chapter 3, this volume). We cannot be bystanders, innocently deploying our methods. Rather, we must take responsibility not only for what we bring into being but also for how we do this, because the two are inseparable. Engaging in digital data sharing methods and practices is about much more than archiving and reusing digital data. It raises ontological, moral and political questions about what realities we inadvertently bring into being through the use of these methods; whether we want or should bring these realities into being; and whether we want or should recognize that we are even doing so. In sum, it raises moral questions about the responsibility we have for the methods we use. 'There is no innocence', write Law and Ury, 'But to the extent social science conceals its performativity from itself it is pretending to an innocence that it cannot have' (2004: 404).

Studying our methods, understanding what they do and what else they are entangled with, is part of our ethical and moral responsibility as researchers. The importance and urgency of this project is difficult to overstate. First, because the digital data sharing movement is changing the ways in which we do qualitative research. Indeed, this *is* its purpose. Digital data sharing methods and practices are being increasingly encouraged, prescribed and regulated in an effort to bring about large-scale behavioural, organizational and cultural change: a new research culture in which digital data sharing will become a normative research practice, and open access to research data a normative (gold standard) data sharing model. Second, as we move into a period of economic austerity and public sector cuts, the economic case for digital data sharing, reuse and recycling will become increasingly compelling. In this context, understanding and justifying the value of primary qualitative research, and its distinctive contribution to knowledge, becomes vital. Third, as we move into an increasingly prescriptive and regulatory research environment we must understand the new methods that we are being encouraged or required to use, including their risks and benefits. Fourth, the digital revolution means that virtually all researchers are working with digital data. Even if our data are generated using non-digital means (for example, through fieldwork, field notes, observations, measurements, conversations), most of us record, store, analyse, exchange and preserve data in digital form. Indeed, we are increasingly encouraged to make use of digital tools, services and facilities for these data manipulation activities. Living in a digital world means that *all* of our methods and practices are being reconfigured through their intra-actions with digital technologies; and understanding the ethical and moral consequences of this becomes critical. Fifth, as is discussed elsewhere in this book (and also see Stanley and Wise, 2010), growth in the regulation of research ethics can, at best, induce a tick-box mentality and lull researchers into a false sense of security that our ethical and moral responsibilities end once we have completed our ethical review forms and submitted them to ethical review boards and committees; at worst, it can be seen to absolve researchers from their moral responsibilities. Paradoxically, the spread of ethical regulation highlighted by Tina Miller in Chapter 2 (this volume) can weaken researchers' personal sense of ethical responsibility over the methods they use, just at a time when new digital and regulatory environments demand heightened ethical and moral vigilance.

Acknowledgements

I thank the editors of this book, and Darcy Thompson, for their comments on earlier drafts of this chapter. I also thank Libby Bishop for facilitating my recent visit to the UK Data Archive, and for her commitment to our ongoing conversations about data sharing. Further thanks go to Odette Parry for many discussions about data sharing since the 1990s. I am grateful to the Society for Research into Higher Education for funding my current research on digital data sharing.

Notes

1 Barad (2007: 384).
2 This project is developing a performative approach to digital data sharing. I am using reserach 'data' and materials from jennifer Platt's pioneering sociological study of the social research process as a case study (Social Realities of research: An Empirical Study of British Sociologists, 1976, Sussex University Press), as well conducting interviews with her.
3 Interestingly, researchers in the field of genomics have questioned the ethics of anonymizing biospescimens in biobanks for the very same reasons (see Kaye et al., 2009; O'Brien, 2009; Greely, 2007).
4 This empirical realist framework dominates understandings of digital data sharing in qualitative research. However, some researchers have criticised this approach and developed social constructionist approaches (see Mauthner and Parry, 2009, for further details).
5 Barad (2007: 396).

References

Alderson, P. (1998) 'Confidentiality and consent in qualitative research', *Network -Newsletter of the British Sociological Association,* 69: 6–7.

Arzberger, P., Schroeder, P., Beaulieu, A., et al. (2004) 'Promoting access to public research data for scientific, economic, and social development', *Data Science Journal,* (3): 135–52.

Baillie, M. (2010) 'Tree-ring patterns are intellectual property, not climate data', *The Guardian,* 11 May.

Barad, K. (2007) *Meeting the Universe Halfway: The Entanglement of Matter and Meaning.* Durham, NC: Duke University Press.

Bishop, L. (2007) 'A reflexive account of reusing qualitative data: beyond primary/secondary dualism', *Sociological Research Online,* 12 (3). Available at: http://www.socresonline.org.uk/home.html (accessed 11 July 2009).

Bishop, L. (2009) 'Ethical sharing and reuse of qualitative data', *Australian Journal of Social Issues,* 44 (3): 255–72.

Bornat, J. (2005) 'Recycling the evidence: different approaches to the reanalysis of Gerontological data', *Forum: Qualitative Social Research,* 6 (1): art. 42.

Carusi, A. and Jarotka, M. (2009) 'From data archive to ethical labyrinth', *Qualitative Research,* 9 (3): 285–98.

Christie, B. (2011) 'Tobacco company makes freedom of information request for university's research', *British Medical Journal,* 343: d5655.

Corti, L. and Thompson, P. (2004) 'Secondary analysis of archive data', in C. Seale, G. Gobo and J.F. Gubrium (eds), *Qualitative Research Practice.* London: Sage. pp. 327–43.

Digital Curation Centre (DCC) (2010) 'Cross council policy overview'. Available at: http://www.dcc.ac.uk (accessed 19 July 2010).

ESRC (2010a) 'Framework for Research Ethics (FRE)'. Available at: http://www.esrc.ac.uk/_images/Framework_for_Research_Ethics_tcm8–4586.pdf (accessed 13 April 2011).

ESRC (2010b) 'ESRC research data policy'. Available at: http://www.esrc.ac.uk/_images/Research_Data_Policy_2010_tcm8–4595.pdf (accessed 20 May 2011).

ESRC (2011) 'Research funding guide September 2011'. Available at: http://www.esrc.ac.uk/_images/Research_Funding_Guide_tcm8–2323.pdf (accessed 5 October 2011).

Griffin, C. (1997) 'Archiving qualitative datasets: social research and the politics of control', *Radical Statistics,* 66: 44–7.

Hammersley, M. (1997) 'Qualitative data archiving: some reflections on its prospects and problems', *Sociology,* 31 (1): 131–42.

Law, J. (2004) *After Method: Mess in Social Science Research.* Abingdon: Routledge.

Law, J. and Urry, J. (2004) 'Enacting the social', *Economy and Society,* 33 (3): 390–410.

Mason, J. (2007) 'Re-using' qualitative data: on the merits of an investigative epistemology', *Sociological Research Online.* Available at: http:// www.socresonline.org.uk/home.html (accessed 7 June 2009).

Mauthner, N. and Doucet, A. (2008) 'Knowledge once divided can be hard to put together again': an epistemological critique of collaborative and team-based research practices', *Sociology,* 42 (5): 971–85.

Mauthner, N., Parry, O. and Backett-Milburn, K. (1998) 'The data are out there, or are they? Implications for archiving and revisiting qualitative data', *Sociology,* 32 (4): 733–45.

Mauthner, N.S. and Parry, O. (2009) 'Qualitative data preservation and sharing in the social sciences: on whose philosophical terms?', *Australian Journal of Social Issues,* 44 (3): 289–305.

Mauthner, N.S. and Parry, O. (in press) 'Open access digital data sharing: principles, policies and practices', *Social Epistemology.*

MRC (2011) 'MRC policy on data sharing and preservation'. Available at: http://www. mrc.ac.uk/Ourresearch/Ethicsresearchguidance/Datasharinginitiative/Policy/index.htm (accessed 10 November 2010).

Mol, A. (1999) 'Ontological politics: a word and some questions', in J. Law and J. Hassard (eds), *Actor Network Theory and After.* Oxford: Blackwell and the Sociological Review. pp. 74–89.

Moore, N. (2007) '(Re)using qualitative data', *Sociological Research Online,* 12 (3). Available at: http://www.socresonline.org.uk/home.html (accessed 15 March 2009).

OECD (2007) 'Principles and guidelines for access to research data from public funding'. Available at: http://www.oecd.org/dataoecd/9/61/38500813.pdf (accessed 16 March 2009).

Parry, O. and N. Mauthner. (2004) 'Whose data are they anyway? Practical, legal and ethical issues in archiving qualitative research data', *Sociology,* 38 (1): 139–52.

Parry, O. and N. Mauthner. (2005) 'Back to basics: who re-uses qualitative data and why?', *Sociology,* 2005 (39): 337–42.

Pearce, F. (2010) 'Climate sceptic wins landmark data victory "for price of a stamp"', *Guardian,* 20 April.

Richardson, J.C. and Godfrey, B.S. (2003) 'Towards ethical practice in the use of archived transcribed interviews', *International Journal of Social Research Methodology,* 6 (4): 347–55.

Rusbridge, C. and Charlesworth, A. (2010) 'Freedom of information and research data: questions and answers: JISC'. Available at: http://www.jisc.ac.uk/foiresearchdata (accessed 23 July 2010).

Ruusalepp, R. (2008) 'A comparative study of international approaches to enabling the sharing of research data'. Available at: http://www.jisc.ac.uk/media/documents/ programmes/preservation/data_sharing_report_main_findings_final.pdf (accessed 17 July 2010).

SHERPA (2009) 'Research funders' open access policies – JULIET'. Available at: http://www. sherpa.ac.uk/juliet (accessed 13 March 2010).

Spivak, G.C. (1988) 'Can the subaltern speak?', in C. Nelson and L. Grossberg (eds), *Marxism and the Interpretation of Culture.* Urbana, IL: University of Illinois Press. pp. 271–315.

Stanley, L. and Wise, S. (2010) 'The ESRC's 2010 framework for research ethics: fit for research purpose?', *Sociological Research Online,* 15 (4): 12. Available at: http://www. socresonline.org.uk/15/4/12.html (accessed 14 November 2011).

UK Data Archive (2011) 'UK data archive – HOME'. Available at: http://www.data-archive. ac.uk/home (accessed 15 November 2011).

Thompson, P. (2003) 'Towards ethical practice in the use of archived transcribed interviews: a response', *International Journal of Social Research Methodology,* 6 (4): 357–360.

Van den Eynden, V., et al. (2011) *Managing and Sharing Data – Best Practice for Researchers.* Colchester: UK Data Archive, University of Essex.

Willinsky, J. (2006) *The Access Principle: The Case for Open Access to Research and Scholarship.* Cambridge, MA: Massachusetts Institute of Technology.

Zimmer, M. (2010) '"But the data is already public"': on the ethics of research in Facebook', *Ethics in Information Technology,* 12: 313–25.

11

Conclusion: navigating ethical dilemmas and new digital horizons

MELANIE MAUTHNER, MAXINE BIRCH,
TINA MILLER AND JULIE JESSOP

Qualitative research continues to evolve and offer new opportunities through which to explore and understand the social world. In this second edition, the ethical dilemmas that we initially identified and discussed through our qualitative research experiences 10 years ago, continue to have resonance for researchers today. Indeed, our concerns then – that as society becomes more complex a broader ethical stance is required – are now re-examined in relation to the changing social landscape and its implications for research design, practice and regulation. The research context has been altered in dramatic ways by the gradual progression of the digital age, which now seeps into many aspects of everyday life. In relation to research practice, new technologies have led to increased regulation and concerns with litigation. These are evidenced through ever more standardized systems of ethical approval alongside ethical tensions arising from the blurred boundaries of virtual, everyday social worlds. The growing pressures of ethical governance, on the one hand, and a host of new mobile digital technologies, on the other, continue to present the researcher with complex situations to negotiate. The growth of ethical governance has done little to lessen the complexity of the ethical dilemmas encountered in practice by qualitative researchers. Rather the ethical tensions between the regulatory ethical frameworks and the inherent complexity of the qualitative research relationship and goals of knowledge production remain similar to those we experienced 10 years ago. Yet virtual worlds present new possibilities that enable social actors to become more visible or hidden, more tangible or abstract. And new digital research tools can offer creative ways to explore sensitive issues, capture personal experiences from diverse groups of participants, and support feminist research ethical principles to *give voice* to others from less powerful and/or marginalized social groups.

As feminists, we continue to challenge and address issues of power across academic and research boundaries (Gillies and Lucey, 2007). But we can also become concerned when power dimensions shift too far in one direction, as elements of more recent research experience and practice seem to indicate is occurring. Challenges to the interpretative authority of the researcher, for example have become more possible through digital media, which potentially counter the preserve of academia. Such actions could, however, also be seen as enabling the democratization of knowledge production. To explore how these ethical dilemmas continue to shape our research experiences, knowledge and practices we conclude by returning to our key, overarching themes of responsibility and accountability, highlighting notions of privacy and protection within shifting boundaries in order to offer new insights and propose ways forward.

Traditionally, the ethical responsibility of protecting those involved in our research has been an important aspect of demonstrating a good professional relationship. Professional codes of conduct alongside peer scrutiny and structures for vetting research designs serve to sanction a researcher's compliance to follow procedures. Ethical regulators have opted for more standardization (as they are concerned about risk management, being sued and intellectual property rights). Researchers are bound by and agree to conform to a set of shared professional expectations and values about their research design, how they will collect data and elaborate and communicate (emerging) ideas. However, many of the chapters in this book question this shared set of professional expectations and associated assumptions that one size fits all.

Elements of qualitative research procedures – informed consent, confidentiality, participation, and rapport – are cross-examined in several of the preceding chapters and illustrated through a range of research examples. The authors discuss the varying dilemmas they have encountered in their research projects to reveal different aspects of ethical responsibility. For example, Tina Miller and Linda Bell in Chapter 4 and Maxine Birch and Tina Miller in Chapter 6 highlight the ethical responsibility on the part of the researcher to continually (re)negotiate aspects of consent and participation *throughout* the life of a research project. These authors offer particular strategies for communicating with research participants and creating space for them to raise their views, negotiating with and between them. This negotiation however is never a simple process and as Linda Bell and Linda Nutt illustrate, in Chapter 5, a researcher can be obliged to consider professional responsibilities outside of the research role. In this particular case it is argued that the statutory duty of social work overrides the primacy of the research relationship. In many other situations, conflicts can arise between the rights of the individual and wider social concerns. Questions such as those posed in the introduction to this book (see p. x) can guide ethical thinking and help to address the balance between personal and social power, asking how those involved will understand the researcher's actions and how such actions will affect the relationships between the parties involved. But as noted earlier this is a changing landscape in which relationships and issues of power are having to be contemplated from shifting and sometimes new positions. The concerns exposed in Jean Duncombe and Julie Jessop's chapter (7) on the ideal of a feminist ethical researcher set against the power dimensions of 'developing rapport' or 'faking friendship' within the research relationship have a heightened resonance in this technologically rich age. Ideas of 'friendship' have become distorted and multi-faceted, for example being 'friends' (sometimes with hundreds of people) on social networking sites such as Facebook. Research 'friendships' may have become easier to establish, but also harder to escape. And so it becomes increasingly important for researchers to identify and question the strategies they may use to 'coerce' participants to reveal and disclose 'good' data and the potentially unethical consequences of such strategies. It is clear then that protocols to standardize 'good', ethical research practices can only go so far. Flexible, research skills and thinking must also be comprehensively taught and developed through practical application, with adequate support and supervisory mechanisms in place. Researchers should be required to think ethically about the particular and often challenging contexts throughout the research process.

While it is important to acknowledge that access to computers, the Internet and other social networking facilities are uneven across the global landscape, it also appears that many researchers make use of digital progress wherever possible. Access to digital tools broadens the scope for increased dialogue between researcher and participant and the varying benefits and risks, advantages and disadvantages can confuse where the researcher's responsibilities lie. Increasingly, offline and online research can interlink in a variety of ways. This may simply involve researchers accessing participants via e-mail and then participating in email conversations throughout the research process. Yet the relatively unproblematic email exchange between researcher and participant can eventually emerge as data for analytical interpretation and public dissemination, a consequence perhaps not envisaged at the start, as explored in Tina Miller's chapter (2). As new forms of writing and narrative conventions expand, the phone text, the public 'blog' for diary entries, the different genres (article, poem, podcast, interview, lecture, etc.) become more accessible in a digital world. Previously accepted procedures to guarantee confidentiality and anonymity become increasingly permeable in this virtual world. Documenting personal information can move from a closed and protected forum into a shared and public arena in which safeguarding privacy (of both the participant and researcher) becomes much more problematic.

There is also the issue of invisible surveillance, which we are all subjected to in late modernity. We leave trails of (potentially indelible) visual and electronic footprints which are collected in all sorts of ways as we go about our daily business. Increasingly our privacy is invaded without our permission, rather it seems to be a taken-for-granted aspect and consequence of – paradoxically – ensuring safe and 'protected' citizenship. Technical experts can identify how many people logged on to a particular web page, how long each person spent viewing that web page and reveal numerous other 'facts' to evidence when and how Internet users engage. The growth of online surveys can use such technical details to provide a subsystem of data – 'paradata' – that can shape future research designs and offer unique insights into survey responses (Heerwegh, 2003). Similarly other administrative data can be joined up and shared in new ways that blur commercial and government data set boundaries and raise questions about the original basis on which participant consent was given as well as confidentiality and anonymity. Even more recently it has been proposed that patient information held by the National Health Service in the UK should be made available to commercial pharmaceutical companies (http://www.bbc.co.uk/news/uk-16026827). So while privacy as an individual citizen may be understood in a particular way, data from that citizen-as-consumer will be subject to the control of internet conglomerates with different ideas of privacy who can redistribute information according to their own rules

(Pariser, 2011). If the public spaces of the Internet become governed through under-standings of consumerism in Western societies the default philosophy, 'metaphysics of consumerism' can influence ethical decision making (Bauman, 2008: 59). In contrast, qualitative researchers have the prospect of using opportunities for transparency made possible through new digital mobile media to encourage the growing trend of democ-ratization. This is especially the case as more of us gain access to (potentially global) platforms and so can express our views in new ways.

New relationships with participants and users of research bring different responsi-bilities for us as researchers, and we must mediate and manage the resulting dynam-ics. As researchers we may have to pay closer attention to our own privacy, to how we can protect ourselves. This shift in power offers users of our research more ways to comment and interact with those of us who produce 'content' as info-knowledge (knowledge in the digital sphere). The environment within which we now construct knowledge is one where barriers are being eroded, namely the boundary between the professional/expert/producer and the participant/consumer/reader, as well as the dividing line between knowledge versus information, and argument versus opinion. Clearly, these changes point to a larger social and political trend that is occurring where the balance of power is shifting not only with regard to research knowledge, but also in all areas of digital production and consumption. Ethically speaking then we need to ask further questions: when do we think about protection? Who do we have in mind? How can we control these varying contexts?

These new questions return us to focus on our responsibility for the production of knowledge. Andrea Doucet and Natasha Mauthner's chapter (8) on 'knowing respon-sibly' reconnects responsibility for the research relationship with the stages of analy-sis and dissemination. While stressing the importance of maintaining relationships with research participants they also highlight the inherent tensions that this process elicits. Research participants are drawn from varying groups and perhaps may not 'fit' with the particular theoretical, epistemological, and political frameworks of the research/researchers. Pam Alldred and Val Gillies's chapter (9) reminds us how the performance of interview methods reinforces the Western model of the subject that affirms normative understandings of subjectivity and personhood. The counterbal-ance for this is to ensure that the varying epistemological, theoretical and political assumptions are made transparent to the reader as well as to the varied communities from where the knowledge has been generated. Stemming from this onus on research-ers to involve users far more at different stages of the process (beyond design and dissemination) is one of the most important consequences of increased democratiza-tion and dialogue in this digital world. As Tina Miller notes in her chapter (2), one participant used his blog (web-log) to make public his views about the book she pub-lished following the research study in which he had participated (Miller, 2011). His view was that interview data should be provided – and imagined – as a *gift:* such a public rejoinder to the research signals a shift in how 'knowing responsibly' may be understood and (could be) practiced.

The question whether online research simply extends methodological tools or signifies an epistemological shift where new social worlds exist for the researcher to investigate is important to consider. The participant from Tina Miller's study demonstrates how online communities can create their own interpretive understandings. The success of 'Mumsnet' and the activity of blogging on mothering (see Doucet and Mauthner, 2012) illustrate a new sophistication in constructing parental concerns and attitudes in an information society. Clearly would-be participants now have new opportunities to intervene in how knowledge is produced. Not only can reader-respondent-users have a clearer presence throughout and beyond a study's life in the digital sphere, new technologies mean that boundaries between who retains autonomy and authority are being challenged and becoming blurred. New technologies also have a global reach and the implications for this within different cultural contexts are only just beginning to be appreciated. Citizens can marshal social media and networking to organize and document protests, to highlight abuses of power and to communicate events to wider audiences (Nash, 2011). The risks now seem greater partly as a consequence of the loss of (some of our) power, especially in relation to protecting ourselves. One example of this is discussed in Natasha Mauthner's chapter on data sharing. In this chapter Natasha highlights the pressure some researchers can experience as they investigate sensitive issues such as climate change when asked to hand over their data and their sources. This growing pressure to deposit data in qualitative research databanks and share it with other researchers raises ethical and moral issues about the responsibility that we take as researchers for the methods we use; for *how* we carry out research and for the contexts in which this occurs and shapes the social realities that we produce.

If we are not careful and thoughtful about the processes of producing knowledge and the multitude of voice-giving channels we may engage or refute, a danger arises in that we might unwittingly reinforce a narrowing of academia, undoing the tenets of making knowledge more accessible and making research count. One criticism of academic knowledge has been that it only reaches familiar audiences. To address this, the balance between academic knowledge production and giving voice to others has to shift – and new technologies can enable changes to be made. Part of our feminist commitment is to involve others in dialogue about our ideas while at the same time holding onto a professionally informed but hopefully not defensive position, but new contexts in which we must reflect upon ethics continue to emerge. For example, in the UK context it will be important to monitor what affects measuring the 'impact' of our research endeavours (a significant new aspect of the next Research Excellence Framework) will have on the democratization of research practices. Who might we feel compelled to draw into our research in order to demonstrate impact and how might our professional autonomy and integrity be affected? Promoting dialogue and exchange of ideas is then a central aim of research and the ways in which this is achieved needs to be continually reflected upon and acknowledged. The growing interactivity that new digital media promote whether among researchers or in other online environments such as the gaming community, for example, leads us to two further thoughts considered below.

On the one hand, it seems to us that researchers need to be equipped to think ethically before, during and beyond the start and ending of their research project because our responsibility and accountability extend beyond these narrow confines. On the other hand, our own thinking and doing and writing about ethics over a decade leads us to advocate 'ethical thinking' as a vital, practical skill that straddles the material and digital worlds, as well as the research and the everyday worlds we live in. In other words, *ethics matters*, not just in research, not just in cyberspace but at the juncture between these worlds when opposing forces and interests clash (as evidenced by ethical misbehaviour/malpractice being deemed criminal in financial, political, medical and environmental contexts). Researchers need to understand issues of copyright, plagiarism and piracy (Levine, 2011) as moral aspects of navigating the information-knowledge available in the digital age. Thus as researchers an integral part of our training is to ask ourselves, what is the best way to investigate a specific topic and to produce responsible, accountable, valid knowledge? In a sense our concern with ethics stems from this, the skills we equip ourselves with are indispensable for our voices as feminist researchers to have authority and to carry weight. As researchers, we care about disseminating our findings, about sharing our knowledge. If we transgress by ignoring these professional/behaviour codes (for example taking the ideas of others and not acknowledging sources), or by refusing to adopt an ethical stance, not only will our peers doubt the value of our work, we will be letting others down who we made a pact with – our participants who 'gifted' their words to us, and the readers of our findings.

As more of us spend more of our time in digital spaces for a greater range of purposes and activities, this ethical toolkit – knowing as a researcher what I can and cannot do, what I should and should not do – becomes imperative. As Tina Miller makes clear in her chapter, new technologies offer new possibilities, new benefits *and* new costs. The problem with increasingly standardized ethical regulation, she suggests, is that it does not always equip the researcher with this kind of practical toolkit. Indeed, *anticipatory,* pre-study regulation only reaches some aspects of the research process, which can be significant (for example, influencing the type of sample recruited). Yet researchers need to be prepared to think ethically throughout the life of their study, including how to protect themselves (rather than just the participant) as the digital sphere as an unregulated public space rivals *professionally disciplined* research spaces. Moreover, she asks whether shifting boundaries (across the research process) and 'answering back' can be viewed as instances of research democratization, of a rebalancing of the power dimensions of earlier research relationships, thus achieving a goal of feminist research.

We find then that we are increasingly working in a new research context with a new set of research dynamics. As Ros Edwards and Melanie Mauthner note (in Chapter 1), ethics is a research skill to help us anticipate and resolve conflict. As researchers, our motivation is to create knowledge that others will be eager to discover just as we have been. We care about the sources we use and how we acknowledge them and as Andrea Doucet and Natasha S. Mauthner make clear in their chapter (8), we care about where our data come from, and we care about the ways in which they are generated. As databanks encourage us to 'gift' or cajole us to archive our datasets so that other (future) researchers can re-use and recycle our material, unseen consequences can be encountered as Natasha S. Mauthner explores in her chapter (10). Digital data sharing methods are being promoted as good science and good research practice on scientific, ethical, moral, economic and political grounds. But we must ask: Good for whom? From whose perspective? And on whose terms? Similarly, we feel that as researchers we ought to give as much attention to who, how and where we decide to interact – whether in cyber or in material spaces – as we do to acknowledging our methods, sources of our ideas, and making ourselves accountable to our funders, respondents and readers.

Spaces where we share, produce, and consume knowledge have mushroomed; opportunities have increased with more and more information on offer and available (as in other consumerist market places). Social networking has been harnessed as a research tool to access online communities such as young people who otherwise may be harder to reach and offer a fuller participative role in the research process (Barratt and Lenton, 2010). At the same time, there are new demands for researchers to network online and create an online research presence. Researchers can create a public/private online presence on social networks, such as Facebook and LinkedIn, that can fall outside of the remit of institutional responsibility and depend upon the individual adoption and adherence to professional codes of practice. New – immediate – spaces for research participation and research presence on the other hand may challenge our notions of data collection, production of 'thick' descriptions, immersion in the data and analysis. For example, data collected using digital Internet sources, where the spoken 'voice' of the participant and the stages of being with and listening/interacting with a participant, recording and transcription are missing in the electronic texts which are downloaded and diminish the temporal, data-familiarizing elements long associated with interpretive, qualitative research. To make ethical decisions, information-knowledge sources are vital as researchers are increasingly working with digital data. But we also need to be able to evaluate the provenance and authority of knowledge-information – questioning how far they are reliable and trustworthy.

Ten years on, the qualitative research landscape is still evolving. We note two movements going in different directions and position ourselves as researchers in a bridging generation. Politically, greater user involvement whether voluntary or because of pressure can only be a good thing. We can see this as a positive – democratizing – development. In terms of training, new researchers need to be increasingly ethically and ICT literate in these issues. We suggest that *ethical thinking* requires both skills and practice, which in an increasingly complex world needs to be developed and reflected upon. Ethical thinking is becoming a practice required by everyone as they negotiate the social world, from the teenager on Facebook to the Mumsnet moderator (http://www.mumsnet.com/) to the academic engaged in qualitative research and knowledge production. In the final section of this chapter we offer a guide for planning and practicing as an ethical researcher drawing upon the nine questions originally developed in Rosalind Edwards and Melanie Mauthner's chapter (1) and developed here alongside others (Rogers and Ludhra, 2011). We also remind ourselves how feminist research has problematized the boundaries of public and private for several decades (Edwards and Ribbens, 1998). These debates are once again highlighted in order to signal the growing ambiguity between online public and private demarcations, even more so with the democratic call for open access and open sources on the Internet.

This is then a time of new – exciting – research horizons and rapid digital and technological shifts which require increased attention to ethical thinking and practices. Ethical thinking as we have noted is a continual process, and based on the issues raised in this book we have formulated a series of questions for researchers to bear in mind as they plan, undertake and disseminate findings/end their research. Reflecting on these questions will enable researchers to develop their ethical practice based on their own particular research approach.

- Methods

Should I simply use methods or study them as well in terms of the effects they might have on the research process e.g. what they *do* when put into practice? How aware am I that new methods and the new ethical, moral and political challenges they give rise to, must be understood in their own right before their widespread implementation?

- Sample

How might my method of accessing a sample raise ethical concerns? What are the implications for my sample/research if specific recruitment (or other) strategies are imposed by an ethics committee? Who are the people involved in my research and (potentially) affected by the ethical dilemmas raised in the research? What can I do to diminish/ anticipate ethical dilemmas in terms of the specific topic of the research and the issues it raises personally and socially for those involved? What strategies can I employ if these arise (e.g. provide information notes on support groups and help-lines)?

- Power, relationships and needs

What is the balance of personal and social power between those involved in the research? How have ethics committee requirements affected my original research intentions? What are the specific social and personal locations of the people involved in my research in relation to each other? What are the needs of those involved and how/are they interrelated? Who am I identifying with, who am I positioning as 'other', and why?

- Actions, practices and consequences

How will those involved understand my actions and are these in balance with my judgment about my own practice? How can I best communicate the ethical dilemmas to those involved, give them room to raise their views, and negotiate with and between them? How collaborative and interactive do I want to be as a researcher? How will my actions affect the relationships between the people involved and beyond the life of the research project? Have I been mindful of silences, gaps and absences in the research process?

- Communication and community

Who do I want to communicate my research to and which research communities and networks do I want to belong to in order to share and disseminate my work? How much engagement and exchange do I want with participants, users and funders of my research? How much control is it possible to retain over my research findings (in this digital age of global reach) and what can I do to protect the ethical and professional integrity of my research intentions (for example, to maintain anonymity and protect participants)?

- Archiving my data for future researchers

Is my moral responsibility to comply with emerging data sharing expectations, requirements and demands: to use prescribed methods in ethically, morally and legally prescribed ways? Or should I preserve my own archive and resist data sharing imperatives?

- Autonomy, values and politics

How can I maintain my professional autonomy as a researcher to carry out research that has philosophical, moral and ethical integrity? How do I decide what constitute legitimate moral concerns? Where exactly do I decide to draw the line around my ethical and moral responsibilities? What shall I consent to and reject, and what shall I agree to compromise on? What are the consequences of my inclusionary and exclusionary practices, of making the specific choices that I do?

The tensions between the range of ethical models, practical and theoretical, that researchers draw upon to negotiate their way through the competing demands of research, impels us to return to and develop ethical research practice as part of a feminist ethics of care. Ten years on, we find this framework continues to be relevant as online research increases. And like us, many other qualitative researchers are proposing that dialogical and relational processes, particularly pertinent for online research, can support and enable a contextually sensitive and flexible approach to ethics (Ess and Jones, 2004; Berry, 2004; Denzin and Lincoln 2008; Hookway, 2008). Our concern has been with the importance of mutual responsibility as conveyed in an ethics of care framework; this is also prioritized and developed in the next publication from the Women's workshop (Held, 2006; Gilligan, 2011; Weller and Rogers, 2012). Drawing upon elements of the ethics of care literature and theorizations in which the personal is linked with the political will, in this technologically rich and materialist world, provide an indispensable toolkit for planning research ethically.

With so many possibilities on the research horizon it is important that researchers explore and reflect upon this constantly evolving area. Many resources are now produced in the UK and are available to guide ethical thinking: the Associations of Internet Researchers (AoIR), for example, offers particular questions when using specific aspects of online research. The Economic and Social Research Council, the Research Development Initiative and the Institute of Education have combined forces to develop an online resource for social scientists – the Research Ethics Guidebook (www.ethicsguidebook.ac.uk). This guidebook deals with processes of ethics approval as well as providing questions that can guide ethical practice in the field. Researchers in the area of health can access a National Research Ethics Service from the National Health Service for similar resources. Further afield the development of guidelines for ethical research practice has also continued, for example the EU-Code for Ethics for Socio-Economic Research (Dench et al., 2004), the National Committee for Ethics in

Social Science Research in Health (NCESSRH) in India (2004) and the National Statement on Ethical Conduct in Human Research in Australia (2007).

There has also been greater attention given to specific areas of ethical guidance when working with particular groups or communities, for example, researching children and/or young people (Alderson and Morrow, 2004; Rodgers and Ludhra, 2011). Research professionals continue to influence integrity and quality in research practice within many national and international projects (Dench et al., 2004) and every university in the UK now has in place its own research ethics protocols. Academic peer-reviewed journals focusing on Internet research and ethics are now available as are Internet sources focusing on a wide range of guidelines for ethical practice in a range of research settings and with a range of participant groups. Our hope is that the debates and examples provided in this book along with the broader ethical research guidance which is emerging in response to changing research environments will enable a more democratized setting in which qualitative research and knowledge production can be ethically conducted.

References

Alderson, P. and Morrow, V. (2004) 'Ethics, social research and consulting with children and young people children', *Youth and Environments,* 16 (2): 148–74.

Ess, C. and Jones, S. (2004) 'Ethical decision-making and internet research: recommendations from the AoIR Ethics Working Committee', in E.A. Buchanan (ed.), *Readings in Virtual Research Ethics: Issues and Controversies.* Idea Group. pp. 27–44.

Barratt, M.J. and Lenton, S. (2010) 'Beyond recruitment? Participatory online research with people who use drugs', *International Journal of Internet Research Ethics,* 3: 69–86.

Bauman, Z. (2008) *Does Ethics Have a Chance in a World of Consumers?* Cambridge, MA: Harvard University Press.

Berry, D.M. (2004) 'Internet research: privacy, ethics and alienation: an open source approach', *Internet Research,* 14 (4): 323–32.

Dench, S., Iphofen, R. and Huws, U. (2004) 'An EU code of ethics for socio-economic research'. Available at: http://www.employment-studies.co.uk/pubs/report.php?id=412 (accessed 3May 2012).

Denzin, N.K. and Lincoln, Y.S. (2008) *The Landscape of Qualitative Research: Theories and Issues,* 3rd edn. Thousand Oaks: Sage.

Doucet, A. and Mauthner, N.S. (2012) 'Tea and tupperware: mommy blogging as care, work, and consumption', In Weller, S. and Rogers, C. (eds), *Critical Approaches to Care: Understanding Caring Relations, Identities and Cultures.* London: Routledge.

Edwards , R. and Ribbens, J. (1998) *Feminist Dilemmas in Qualitative Research: Public Knowledge and Private Lives.* London: Sage.

Gillies, V. and Lucey, H. (eds) (2007) *Power, Knowledge and the Academy: The Institutional is Political.* London: Palgrave Macmillan.

Gilligan, C. (2011) *Joining the Resistance.* Cambridge: Polity Press.

Heerwegh, D. (2003) 'Explaining response latencies and changing answers using client-side paradata from a web survey', *Social Science Computer Review,* 21 (3): 360–73.

Held, V. (2006) *The Ethics of Care Personal, Political, and Global.* Oxford: Oxford University Press.

Hookway, N. (2008) 'Entering the blogosphere': some strategies for using blogs in social research', *Qualitative Research*, 8: 91–113.

Levine, R. (2011) *Free Ride: How the Internet is Destroying the Culture Business and How the Culture Business Can Fight Back.* London: Bodley Head.

Miller, T. (2011) *Making Sense of Fatherhood: Gender, Caring and Work.* Cambridge: Cambridge University Press.

Nash, V. (2011) 'Facebook revolutions?', *Oxford Today*, 23 (3). Available at: http://www.mumsnet.com/

National Committee for Ethics in Social Science Research in Health (NCESSRH) Members (2004) http://www.fabtp.com/wp-content/uploads/2010/07/NCESSRH-Guidelines.pdf (accessed 3 May 2012).

Pariser, E. (2011) *The Filter Bubble: What the Internet is Hiding From You.* London: Viking.

Rogers, C. and Ludhra, G. (2011) 'Research ethics: participation, social difference and informed consent', in S. Bradford and F. Cullen (eds), *Research Methods for Youth Practitioners.* London: Routledge. pp. 43–65.

Weller, S. and Rogers, R. (eds) (2012) *Critical Approaches to Care Understanding Caring Relations, Identities and Cultures.* London: Routledge.

Websites

Economic and Social Research Council
http://www.esrcsocietytoday.ac.uk/about-esrc/information/research-ethics.aspx
The Research Ethics Guide Book: a guide for social scientists
http://www.ethicsguidebook.ac.uk/
National Research Ethics Service
The National Statement on Ethical Conduct in Human Research Australia (2007).
http://www.nhmrc.gov.au/guidelines/publications/e72

Author index

Page numbers in *italics* represent tables. Page numbers followed by b represent box. Page numbers followed by n represent endnotes.

Subject index

Page numbers in *italics* represent tables. Page numbers followed by b represent box. Page numbers followed by n represent endnotes.

daily life dilemmas 19
data analysis 151; processes 122–39
data collection 29–42, 151
data management plans 157
data protection 160
data set 167
data sharing 157–75, 183, 185; debates
170–1; moral responsibility 164–5;
movement 167, 172–3; policies 159–60,
see also digital data sharing
data suppliers 170
data users 170
decision-making 1, 37, 68, 148, 150,
160, 180
deconstruction 55–6, 96, 142
deontological model 19
Department of Health (UK) 78; *Research
Governance Framework* 4
depression 70, 132; anti-depressants 70b, *see
also* postnatal depression
descriptive norms 144
developing countries 147
difference 22, 46, 129–31, 141
digital archives 157, 167, 182
digital data sharing 7, 9, 11, 30, 157–75,
183; anonymizing data 165–6; informed
consent 162–5; problems 161–2;
responsibility 170–3; reuse 167–70;
sharing imperative emergence 159–61,
see also data sharing
digital revolution 173
digital technology 158, 166, 173, 177–87
discourse analysis 142
discourse ethics 23
discovery context 136
diversity 48
doctoral research 80–5
domestic labour division 129

ecological thinking 136n
Economic and Social Research Council
(ESRC) 4, 14, 158, 161–3, 167, 185;
Datasets Policy 161, 167, 170; *Research
Data Policy* 159; *Research Ethics
Framework* 163; *Research Funding
Guide* 167
education 147; professional 76–7, 80, 85–8,
91n, *see also* higher education
egalitarian research 62
email 32–3, 36, 179
emancipation politics 47–8
emotions 10, 18–20, 23, 25, 45, 83, 85, 111–19,
126, 152; emotion work 108, 112;
interviewing 115–19; management 110
empathy 25, 85, 108, 111–15, 117, 119

empirical realist 167
empiricism 16, 44–5, 91n
employment 10, 76, 125, 129
empowerment 49–56, 71
enlightenment 53
Environmental Information Regulations
Act (2004) 159
Environmental Information Regulations
(EU) 169
epistemic responsibility 123, 134–5
epistemic violence 168
epistemological accountability 134
epistemological communities 128
epistemology 10, 18, 43–4, 72, 77, 90,
122–39, 141; debates 44–7
epistemology and methodology 122–39;
reflexivity 130–4; research subject
relationships 127–30
essentialism 47–8
ethical covenant 103
ethical dilemmas 1–2, 5–6, 9–11, 19–20,
23, 26–7, 31, 44–9, 53, 57, 177–87;
consent 61–75; data collection 122–39;
experience 51; participant access 63–4;
practitioner-researchers 76–93; rapport
108–21
ethical governance 38–9, 177
ethical judgement 25
ethical models 19–22, *21*
ethical narratives 97–103
ethical skills 19–20
ethical talk sessions 101–2
ethical training 34
ethicism 15–16
ethics of care 6, 9, 15–18, 21–7, 90,
96, 129, 185; practical guidelines
25–7
ethics committees 1–2, 14, 17, 20, 29–42,
62–3, 68, 71–3, 79–80, 87, 145, 184;
medical/health 32
ethics creep 3, 30
ethics of justice 21
ethics of responsibility 95, 103
ethnicity 61, 63, 73
ethnographic studies 98
ethnography 22, 24, 97–100
Europe 3
European Union (EU) 169, 186
evidence-based practice 88–90
exploitation 86, 100, 103, 118, 145
expressive-collaborative model 96–7, 103

Facebook 4, 178, 183
'faking friendship' 108–21
false consciousness 54, 142

London 169
longitudinal research 69–72, 96, 102

social networks 4, 63, 178, 181, 183
social problems 7
social research 2–4, 11, 14–15; ethical
    concerns 18–19; modernism 141;
    rise in concern 15–18
social values 19
social work 76, 81, 83–5, 178; clients 79;
    code of practice ethics 79; intervention
    89; professional discourse 81–2; studies
    85–8
student-practitioners 79, 85–8
subject/object split 145
subjectivity 140–56, 180
successor science 45
surveillance (invisible) 179

technology 96; new 2–5, 7–11, 29–42, 177,
    181–2; research tool innovations 3,
    29–42
therapy study 97, 102
thinking ethically 1, 4–5, 182–3
transcription 151–3
Transition to Fatherhood study 31–7, 39–40
Transition to Motherhood study 31–2, 34,
    39–40
transparency 135, 157, 180
tree-ring data 169
truth 10, 43, 45–6, 48–9, 51, 55, 147

UK Data Archive (UKDA) 157, 162,
    165–6

unitary rational subject 153
United Kingdom (UK) 3–4, 14, 17, 31–2,
    61–2, 129, 159, 179, 181, 185;
    Department of Health 4, 78;
    southern England 61, 68, 97;
    universities 4, 17, 160, 186
universalistic principles 20
university research ethics committees
    (URECs) 31–6
utilitarianism 23; ethics of consequences
    model 19

value principles 86
verbal consent 71
violent men 61, 65, 73–4n, 118; women
    partners 65–8
virtue ethics of skills model 19–20
voice-as-empowerment approach 53
voluntary sector 76

women's groups 67
women's liberation movement 52
Women's Workshop on Qualitative/
    Household Research 7, 185
working-class 116, 149
World War II 3
written consent 71

youth 103–4, 143, 150, 183, 186, *see also*
    children
youth training schemes (YTS) 115